Readings
in
Asian Literatures
from Antiquity
to the Fifteenth Century

An Anthology

❖

Prepared by the Committee
on the World Humanities Courses
of The City College
of the City University of New York

KENDALL/HUNT PUBLISHING COMPANY
2460 Kerper Boulevard P.O. Box 539 Dubuque, Iowa 52004-0539

Typography by: Graphlink
of Setauket, NY

Cover Design by: David R. Leaman

Copyright © 1992 by World Humanities Core Committee, The City College of
The City University of New York

Library of Congress Catalog Card Number: 92-85564

ISBN 0-8403-8164-6

Printed in the United States of America

10   9   8   7   6   5   4   3   2   1

Contents

Chinese Literature

✆

Indian Literature

✆

Islamic Literature

Japanese Literature

XI

✧

Acknowledgements

Sources of Chinese Tradition
From SOURCES OF CHINESE TRADITION Vol. I, edited by William T. De Bary, c 1960 Columbia University Press, New York. Reprinted by permission of the publishers.

Near the East Gate; Random Pleasures: Nine Quatrains; Upon a Brook; Reading the Collected Works of Li Po and Tu Fu: A Colophon
From SUNFLOWER SPLENDOR: 3000 YEARS OF CHINESE POETRY, edited by Wu-Chi Liu & Irving Yucheng Lo. c 1975 by Wu-Chi Liu & Irving Yucheng Lo. Published by Indiana University.

In the Meadow There's A Dead Deer; Please, Chung Tzu;Decline and Growth Have No Fixed Time; The Way Has Declined Almost a Thousand Years; Anxious, Seeking, the Bird Lost from the Flock; I Built My Hut Beside a Traveled Road; The Fall Chrysanthemums Have Lovely Colors; At Yellow Crane Tower; Moonlight Night; A Traveler At Night Writes His Thoughts
From THE COLUMBIA BOOK OF CHINESE POETRY by Burton Watson. c 1984 Columbia University Press, NY. Reprinted by permission of the publisher.

The Fourth Month
Trans. by C. H. Wang. Reprint with permission.

The Autumn Wind
Trans. by Ronald C. Miao. Reprinted with permission.

A Speeding Carriage Climbs Through Eastern Gate
Trans. by Charles Hartman. Reprinted with permission.

They Fought South of the Walls
Trans. by Hans H. Frankel. Reprinted with permission.

Substance, Shadow and Spirit; From Twenty Poems After Drinking Wine
From THE POETRY OF T'AO CH'IEN by James Robert Hightower. c 1970 Oxford University Press. Reprinted with permission of Oxford University Press.

Passing Ch'ien-hsi as Military Advisor Miscellaneous Poems, Six Selections; A Man Has No Roots; Bright Sun Lights Over the Western Bank; Bright Blossoms Seldom Last Long; A Noble Ambition Spand the Four Seas; When I Was Young and in My Prime; Years Ago, When I Heard the Words of My Elders; No One Lives Past a Hundred; Four Untitled Poems; No Word; The Old Man of Hsin-feng with the Broken Arm; Tune: The Beautiful Lady Yu; Tune: Telling of Innermost Feelings
Trans. by Eugene Eoyang. Reprinted with permission.

Four Recollections; The Fishing Rod
Trans. by Richard B. Mather. Reprinted with permission.

I Say Goodbye to Fan An-ch'eng
Trans. by Lenore Mayhew & William McNaughton. Reprinted with permission.

I Saw Another Man Die
Trans. by Edward H. Schafer. Reprinted with permission of Phyllis Brooks Schafer.

A Visit to the Broken Hill Temple; Calling On a Taoist Priest; They Fought South of the Walls; Written on Behalf of My Wife
Trans. by Joseph J. Lee. Reprinted with permission.

The Elegant Women; I Spent the Night in a Room by the River
Trans. by Mark Perlberg. Reprinted by permission.

Laments for Lu Yin
Trans. by Stephen Owen. Reprinted with permission.

Poem on Losing One's Teeth; The Pond in a Bowl, Five Poems
From GROWING OLD ALIVE, POEMS BY HAN YU, copyright by Kenneth Hanson, 1978. Copper Canyon Press. Reprinted by permission of Kenneth Hanson.

For Lotus Flower
Trans. by Eugene Eoyang & Irving Y. Lo. Reprinted with permission.

Fisherman on a Southern Stream
Trans. by Robin D. S. Yates. Reprinted with permission.

Tune: Telling of Innermost Feelings; Tune: Pleasure of Returning to the Fields: A Prelude
Trans. by James J. Y. Liu. Reprinted with permission.

Tune: Crows Crying at Night
Trans. by Daniel Bryant. Reprinted with permission.

Song of the Crow Pecking at My Scarred Donkey; Elegy for a White Cock; Master Liu Painted a Portrait of Me
Trans. by Jonathan Chaves. Reprinted by permission.

Summertime
Trans. by Michael E. Workman. Reprinted by permission.

Written on the Wall of Halfway Mountain Temple
Trans. by Jan W. Walls. Reprinted with permission.

Replying to a Poem by Li T'ien-Lin
Trans. by Sherwin S. S. Fu. Reprinted with permission.

In a Boat on a Summer Evening, I Heard the Cry of a Water Bird
From THE OLD MAN WHO DOES AS HE PLEASES, SELECTIONS FROM THE POETRY & PROSE OF LU YU. c 1973 Columbia Univ. Press, NY. Reprinted by permission of the publishers.

Tune: Full River Red; Lament of a Soldier's Wife; Sunflower
Trans. by Irving Y. Lo. Reprinted with permission.

Tune: Song of Great Virtue, Spring; Tune: Song of Great Virtue, Winter, Two Songs; Tune: A Sprig of Flowers—Not Bowing to Old Age
Trans. by Jerome P. Seaton. Reprinted with permission.

Tune: Wild Geese Have Come Down: Song of Victory; Tune: Slow Chant—Kao-tsu's Homecoming
Trans. by Sherwin S. S. Fu. Reprinted with permission.

Sakuntala and the Ring of Recollection
From THEATER OF MEMORY: THE PLAYS OF KALIDASA, ed . by Barbara Stoler Miller. c 1984 Columbia University Press, NY. Reprinted by permission of publisher.

Fables of Bidpai; The Lion and the Ox; The Monkey and the Tortoise
From KALILA WA DIMNA: FABLES FROM A 14TH CENTURY ARABIC MANUSCRIPT by Esin Atil. Published by Smithsonian Institution Press. c 1981 Smithsonian Institution.

Samarkand
From THE ASSEMBLIES OF AL-HARIRI Vol. 2 Trans. by Dr. F. Steingas. (1896)

Rustam & Sohrab
From THE SHAHNAMA OF FIRDAUSI Trans. by A. G. Warner & E. Warner. Reprinted with permission of Routledge Ltd.

The Bird Parliament
From THE CONFERENCE OF THE BIRDS Trans. by S. C. Nott. Reprinted with permission of Routledge Ltd.

Women of Memphis
From YUSEF & ZULAIKHA Trans. by Ralph T. H. Griffith (1882).

Song of a Lady from Mie; When Emperor Tenji; An Exchange of Tanka with Lady Ishikawa; Longing for His Son, Furuhi; In Praise of Saki; Tegona of Mama; Looking at Mount Fuji in the Distance; Climbing Kasuga Field; Song; Two Tanka; Love's Complaint; Eighteen Tanka Written to Otomo no Yakamochi; Tanka; Three Anonymous Tanka with Stories; On Love; On the Roads of Yamashiro; Twenty-three Anonymous Tanka on Love; From the Kokinshu; Eighteen Tanka; On Vacation: A Poem to Record My Thoughts; Twenty-four Tanka on Love; Elegies for Her Daughter; Matters I Want Settled: Three Tanka; Four Songs; Women Are at Their Best; One Long Pine Tree; Since I No Longer Think; Did I Hear You Ask; An Outline for Composing Tanka; TEIKA, A No Play
From THE COUNTRY OF EIGHT ISLANDS by Hiroki Sato & Burton Watson. c 1981 by Hiroki Sato & Burton Watson. Used by permission of Doubleday, a division of Bantam Doubleday Dell Publishing Group, Inc.

On Passing the Ruined Capital at Omni; Composed When the Sovereign Journeyed to the Yoshino Palace; Composed When the Sovereign Journeyed to the Yoshino Palace; A Poem Written by Kakinomoto no Hitomaro; Written on Parting from His Wife; Love: Topic Unknown; Love Abe no Kiyoyuki; Love: Topic Unknown; Spring: Topic Unknown; Spring, Composed on the First Day of Spring; Spring, On a Snowfall; Spring, Composed by Command; Spring, On Seeing Cherry Blossoms; Spring; Laments; Autumn. Written as an Autumn Poem; Autumn. Written as an Autumn Poem; Love. A Poem on Love; Spring. Written for a Five-poem Sequence; Summer. A Poem on the Topic Cuckoo; Autumn. Written as Part of a Hundred-poem Sequence; Winter. Topic Unknown; Winter. Among Poems Presented to Cloistered Prince Shukaku; Winter. Written for the Poem Contest; Laments. Written in the Autumn; Love. Sent to a Woman on a Rainy Day; Autumn. Topic Unknown; Autumn. Topic Unknown; Autumn. Topic Unknown; Autumn. Topic Unknown
From TRADITIONAL JAPANESE POETRY: AN ANTHOLOGY, trans. with an introduction by Steven D. Carter. With permission of the publishers, Stanford University Press c 1991 by the Board of Trustees of the Leland Stanford Jr. University.

An Account of My Hermitage
From YOSHITSUNE: A 15TH CENTURY JAPANESE CHRONICLE trans. by Helen Craig McCullough.

A Tale of Brief Slumbers
From TALES OF TEARS & LAUGHTER: SHORT FICTION OF MEDIEVAL JAPAN trans. by Virginia Skord c 1991 University of Hawaii Press. Reprinted by permission.

Preface

This anthology provides a selection of readings from Asian cultures, with emphasis on works from China and Japan, but also with materials from India, Persia, and Arabia. Readers of this volume will find examples of poetry, drama, and prose written from antiquity to the fifteenth century, with the bulk of the offerings dating from a period corresponding to the Middle Ages in Europe. The anthology thus makes no pretense at presenting samples of all Asian literatures, or even all the major writers of the literatures and periods that are included.

Its objects are more modest, though not less vital. The book sets out to help readers unfamiliar with Asian literatures to gain a taste for them, to understand certain of their traditions, and to see how their writers address questions that occupy authors at all times, in all places. Finally, and most importantly, this collection seeks to bring readers simply to enjoy a body of stories, poems, and plays they may never before have encountered.

By definition, an anthology must select from among an array of materials that is certain to include more than can possibly be contained in the book. Decisions on what to include, what to exclude, are sure to be difficult, as the compilers of this book have found. Nevertheless, the editors have been guided by two principles: The first was that the selections conform to the objects of the book; and, because the immediate context for this book is a particular course at The City College, the second was that the readings be teachable.

The initial course in City College's required World Humanities sequence is "an introduction to world literature...from antiquity to the seventeenth century." As a course that includes literature written in a variety of languages, its texts are often literature in translation. The problems of reading translations are both too extensive and too familiar either to permit or require their elaboration here. The editors wish only to point out that they are painfully familiar with them and that they have tried to select translations that are readable and that capture something of the literary spirit of the originals.

This anthology has been assembled from selections taken from a variety of sources. Except for occasional minor alterations, the translations are reprinted exactly as they appear in those sources, together with accompanying footnotes and (where available) transliterations. The editors have also reprinted introductory comments found in the books they have drawn on. Readers seeking more information about the poets and poems in this anthology are urged to consult this book's sources, as well as the titles to be found elsewhere in this book under "Suggestions for Further Reading."

In accomplishing their task, the editors have been guided by the Committee on the World Humanities Courses: Gary S. Bloom, Barbara Brooks, James de Jongh, Jeanette Gatty, John E. Geary, Diana R. Gordon, Marshall Hurwitz, Geraldine Murphy, Beatrice G. Popper, Martin Tiersten, Chudi P. Uwazurike, and Jo-Ann D. Wyke-Hamilton.

In addition, they have been helped by the suggestions of many of their other colleagues on the City College faculty, including Roger E. Boxill, John DeWind, Sidney Feshbach, Arthur Ganz, Robert Ghiradella, Leon M. Guilhamet, Leo Hamalian, K.D. Irani, Penelope Karageorge, Thomas Lee, Norman Levine, Barbara Ungar, and Steven S. Urkowitz.

Particular thanks go to Faye Yuan Kleeman, of the Department of Asian Studies, for her careful review of an early draft of the manuscript and for bringing additional sources and alternative translations to the attention of the editors.

The editors are deeply grateful for all the recommendations they have received, but—in keeping with an ancient and honorable academic tradition—they hasten to assure the world that their advisors are to be held blameless for such faults as this book may contain.

The editors wish to encourage those who have suggestions on how to improve this collection to communicate them to Saul N. Brody, Department of English, The City College, New York N.Y. 10031.

The Editors

Saul N. Brody, *Editor-in Chief*

Joshua Wilner

The City College
June, 1992

Chinese Literature

Introduction
by Burton Watson

Poetry has been many things to the Chinese over the long centuries of their history—a hymn to ancestral spirits, a celebration of the beauties of nature, an expression of friendship or a pleasant accompaniment to a social gathering, a medium for airing political criticisms, for venting grief, for advancing a courtship. It has been composed by emperers and their ladies-in-waiting, by monks and generals, city dwellers and farm folk, but above all by the scholar-officials, men who had received a thorough education in the classics of the language and who, often after passing civil service examinations, were assigned posts in the complex bureaucracy that governed the vast nation. Whatever level of society it may have sprung from, poetry is woven into the life and history of the Chinese people, and perhaps no other facet of their traditional culture possesses such universal appeal.

Two things about the Chinese poetic tradition are immediately striking — its great antiquity and its remarkable continuity... Moreover, they draw upon an oral tradition whose origins are probably as old as the Chinese people themselves. Though there are few works from the centuries immediately following [an] early anthology [compiled around 600 B.C.], for the period from around 300 B.C. down to the present century, the stream of poetic output is virtually unbroken. The discovery in the first century A.D. of a method of making paper, and the invention of printing about seven centuries later, greatly aided the dissemination and pres-ervation of literary works, with the result that, the Chinese being among the world's most indefatigable compilers and transmitters of texts, the volume of poetry handed down from the past is truly staggering....

Here I would like first to describe the outstanding character-istics and themes of Chinese poetry as a whole, and then proceed to examine its principal forms in the early period.

One of the first things that is likely to strike the Western reader about Chinese poetry is its remarkable degree of accessibility. To be sure, like any great poetic tradition with a long history of development, that of China has its particular conventions, some of which may seem strange to the reader at first. For example, its treatment of romantic love — a theme it takes up rather less frequently than does the poetry, say, of Europe or Japan — tends, particularly in later centuries, to be presented almost exclusively from the woman's point of view and to place great emphasis upon the pathos and helplessness of her situation. Another set of conventions is found in poetry dealing with the imperial court, in which the ruler is likened to Heaven, his ladies-in-waiting to fairy maidens of the sky, and his favor to the life-giving rain or dew.

In addition to such conventions and stereotypes, Chinese poetry, like that of the West, has its body of myths and legends that it draws upon, and is especially fond of employing allusions to the famous events and personages of the nation's lengthy past. All such mythical and historical allusions, of course, require some degree of explanation to be intelligible to the foreign reader.

But, as has been so frequently remarked, the Chinese poetic tradition is on the whole unusually humanistic and commonsensical in tone, seldom touching on the supernatural or indulging in extravagant flights of fancy or rhetoric. For this reason, even works that are many centuries removed from us in time come across with a freshness and immediacy that is often quite miraculous. The Chinese poetic world is one that is remarkably easy to enter because it concentrates to such a large degree on concerns that are common to men and women of whatever place or time.

Closely allied to this tone of reasonableness that marks Chinese poetry is its air of restraint and decorum. There are no epic poems in the language, and little of the ebullient celebration of heroic deeds and feats of arms that we associate with the epic poetry of India or the West. War and violence are rather seldom touched on, and when they are, it is more often to deplore than to glorify them. Erotic themes likewise are treated in a highly restrained manner. Sexual appeal is suggested by descriptions of dress, makeup, or articles of personal use rather than of the body itself, and anything approaching the indecent is so heavily cloaked in euphemisms that it could be titillating only to the highly initiated. All of this reflects the pervading influence of Confucianism, with its emphasis upon civil rather than military arts and virtues and its somewhat puritanical outlook.

Another important characteristic of Chinese poetry is its frequently personal and occasional nature. The Chinese have for the most part regarded poetry not as the product of any one particular group in society or personality type, not as the fruit of rare genius or divine inspiration, but as something that almost anyone with a grasp of the rules of prosody and a genuine desire for self-expression can compose. Particularly among scholars and government officials, poetry was an indispensable accompaniment of daily life. Poems were customarily composed as part of the entertainment at banquets and outings or exchanged among friends at times of parting. At other times, one might write poems to describe the events of his daily life, to record the scenes of a journey, to give vent to grief or frustration, or simply to dispel boredom or polish up one's literary skills. The practice of drawing lots to determine what rhymes one was to use when composing poems with a group of friends, or of "harmonizing" with the rhymes of someone else's poem — either employing the same rhyme categories as the original poem, or using the exact same rhyme words — added an element of challenge to the composing of poetry and gave it a gamelike quality.

Chinese occasional poetry — that is, poetry inspired by or written to commemorate a particular occasion — is much like the occasional poetry of the West. But whereas the Western poet in such circumstances usually tries to invest his poem with some sense of a universal truth transcending the occasion, the Chinese poet is more often content to try to capture the particular truth or sentiment that came to him on that occasion. For this reason, he frequently prefaces his poem with a headnote describing the precise time, place, and circumstances that prompted its composition. There is less sense than in the West of a poem as possessing a life of its own apart from that of its creator, more of the poem as a form of autobiography, shedding light on the life of the poet and at the same time yielding up its full meaning only when read in the context of that life. The poem is the voice of the poet not self-consciously addressing posterity or the world at large, but speaking quietly to a few close friends, or perhaps simply musing to himself.

But, although there is this very important personal and intimate side to Chinese poetry, and it is the side which, because of its engaging understatement and freedom from pretension, is likely to appeal most to present-day Western readers, there is also a more public side to poetry in China. The earliest anthology of Chinese poetry, the *Shih Ching* or *Book of Odes*, was believed to have been compiled by the sage Confucius, who made clear that what he valued in poetry were its moral and didactic elements. From early times, Confucian scholars have seen poetry as playing a vital role in the ordering of the state, functioning as a vehicle through which the officials and common people might celebrate the virtue of a just ruler or, as is more likely to be the case, decry the hardships inflicted by an unjust one. This view of poetry as a medium for social and political complaint has led to the composition of many moving and impassioned works, realistic descriptions of the griefs of the tax-burdened farmers, outcries against military conscription and the ills of war, and attacks on social injustice in its many guises.

According to Confucian theory, the ruler was expected to welcome such complaints as expressions of loyal concern on the part of his subjects. But in an authoritarian governmental system such as that of imperial China, reasonable complaint was in practice all too often interpreted as treasonable impertinence, and countless officials found themselves summarily demoted and "exiled" to minor office in some remote province as a result of their poetic criticisms. It is a tribute to the courage and integrity of the Chinese poet-officials that, in spite of such risks, so many of them continued over the centuries to pour out their remonstrances in poetry.

The fondness of the Confucian scholars for poetry of didactic and political import at times led them to discover political meaning in places where it was almost certainly never intended. Thus, for example, they interpreted the simple love and courtship songs of the *Book of Odes* as allegories of the loyal minister's devotion to his sovereign, or saw in the crude ditties sung by children in the street the prophecies of impending events in the world of politics. On the other hand, countless Chinese poems were in fact intended to have political significance, even though it may not be immediately apparent in the surface meaning of the poem.... Such allegorical levels of meaning are often difficult to identify, particularly at this far remove in time. But it is well to keep in mind that a seemingly ingenuous poem of objective description may have had a quite different significance for the poet and his associates. Most Chinese poets of early times wrote not for the reading public at large, but primarily for the members of their own coterie, and it was enough if the members of that group grasped the full import of the work.

Another important theme of traditional Chinese poetry to be touched on here is that of the beauties of nature, particularly as seen in remote mountain areas, a theme that is of prime importance in Chinese painting as well. Here again there are conventions and symbolisms at work which we should be aware of. Thus, to give a few examples at random, pines and cranes are traditionally suggestive of longevity; orchids — the modest, unshowy Oriental variety — stand for the retiring gentleman of upright character; plum blossoms, because they open so early in the spring, symbolize fortitude; bamboos symbolize integrity, etc.

In the very early period of Chinese history, when large areas of the country were still in a state of wilderness, the natural landscape was often looked on as dark and threatening, the abode of fierce beasts and nature spirits of doubtful benignancy. But as more lands were opened up for cultivation and population pressures built up, the more isolated mountain and valley regions came to seem increasingly inviting. In contrast to the cities, which represented wealth, power, and the corrupting influences that seem inevitably to accompany them — the world of "red dust," as the Chinese call it — the mountains offered a realm of safety, serenity, and freedom from care, where one might savor the unspoiled grandeur of the landscape, pursue the life of a Taoist or Buddhist practitioner, or search for medicinal herbs to prolong life. It is no wonder that the poet officials, shackled to their posts and ever in danger of encountering sudden reversals of fortune or even execution, should have dreamed so often of escaping to these carefree realms. And when, as frequently happened, civil strife erupted in the nation or foreign invaders swept down from the north or west, flight to the hills became almost the only hope for survival.

All these connotations — safety, longevity, spiritual peace, emancipation — underlie the traditional Chinese attitude toward nature and the life that is lived in the midst of natural surroundings. And added to these, as in the West, is an element of mysticism and religious feeling, a sense that in such a setting one is on the threshold of the supernatural. But, whereas the Western poet customarily looks upon nature as the eloquent handiwork of a Supreme Being who exists above and apart from his creation, the Chinese poet, imbued with the nondualism of Taoism and Buddhism, sees nature as the embodiment of the Absolute itself. Every element in the landscape from the most sublime to the lowliest, is equally a manifestation of the Tao. And man, far from being the lord and caretaker of creation, is simply another one of the elements in it.

Finally, a word must be said about the theme of death. Though the poems in the *Book of Odes*, as will be noted later, are almost superstitious in their avoidance of the subject, by Han times the terrifying brevity and uncertainty of human life and the fear of death — the "claw coming out of the earth," to borrow Robert Payne's striking phrase[1] — had become a major theme in Chinese poetry.

In the face of such fear, many writers could only urge that we make the most of the little time given us. As one of the famous series of anonymous poems known as "The Nineteen Old Poems of the Han" puts it: "If the day is short and you hate the long night,/why not take the torch and go wandering?" In time, however, more thoughtful poets came forward with three possible ways to solve, or in some sense alleviate, the problem of human mortality.

The first, drawing upon ancient beliefs of the folk religion, particularly those associated with popular Taoism, suggests that, through the use of rare herbs or other semimagical means, one can attain the status of a *hsien* or immortal spirit, or at least greatly prolong the span of life. The art and literature of early China abound in descriptions and depictions of such immortals, cavorting in the mountain fastnesses that are their habitat or winging to the sky on the back of a white crane.

Confucianism, with its stress on humanism and rationalism, understandably took a dim view of such beliefs. Confucian-minded writers offered in their place more sober and socially responsible kinds of immortality, that achieved biologically through the perpetuation of the family, and the less certain hope of being remembered by posterity because of one's outstanding deeds or character. "A shining name — let that be the prize!" declares another of the poems in the series just mentioned.

But virtue, as the poets themselves glumly noted, too often fails to receive its just recognition, and the Chinese annalists, for all their proverbial diligence, can hardly be counted on to get down all the names of those who deserve remembrance. Thus in time a third solution to the problem began to take shape, one that is far subtler than the others and founded on the Taoist and Buddhist concepts of nondualism already alluded to above. The individual is indeed fated to perish when his allotted years come to an end. But if he can somehow transcend or set aside his individuality and

1. Robert Payne, ed., *The White Pony: An Anthology of Chinese Poetry* (New York: The New American Library, 1947), p. xi.

merge himself with the ceaselessly recurring life of nature as a whole, he can in a sense free himself from bondage to the conventional concepts of life and death and become as eternal as the universe itself.

Sometimes, as in T'ao Yüan-ming's poem "Substance, Shadow, and Spirit," such philosophical ideas are set forth in a systematic manner, though more often, particularly in the case of the last view mentioned, they are merely hinted at. Many Chinese poems are frank celebrations of the sensual pleasures of life, albeit conscious of how fleeting such pleasures may prove to be. Others are works of high moral and artistic seriousness, intended in some way to better the state of mankind, and at the same time to insure a measure of literary immortality to the author. But others — often among the finest works in the language — are quite different from these in nature, exercises in quietude and anonymity in which the poet deliberately seeks to divest himself of his personality, even of his humanity, in an effort to become one with the countless other forms of being around him.

The question of just how satisfactory any of these solutions I have outlined may have been to the poets who embraced them is outside the scope of our inquiry here. But we ought to be aware of these varieties of philosophical orientation so that we can properly appreciate the tenor of a given poet's work. And not look for moralizing from someone who is concerned only with sensibility, or displays of ego from one whose whole aim is the shedding of ego.

Having noted some of the principal themes and characteristics of Chinese poetry, I would like to say something about its forms. Nearly all the works contained in the present anthology....employ the *shih* form, a term we have already encountered in the title of the earliest anthology, the *Shih ching* or *Book of Odes*. It was originally a song form, and continued in later centuries to be essentially lyric in nature, though at times employed for narrative and descriptive poetry as well.

In its earliest from in the *Book of Odes*, it customarily uses a line made up of four characters. Since one character represents one syllable, and since classical Chinese is basically monosyllabic, this means in effect that there are usually four words to a line. Lines tend to be end-stopped, with few run-on lines except in the final couplet, so that the effect is of a series of brief and compact utterances or images.

In later centuries, the old four-character line of the *Book of Odes* for the most part dropped out of use, being replaced by versions of the *shih* that use a five-character or seven-character line. Rarely, poems with a three-character or six-character line are found, as well as those in the so-called "mixed line" form that uses lines of varied lengths.

End rhyme is employed from the earliest times, usually appearing at the end of the even-numbered lines. Occasionally rhymes on the odd-numbered lines are also used, as well as rhymed couplets. In short poems a single rhyme is customarily used throughout; in longer poems the rhyme may change as often as the poet wishes. In addition to end rhyme, much use is made of alliteration, internal rhyme, and onomatopoetic words descriptive not only of sounds but of actions and moods as well.

Though Chinese was probably a tonal language from very early times, we are not certain what role tone played in the prosody of ancient Chinese poetry. From around the sixth and seventh century, a new type of *shih* poetry evolved that took careful account of the tone of the words used in compostion. This new, tonally regulated type of verse came to be known as *chin-t'i-shih* or "modern style *shih*," and the older, unregulated type was referred to as *ku-shih* or "old style" *shih*....

For purposes of prosody, the four tones of medieval Chinese were classified into two categories: level tones, in which the voice remains on an even level, and deflected tones, in which the voice dips or rises in pronouncing the syllable. The rules for tonal regulation, or tonal parallelism, as it is sometimes called, are highly complex and need not be described in detail here. In principal they decree that a single line shall not have more than two, or at the very most three, syllables or words in succession that belong to the same tonal category, and that in the second line of a couplet the words in key positions shall be opposite in tone to the corresponding words in the first line of the couplet. This latter results in the second line of the couplet producing, in terms of tone, a mirror image of the first line.

All of these rules and devices no doubt insured that traditional Chinese poetry had a highly patterned and pleasing aural effect.

However, because of the extensive changes that have taken place in pronunciation over the centuries, it is difficult to reconstruct the exact effect today.

Along with such euphonic devices as rhyme and tonal parallelism, Chinese poetry employs numerous rhetorical devices such as simile, metaphor, personification, etc. in the manner of Western poetry, though usually with greater restraint, and makes extensive use of verbal parallelism. Such parallelisms customarily appear in the form of couplets in which both lines follow exactly the same syntactical pattern; thus nouns, verbs, adjectives, etc. in the upper line are matched by identical parts of speech in the lower line, number words are matched with number words, color words with color words, etc.

Let me illustrate some of these points by quoting a typical poem in *shih* form. It is by Liu Tsung-yüan (773-819), a well-known T'ang official, poet, and prose writer, and is entitled "River Snow." The poem is in the *chüeh-chü* or quatrain form, one of the "modern style" or tonally regulated forms which consists of four lines made up of five, seven, or in rare cases six characters each. This particular example uses a five-character line. The transcription of the original given here represents the pronunciation used in modern standard Chinese, which is quite different from the pronunciation of T'ang times, when the poem was written. For example, in T'ang pronunciation, the rhyme words *chüeh, mieh,* and *hsüeh* all ended in a final "t," giving them a gently plosive effect that is lost in modern pronunciation. The mark O indicates syllables that belong to the level tone category, the mark ▲ , those that belong to the deflected category.

As will be seen, the first two lines observe strict verbal parallelism. Interestingly, the poet summons up images of flying birds and well-traveled paths, only to negate them by telling us that they have been obliterated by the heavy snow. The third line is a run-on line, requiring the final line to complete the sense. Against a background of all-enveloping gray, the old man, muffled up in straw cloak and broad hat, sits alone in his little boat, apparently so immersed in his fishing and so at home on the river that he does not even notice the cold. The poem, because of its hushed atmosphere and air of mystery, has been a favorite subject for illustration by Chinese painters.

Liu Tsung-yüan, River Snow (5-ch. *chüeh-chü*)

○	○	▲	○	▲
Ch'ien	*shan*	*niao*	*fei*	*chüeh*

▲	▲	○	○	▲
wan	*ching*	*jen*	*tsung*	*mieh*

○	○	○	▲	○
ku	*chou*	*so*	*li*	*weng*

▲	▲	○	○	▲
tu	*tiao*	*han*	*chiang*	*hsüeh*

From a thousand hills, bird flights have vanished;
on ten thousand paths, human traces wiped out:
lone boat, an old man in straw cape and hat,
fishing alone in the cold river snow.

In addition to the *shih*, there are two other poetic forms that were of importance during the period treated here. The first is the *fu* or rhyme-prose form, which came to prominence in the second century B.C. and continued to be of major significance down to T'ang times. The *fu* employs lines of varying lengths, arranged usually in blocks of lines of a uniform length that alternate with one another. A strong preference for four-character and six-character lines is apparent, and many poems are made up entirely of such lines. The poem often begins with an introduction in prose and contains prose interludes; in many cases it concludes with a reprise or recapitulation in verse. End rhyme is used throughout in the verse portions, as well as extensive alliteration and assonance. Many of the early *fu*, written by poets associated with the court, are given over to lavish depictions of imperial hunts and entertainments or the splendors of the capital cities, and run to considerable length....Rhetorical devices such as parallelism and allusion abound in the *fu*, and the language tends to be learned and ornate...

Around the ninth and tenth centuries, a new poetic form came into vogue, the *tz'u* or "lyric meter." The earliest *tz'u*, anonymous works that originated on the popular level, were lyrics composed to fit Chinese tunes imported from Central Asia, and usually dealt with romantic lovers or other themes common in the folk song tradition. Later, the form was taken up by members of the educated class and used to treat a variety of subjects.

As pointed out by David Lattimore, among others, classical Chinese poetry was only successfully translated into English when the translators were willing to set aside the rhymes and meters of traditional English verse, as well as Western concepts of what constitutes poetic diction and subject matter. and create a freer form that would permit the power and expressiveness of the originals to shine through.[2] This act of creation, as is well known, was brought about largely through the efforts of Pound, Waley, and other translators of their ilk in the early decades of the present century, and all of us who work in the field today stand immensely in their debt. As a result of their pioneering efforts, the poetry of premodern China, though perhaps not always fully or correctly understood, has come to be widely admired in the West, and in fact has become a major influence on contemporary poets writing in English.

At the present time, some translators of Chinese poetry into English continue to press in the direction of even greater freedom, while others experiment in the reintroduction of rhyme and other formal elements that were earlier jettisoned. My own belief is that all types of innovation and experiment are to be welcomed, for from them hopefully will evolve even more effective methods for bringing the beauties of Chinese poetry over into English....

The Chinese have customarily looked upon poetry as the chief glory of their literary tradition, particularly poetry in the *shih* form and have take enormous pains to preserve it in countless editions and anthologies, many of them elaborately annotated. Other literary genres may show off more of the intellectual and philosophical aspects of the Chinese personality, or give greater scope to its fondness for pomp and ornateness, for mystery, fantasy, or rollicking fun.

2."Chinese Poetry and the American Imagination" (excerpts from a panel discussion attended by poets and scholars), *Ironwood 17* (Tucson: Ironwood Press, 1981), p. 38.

But no other type of literary expression so clearly reveals the basic humanism and realism of the Chinese, their abiding concern with the world that confronts us day to day. In poetry to a greater degree than in any other genre of traditional Chinese literature, they have faced that world, and themselves in it, and through the act of describing it in carefully ordered language, have calmly, and even at times with a certain elation, learned to come to terms with it.

From *Lao Tzu* (*Tao-te Ching*) (mid 3rd cent. B.C.)

Taoism
by Y.P. Mei and others

Next to Confucianism the most important and influential native philosophy of the Chinese has undoubtedly been that of the Taoist school. No other doctrine of the ancient period except Confucianism has for so long maintained its vigor and attractiveness to the Chinese mind. In many ways the doctrines of Confucianism and Taoism complement each other, running side by side like two powerful streams through all later Chinese thought and literature, appealing simultaneously to two sides of the Chinese character. To the solemn, rather pompous gravity and burden of social responsibility of Confucianism, Taoism opposes a carefree flight from respectability and the conventional duties of society; in place of the stubborn Confucian concern for things human and mundane it holds out a vision of other, transcendental worlds of the spirit. Where the Confucian philosophers are often prosaic and dull, moralistic and commonsensical, the early Taoist writings are all wit and paradox, mysticism and poetic vision. As the two streams of thought developed in later ages, Confucianism has represented the mind of the Chinese scholar-gentleman in his office or study, being a good family man, a conscientious bureaucrat, and a sober, responsible citizen; Taoism has represented the same gentleman in his private chamber or mountain retreat, seeking surcease from the cares of official life, perhaps a little drunk, but more likely intoxicated by the beauties of nature or of the world of the spirit.

Without this Taoist leaven of poetry and mysticism Chinese literature and thought would undoubtedly be a much poorer and shallower affair. But this very preoccupation with mystic worlds has proved to be the greatest weakness of the Taoists. After a brilliant beginning Taoism tended to become appropriated by those who wandered off on an interminable search for the secret of eternal life, which led them into such a slough of superstitious hocus-pocus that they eventually lost credit in the eyes of the intellectual class. The early classics of the Taoist school never ceased to be read by the educated, and to exert an influence upon the formation of their ideas. Indeed many of the most important elements of Taoist teaching were absorbed into Confucianism and Chinese Buddhism. But the Taoist school itself became more and more a cult of popular religion, adopting rites and organizational forms from the Buddhist church, absorbing all sorts of popular superstitions and demon lore, until it became an object of ridicule among educated Chinese.

Metaphysics and Government in the Lao Tzu

The Taoist school is often referred to as the "Teachings of the Yellow Emperor and Lao Tzu" or of "Lao Tzu and Chuang Tzu." The Yellow Emperor is a purely legendary figure, but we possess two books attributed to the other two fathers of the sect, Lao Tzu and Chuang Tzu. Chuang Tzu seems to have been an actual historical person, but who the philosopher called Lao Tzu was, when he lived, or what his connection was with the text that we have, have been questions of doubt since the first history of the ancient period was written. The tales of the philosopher-recluse Lao Tzu need not concern us here, however; what is important is the book—one of the shortest, most provocative, and inspired works in all Chinese literature. Though the quietism, mysticism, and love of paradox that distinguish this work probably represent very old strains in Chinese thought, whether the book itself is any earlier than the third century B.C. is a question still much debated by scholars.

In a sense, the *Lao Tzu* (or*Tao-te ching*) like so many of the works of this period of political chaos and intellectual ferment, proposes a philosophy of government and a way of life for the ruling class, probably the only people who could read its pages. Yet its point of view and approach to the problems of government are vastly broader than this statement would at first suggest. For the teaching of the *Lao Tzu* is based upon a great, underlying principle, the Way or Tao (from which the name of the Taoist school derives) which is the source of all being and governor of all life, human and natural, and the basic, undivided unity in which all the contradictions and distinctions of existence are ultimately resolved. Much of the book deals with the nature and workings of this first principle, while admitting that it must remain essentially indescribable and known only through a kind of mystic intuition. The way of life which accords with this basic Tao is marked by a kind of yielding passivity, an absence of strife and coercion, a manner of action which is completely spontaneous, effortless,and inexhaustible.

In the human sphere the *Lao Tzu* describes the perfect individual, the sage, who comprehends this mystic principle of Tao and orders his own life and actions in accordance with it, humbling himself, pursuing a course of quietude and passivity, free from desire and strife. It is clear that the sage is conceived of as the ideal ruler, for the *Lao Tzu* gives definite instructions as to how the sage is to conduct his government. He is to cease from meddling in the lives of people, give up warfare and luxurious living, and guide his people back to a state of innocence, simplicity, and harmony the Tao, a state that existed in the most ancient times before civilization appeared to arouse the material desires of the people and spur them to strife and warfare, and before morality was invented to befuddle their minds and beguile them with vain distinctions.

But such is the vagueness and ambiguity of the *Lao Tzu* text and the subtlety of its thought that it may yield different interpretations and be approached on very different levels. There have been times in Chinese history, notably at the beginning of the Han dynasty, when men attempted to translate the doctrines of the *Lao Tzu* into action through government policies embodying an extreme laissez-faire attitude. But the teachings of the *Lao Tzu* may also be understood as the creed of the recluse, the man of superior wisdom and insight who, instead of taking a part in society, chooses to retire from public life in order to perfect his own purity and intelligence. It is this interpretation of the *Lao Tzu* that has most often prevailed in later Chinese thought. This, perhaps, is largely because of the influence of the second great Taoist teacher, Chuang Tzu, the author of numerous stories about sages and worthies who were entreated by the rulers of their time to accept high political positions, but who rejected all such offers in favor of seclusion and self-cultivation. It is for this reason that Taoism has so often been the philosophy and consolation of the Chinese gentleman in retirement, of the political failure, and of the scholar who abandons human society in search of a mystic harmony with the world of nature.

The style of *Lao Tzu* is quite unlike that of the works of the other schools. The text appears to be a combination of very old adages or cryptic sayings, often in rhyme, extended passages of poetry, and sections of prose interpretation and commentary. There is extensive use of parallel constructions and neatly balanced phrases; the statements are laconic and paradoxical, intended not to convince the mind by reasoning but to startle and capture it through poetic vision. The writer makes striking use of symbols such as water, the symbol of a humble, self-effacing force that is in the end all-powerful, or the female and the mother, symbol of passivity and creation. It is this symbolism, this paradoxical, poetic view of life which have won for the work the tremendous popularity and influence which it has exercised through the centuries of Chinese literature, and these same appealing qualities that have made it the Chinese work most often translated into foreign languages.

1

The Tao [Way] that can be told of
 Is not the eternal Tao;
The name that can be named
 Is not the eternal name
Nameless, it is the origin of Heaven and earth;
Namable, it is the mother of all things.

Always nonexistent,
 That we may apprehend its inner secret;
Always existent,
 That we may discern its outer manifestations.
These two are the same;
Only as they manifest themselves they receive different names.

That they are the same is the mystery.
Mystery of all mysteries!
The door of all subtleties.

. . . .

3

Refrain from exalting the worthy,
  So that the people will not scheme and contend;
Refrain from prizing rare possessions,
  So that the people will not steal;
Refrain from displaying objects of desire,
  So that the people's hearts will not be disturbed.

Therefore a sage rules his people thus:
  He empties their minds,
  And fills their bellies;
  He weakens their ambitions,
  And strengthens their bones.

   He strives always to keep the people innocent of knowledge and desires, and to keep the knowing ones from meddling. By doing nothing that interferes with anything (*wu-wei*), nothing is left unregulated.

4

 The Tao is empty [like a bowl],
It is used, though perhaps never full.
It is fathomless, possibly the progenitor of all things.
It blunts all sharpness,
It unties all tangles;
It is in harmony with all light,
It is one with all dust.
Deep and clear it seems forever to remain.
I do not know whose son it is,
A phenomenon that apparently preceded the Lord.

5

Heaven and earth are not humane:
  To them all things are as straw dogs.
The sage is not humane:
  To him all the people are as straw-dogs.

. . . .

8

The highest good is like water. Water benefits all things generously
and is without strife. It dwells in the lowly places that men disdain.
Thus it comes near to the Tao.
The highest good loves the [lowly] earth for its dwelling.
It loves the profound in its heart,
It loves humanity in friendship,
Sincerity in speech, order in government,
Effectiveness in deeds, timeliness in action.
Since it is without strife,
It is without reproach.

. . . .

10

In keeping your soul and embracing unity,
  Can you forever hold fast to the Tao?
In letting out your vital force to achieve gentleness,
  Can you become as the new-born babe?
In cleansing and purifying your mystic vision,
  Can you be free from all dross?
In loving the people and governing the land,
  Can you practice nonaction (*wu-wei*)?
In opening and shutting the gates of heaven,
  Can you play the part of the female?
In perceiving all and comprehending all,
  Can you renounce all knowledge?

To beget, to nourish,
  To beget but not to claim,
  To achieve but not to cherish,
  To be leader but not master—
This is called the Mystic Virtue (*te*).

. . . .

14

You look at it, but it is not to be seen;
  Its name is Formless.

You listen to it, but it is not to be heard;
  Its name is Soundless.
You grasp it, but it is not to be held;
  Its name is Bodiless.
These three elude all scrutiny,
  And hence they blend and become one.

Its upper side is not bright;
  Its under side is not dim.
Continuous, unceasing, and unnamable,
  It reverts to nothingness.

It is called formless form, thingless image;
  It is called the elusive, the evasive.
Confronting it, you do not see its face;
  Following it, you do not see its back.

Yet by holding fast to this Tao of old,
  You can harness the events of the present,
  You can know the beginnings of the past—
Here is the essence of the Tao.

                    . . . .

                    16

Attain utmost vacuity;
  Hold fast to quietude.
While the myriad things are stirring together,
  I see only their return.
For luxuriantly as they grow,
Each of them will return to its root.

To return to the root is called quietude,
  Which is also said to be reversion to one's destiny.
This reversion belongs with the eternal;
  To know the eternal is enlightenment;
  Not to know the eternal means to run blindly to disaster.

He who knows the eternal is all-embracing;
  He who is all-embracing is impartial,
  To be impartial is to be kingly,
  To be kingly is to be heavenly,
  To be heavenly is to be one with the Tao,
  To be one with the Tao is to endure forever.
Such a one, though his body perish, is never exposed to danger.

17

The best [government] is that whose existence only is known by the people. The next is that which is loved and praised. The next is that which is despised....

18

It was when the Great Tao declined,
  That there appeared humanity and righteousness.
It was when knowledge and intelligence arose,
  That there appeared much hypocrisy.
It was when the six relations lost their harmony,
  That there was talk of filial piety and paternal affection.
It was when the country fell into chaos and confusion,
  That there was talk of loyalty and trustworthiness.

19

Banish sageliness, discard wisdom,
  And the people will be benefited a hundredfold.
Banish humanity, discard righteousness,
  And the people will return to filial piety and paternal affection.
Banish skill, discard profit,
  And thieves and robbers will disappear.

These three are the ill-provided adornments of life,
  And must be subordinated to something higher:—
See the simple, embrace primitivity;
  Reduce the self, lessen the desires.

. . . .

21

The expression of Vast Virtue *(te)*
  Is derived from the Tao alone.
As to the Tao itself,
  It is elusive and evasive.
Evasive, elusive,
  Yet within it there are images.
Elusive, evasive,
  Yet within it there are things.
Shadowy and dim,
  Yet within it there is a vital force.
The vital force is very real,
  And therein dwells truth.

From the days of old till now,
  Its name has never ceased to be,
  And it has witnessed the beginning of all things.
How do I know the shape of the beginning of all things?
  Through it.

. . . .

25

There was something nebulous yet complete,
  Born before Heaven and earth.
Silent, empty,
  Self-sufficient and unchanging,
  Revolving without cease and without fail,
  It acts as the mother of the world.

I do not know its name,
  And address it as "Tao."
  Attempting to give it a name, I shall call it "Great."
To be great is to pass on.
  To pass on is to go further and further away.
  To go further and further away is to return.

Therefore Tao is great, Heaven is great, earth is great,
  And the king is also great.
These are the Great Four in the universe,
  And the king is one of them.
Man follows the ways of earth,
  Earth follows the ways of Heaven;
  Heaven follows the ways of Tao;
  Tao follows the ways of itself.

. . . .

28

He who knows the masculine but keeps to the feminine,
  Becomes the ravine of the world.
Being the ravine of the world,
  He dwells in constant virtue,
  He returns to the state of the babe.

He who knows the white but keeps to the black,
  Becomes the model of the world.
Being the model of the world,
  He rests in constant virtue,
  He returns to the infinite.

He who knows glory but keeps to disgrace,
  Becomes the valley of the world.
Being the valley of the world,
  He finds contentment in constant virtue,
  He returns to the uncarved block.[1]

The cutting up of the uncarved block results in vessels,
  Which, in the hands of the sage, become officers.
Truly, "A great cutter does not cut."

. . . .

1. The "uncarved block" is a favorite figure used by the author of the *Lao Tzu* in referring to the original state of complete simplicity which is his highest ideal.

32

Tao is eternal, nameless. Though the uncarved block seems small, it may be subordinated to nothing in the world. If kings and barons can preserve it, all creation would of itself pay homage, Heaven and earth would unite to send sweet dew, and the people would of themselves achieve peace and harmony.

Once the block is cut, names appear. When names begin to appear, know then that there is time to stop. It is by this knowledge that danger may be avoided.

[The spontaneous working of] the Tao in the world is like the flow of the valley brooks into a river or sea

. . . . .

34

The great Tao flows everywhere:
  It can go left; it can go right.

The myriad things owe their existence to it,
  And it does not reject them.

When its work is accomplished,
  It does not take possession.
It clothes and feeds all,
  But does not pose as their master.

Ever without ambition,
  It may be called small.
All things return to it as to their home,
  And yet it does not pose as their master,
  Therefore it may be called Great.

Because it would never claim greatness,
  Therefore its greatness is fully realized.

. . . .

37

Tao invariably does nothing (*wu-wei*),
  And yet there is nothing that is not done.

If kings and barons can preserve it,
  All things will go through their own transformations.
When they are transformed and desire to stir,
  We would restrain them with the nameless primitivity.

Nameless primitivity will result in the absence of desires,
Absence of desires will lead to quietude;
The world will, of itself, find its equilibrium.

. . . .

40

Reversal is the movement of the Tao:
Weakness is the use of the Tao.
All things in the world come into being from being;
Being comes into being from nonbeing.

. . . .

42

Tao gave birth to One: One gave birth to Two; Two gave birth to Three; Three gave birth to all the myriad things. The myriad things carry the yin[2] on their backs and hold the yang in their embrace, and derive their harmony from the permeation of these forces.

To be "orphaned," "lonely," and "unworthy" is what men hate, and yet these are the very names by which kings and dukes call themselves.

Truly, things may increase when they are diminished, but diminish when they are increased.

What others teach I also teach: "A man of violence will come to a violent end."[3] This I shall regard as the parent of all teachings.

43

The most yielding of things outruns the most unyielding.
Having no substance, they enter into no-space.

---

2. Yin is the passive, negative, or female principle of the universe; yang is the active, positive, or male principle.
3. An ancient saying.

Hence I know the value of nonaction (*wu-wei*). The instructiveness of silence, the value of nonaction— few in the world are up to this.

. . . .

48

To seek learning one gains day by day;
To seek the Tao one loses day by day.
  Losing and yet losing some more,
  Till one has reached doing nothing (wu-wei).
Do nothing and yet there is nothing that is not done.
To win the world one must attend to nothing.
When one attends to this and that,
  He will not win the world.

. . . .

51

Tao gives them birth;
  Virtue *(te)* rears them.
They are shaped by their species;
  They are completed by their environment.
Therefore all things without exception exalt Tao
          and honor Virtue.
Tao is exalted and Virtue is honored,
  Not by anyone's command, but invariably and spontaneously.

Therefore it is Tao that gives them birth;
It is Virtue that rears them, makes them grow, fosters them,
          shelters them.

To give life but not to own,
To achieve but not to cherish,
to lead but not to be master—
  This is the Mystic Virtue!

. . . .

65

The ancient masters in the practice of the Tao did not thereby try to enlighten the people but rather to keep them in ignorance. If the people are difficult to govern, it is because they have too much knowledge. Those who govern a country by knowledge are the country's curse. Those who do not govern a country by knowledge are the country's blessing. To know these two rules is also to know the ancient standard. And to be able to keep the standard constantly in mind is called the Mystic Virtue.

Penetrating and far-reaching is Mystic Virtue! It is with all things as they run their course of reversal, until all reach Great Harmony.

. . . .

67

All the world says that my Tao is great, yet it appears impertinent. But it is just because it is great that it appears impertinent. Should it appear pertinent, it would have been petty from the start.

Here are my three treasures. Keep them and cherish them. The first is mercy; the second is frugality; the third is never to take the lead over the whole world. Being merciful, one has courage; being frugal, one has abundance; refusing to take the lead, one becomes the chief of all vessels. If one abandons mercy in favor of courage, frugality in favor of abundance, and humility in favor of prominence, he will perish.

Mercy will be victorious in attack and invulnerable in defense. Heaven will come to the rescue of the merciful one and with mercy will protect him.

. . . .

78

Of all things yielding and weak in the world,
  None is more so than water.
But for attacking what is unyielding and strong,
  Nothing is superior to it,
  Nothing can take its place.

That the weak overcomes the strong,
  And the yielding overcomes the unyielding,
Everyone knows this,

But no one can translate it into action.
Therefore the sage says:
"He who takes the dirt of the country,
     Is the lord of the state;
He who bears the calamities of the country,
     Is the king of the world."
Truth sounds paradoxical!

    . . . .

80

Let there be a small country with a few inhabitants. Though there be labor-saving contrivances, the people would not use them. Let the people mind death and not migrate far. Though there be boats and carriages, there would be no occasion to ride in them. Though there be armor and weapons, there would be no occasion to display them.

Let people revert to the practice of rope-knotting [instead of writing], and be contented with their food, pleased with their clothing, satisfied with their houses, and happy with their customs. Though there be a neighboring country in sight, and the people hear each other's cocks crowing and dogs barking, they would grow old and die without having anything to do with each other.

(Tr. Y.P. Mei)

From the *Analects* (uncertain date)

Confucius
By Y. P. Mei and others

If we were to characterize in one word the Chinese way of life for the last two thousand years, the word would be "Confucian." No other individual in Chinese history has so deeply influenced the life and thought of his people, as a transmitter, teacher, and creative interpreter of the ancient culture and literature, and as a molder of the Chinese mind and character. The other ancient philosophies, the religious systems of Taoism and Buddhism, all have known their days of glory and neglect; but the doctrines of Confucianism, since their general recognition in the first century before Christ, have never ceased to exert a vital influence on the nation down to our own century. Many Chinese have professed themselves to be Taoists, Buddhists, even Christians, but seldom have they ceased at the same time to be Confucianists. For Confucianism since the time of its general acceptance has been more than a creed to be professed or rejected; it has become an inseparable part of the society and thought of the nation as a whole, of what it means to be a Chinese, as the Confucian Classics are not the canon of a particular sect but the literary heritage of a whole people.

Considering his tremendous influence and importance, the life of Confucius is peculiarly human and undramatic. He was born in 551 B.C. in the small feudal state of Lu in modern Shantung province. His family name was K'ung, his personal name Ch'iu. "Confucius" is the Latinized form of "K'ung Fu-tzu" or "Master K'ung," the title commonly used in referring to him in Chinese. It is probable that his ancestors were members of the lesser aristocracy who had, however, sunk to a position of poverty and insignificance by the time of his birth. His father died when he was very young, leaving him to struggle alone with the problem of securing an education and making his way in the world.

The world he faced was not a bright one. China was divided into a number of small feudal states which were constantly bickering or making war upon each other or upon the barbarian tribes that pressed the Chinese people on all sides. The kings of the central court of the Chou dynasty, who had once given peace and stability to the nation, were weak and ineffective before the might of the more powerful feudal lords. Kings were ordered about by their vassals, rulers deposed or assassinated by their ministers, fathers slain by their sons. All was violence and disorder among the ruling class and there seemed to be no higher power, temporal or spiritual, to which men might appeal.

With energy and utter selflessness, Confucius set about to bring order and peace to his age. He believed that his place was in the world of politics and with almost pathetic persistence he sought through the states of China for a ruler who would be willing to employ him and his ideas in the government. He managed to find employment for a while in his native state of Lu and, according to tradition, rose to a fairly high position. But his success was short-lived; on the whole his political career was a failure, and more and more he turned his attention to the teaching of young men who, he hoped, might succeed in public life where he had failed. Judging from all accounts he was a teacher of rare enthusiasm and art; he was said to have had some three thousand students, of whom seventy-two were close personal disciples or known for their virtue. In his old age he retired to devote himself, so tradition says, to the editing of the texts of the Confucian Classics. He died in 479 BC....

Confucius and his teachings were little respected and less practiced by the men of his day, and for centuries the Confucian school remained only one among many rival schools of philosophy with its greatest strength in the area of Confucius' native state of Lu. But gradually Confucius' humanism began to triumph over the superstition and mysticism of other doctrines, his idealistic emphasis on virtue, kindness, and learning to attract more men than the harsh and cynical philosophies of other states. At last, in the second century B.C., Confucianism was declared the official creed of the nation and the Classics became the principal, if not the sole, study of all scholars and statesmen. Through the centuries the teachings of Confucius continued not only to be revered in China, but also to exert a tremendous influence in Korea, Japan and Annam. Confucius was given the title "Supreme Sage and Foremost Teacher" and his tomb and temple in Ch'ü-fu in Shantung became a kind of Mecca for all educated Chinese, while a Confucian temple on less elaborate scale was established in every county seat throughout the land. Under the Nationalist regime his birthday was (and still is on Taiwan) observed as Teachers' Day, a national holiday.

There is a large body of literature in Chinese, of varying degrees of reliability, on the life and teachings of Confucius. Among this the most important work is the record of the Master's activities and conversations compiled probably by his disciples' disciples, the *Analects*. This work is in twenty chapters and 497 verses, some consisting of the briefest aphorisms. From the time when Confucianism became widely accepted, the laconic and provocative sentences of this work, difficult though they often are to interpret, have exercised a profound influence upon the thought and language of the peoples of East Asia, while for the last eight hundred years it has been a basic text in Chinese education known to every schoolboy.

Once when Tzu Lu, Tseng Hsi, Jan Yu, and Kung-hsi Hua were seated in attendance upon him, Confucius said: "You no doubt consider me a day or so your senior, but let us not mind that. When out of office you say among yourselves that your merits are not recognized. Now suppose some prince were to recognize your merits, what would be your wishes?" Tzu Lu without hesitatin replied: "Take a kingdom of a thousand chariots, hemmed in by great powers, oppressed by invading troops, and suffering from famine in addition—I should like to take charge of it. In three years' time I could make it brave and make it understand the right course to pursue." Confucius smiled at him. "And how about you, Ch'iu [Jan Yu]?" "Take a district of sixty or seventy *li*[1] square," answered Jan Yu, "or say, one of fifty or sixty *li* square. I should like to take charge of it. In three years' time I could make its people live in abundance; but as for the promotion of rites (*li*) and music, I should have to leave that to a real gentleman." "And how about you, Ch'ih [Kung-hsi Hua]?" "Not that I say I could do it," he answered, "but I should like to be trained for it. At the ceremonies in the Ancestral Temple [of the Imperial House] or at the conferences of the princes, I should like to wear the ceremonial cap and gown, and be a minor official assisting in the ceremony." "And how about you, Tien [Tseng Hsi]?" Tseng Hsi paused in his playing of the zither. Putting it aside he rose and replied: "I am

1. A *li* is equal to about one-third of an English mile.

afraid my wishes are entirely different from those cherished by these three gentlemen." "What harm is there in that?" said Confucius. "We are just trying to let each express his desire." Then he said: "In the latter days of spring, when the light spring garments are made, I would like to take along five or six grown-ups and six or seven youths to bathe in the River Yi, and after the bath go to enjoy the breeze in the woods among the altars of Wu-yi, and then return home, loitering and singing on our way." Confucius heaved a deep sigh and said: "You are the man after my own heart." [XI:25]

Ch'ang-chü and Chieh-ni were cultivating their fields together. Confucius was passing that way and told Tzu Lu to go and ask them where the river could forded. Ch'ang-chü said: "Who is that holding the reins in the carriage?" Tzu Lu said: "It is K'ung Ch'iu [Confucius]." He said: "You mean K'ung Ch'iu of the state of Lu?" "Yes," Tzu Lu replied. Ch'ang-chü said: "If it is he, then he already knows where the ford is." Tzu Lu then turned to Chieh-ni. Chieh-ni asked: "You are a follower of K'ung Ch'iu of Lu, are you not?" He said: "That is so." Chieh-ni said: "The whole world is swept as by a torrential flood, and who can change it? As for you, instead of following one who flees from this man and that, you would do better to follow one who flees the whole world." And with that he went on covering the seed without stopping. Tzu Lu went and told Confucius, who said ruefully: "One cannot herd together with birds and beasts. If I am not to be a man among other men, then what am I to be? If the Way (*Tao*) prevailed in the world, I should not be trying to alter things." [XVIII:6]

(Tr. Y.P. Mei)

From *Shih Ching*
(ca. 1000-ca. 600 B.C.)

Near the East Gate

Near the East Gate
Young women go
Like so many clouds all day:
Like drifting clouds
A thought of them
Soon blows away.

> There. White robe
> and a blue scarf—
> she makes my day.

Near the Great Tower and Wall   10
Go slender girls
Like reeds by river's edge:
Like bending reeds
A thought of them
Soon passes by.

> There. White robe
> and a purple scarf—
> she makes me rejoice.

(Tr. Heng Kuan)

In the Meadow There's a Dead Deer

(A girl secretly seduced is compared to a deer stealthily shot
and concealed with rushes; the last stanza depicts the seduction.)

In the meadow there's a dead deer,
with white rushes cover it:

there's a girl with thoughts of spring
and fine man who tempts her.

In the woods are the scrub oaks,
in the meadow a dead deer:
in white rushes wrap and bind it.
There's a girl fair as jade.

Go slow — gently, gently!
Don't muss my waist cloth,   10
don't make the dog bark!

(Tr. Burton Watson)

Please, Chung Tzu

(A young woman pleads with an overzealous suitor.)

Please, Chung Tzu,
don't leap into my village,
don't break the willows they planted.
Not that I mind about them —
I'm afraid of my father and mother.
You're a love, Chung,
but the word of my father and mother —
that's something to be scared of!

Please, Chung Tzu,
don't jump over my wall,   10
don't break the mulberries they planted.
Not that I mind about them —
I'm afraid of my older brothers.
You're a love, Chung,
but the word of my older brothers —
that's something to be scared of!

Please, Chung Tzu,
don't jump into my garden,
don't break the spindle trees they planted.
Not that I mind about them —   20
I'm afraid of a lot of talk from others.
You're a love, Chung,
but a lot of talk from others—
that's something to be scared of!

(Tr. Burton Watson)

The Fourth Month

The fourth month: summer already;
In the sixth month I drag in the heat.
My ancestors: were they not men?
How can they continue to see me suffer?

The autumn days are chilly, cold:
All plants and grasses decay.
Tumults and wandering have made me very sick;
What shall I do, how can I go home?

The winter days are fierce and bitter.
Whirlwinds: a gust blasts against another.   10
Nobody gets less than how much he desires—
Why do I alone have to undergo such troubles?

On the mountains there are fine trees:
This is chestnut and that is plum;
And now, that is torn up and this is cut—
I wonder what crime they have committed.
Look at the steamwater from a spring:
Now clear, now polluted!
Yet I have to meet calamities every single day.
How can I wait to become better off?   20

Immense waters flow, the Chiang and the Han,[1]
Main-threads of the Southern Land.
I have drained my vigor to serve,
But why don't I have some support?

Neither am I an eagle, a falcon,
That can flap and soar up to heaven;
Nor am I a sturgeon, a snout-fish,
That can plunge to hide in the deep.

On the mountains there are brackens,
In the swampgrounds, red thorns.   30
I, a gentleman, have made the song,
In order to release my sorrows.

(Tr. C. H. Wang)

The Autumn Wind

Autumn winds rise,
    white clouds fly,
Grass, trees are yellow and sere,
    geese return south.
The orchids are resplendent,
    the chrysanthemums, fragrant;
Tenderly I think of the lovely one,
    I cannot forget her.
Sailing in a pavilion boat,
    we cross the Fen River,[1]

1. I.e., the Han River, which flows into the Yangtze (the Chiang) near modern Hankow, Hupeh.

1. A major river in Shansi which flows southwest into the Yellow River.

Cutting across the current,
   white ripples scatter.
Fife and drums play,
   the oarsman's song begins;   10
As joys reach their end,
   sorrows multiply.
Brief is the vigor of youth—
   helpless before old age!

(Tr. Ronald C. Miao)

Anonymous (uncertain dates)
From *Nineteen Poems in Ancient Style*

A Speeding Carriage Climbs Through Eastern Gate

a speeding carriage climbs through eastern gate
to view far off the tombs past northern wall
white poplar's leaves all a rustle
evergreens line the broad ways

below these are men long dead
come through dark to endless dusk
sunken in sleep under Yellow Springs[1]
never waking for a thousand years or forever

yin and *yang*[2] turn round in ceaseless flow
spans of years like morning dew   10
men's lives go fast like stops overnight
old age lacks the fixity of iron or stone

eons on end we saw them off
no saint nor sage that found escape
some took drugs to find the potions were wrong

better to drink good wine
and clothe yourself in satins and silks

                                        (Tr. Charles Hartman)

---

1. I.e., the nether world, also referred to as the Nine Springs.
2. *Yin* ("dark") and *Yang* ("light") represent respectively the female and the male principles of the universe.

"They Fought South of the Walls"

They fought south of the walls,
They died north of the ramparts.
Lying dead in the open, they won't be buried,
    the crows may eat them.

Tell the crows for me:
Please enjoy a sumptuous meal!
Lying dead in the open, they surely
    won't be buried.
How can their rotting flesh get away from you!

The water runs deep and clear,
The rushes and reeds are dark.
The brave war steeds have died in battle,   10
The worthless nags neigh, running hither
    and thither.

The bridges have been made into buildings,
How can one go south?
How can one go north?
The grain is not harvested, how shall our lord eat?
And we who want to be loyal vassals, how
    can we succeed?

I think of you, fine vassals.
fine vassals, indeed one should think of you.
In the morning you went out to attack,
In the evening you didn't come back for the night.   20

                    (Tr. Hans H. Frankel)

T'ao Ch'ien (372?-427?)

Substance, Shadow, and Spirit

Noble or base, wise or stupid, none but cling tenaciously to life.
This is a great delusion. I have put in the strongest terms the
complaints of Substance and Shadow and then, to resolve the
matter, have made Spirit the spokesman for naturalness. Those
who share my tastes will all get what I am driving at.

I

Substance to Shadow

Earth and heaven endure forever,
Streams and mountains never change.
Plants observe a constant rhythm,
Withered by frost, by dew restored.
But man, most sentient being of all,   5
In this is not their equal.
He is present here in the world today,
Then leaves abruptly, to return no more.
No one marks there's one man less—
Not even friends and family think of him;   10
The things that he once used are all that's left
To catch their eye and move them to grief.
I have no way to transcend change,
That it must be, I no longer doubt.
I hope you will take my advice: 15
When wine is offered, don't refuse.

II

Shadow to Substance

No use discussing immortality
when just to keep alive is hard enough.
Of course I want to roam in paradise,
But it's a long way there and the road is lost.

In all the time since I met up with you   5
We never differed in our grief and joy.
In shade we may have parted for a time,
But sunshine always brings us close again.
Still this union cannot last forever—
Together we will vanish into darkness.   10
The body goes; that fame should also end
Is a thought that makes me burn inside.
Do good, and your love will outlive you;
Surely this is worth your every effort.
While it is true, wine may dissolve care   15
That is not so good a way as this.

III
Spirit's Solution

The Great Potter cannot intervene—
All creation thrives of itself.
That Man ranks with Earth and Heaven
Is it not because of me?
Though we belong to different orders,   5
Being alive, I am joined to you.
Bound together for god or ill
I cannot refuse to tell you what I know:
The Three August Ones were great saints
But where are they living today?   10
Though P'eng-tsu lasted a long time
He still had to go before he was ready.
Die old or die young, the death is the same,
Wise or stupid, there is no difference.
Drunk every day you may forget,   15
But won't it shorten your life span?
Doing good is always a joyous thing
But no one has to praise you for it.
Too much thinking harms my life;
Just surrender to the cycle of things,   20

give yourself to the waves of the Great Change
Neither happy nor yet afraid.
And when it is time to go, then simply go
Without any unnecessary fuss.

(Tr. James Robert Hightower)

From Twenty Poems After Drinking Wine
Preface

Living in retirement here I have few pleasures, and now the nights are growing longer; so, as I happen to have some excellent wine, not an evening passes without a drink. All alone with my shadow I empty a bottle until suddenly I find myself drunk. And once I am drunk I write a few verses for my own amusement. In the course of time the pages have multiplied, but there is no particular sequence in what I have written. I have had a friend make a copy, with no more in mind than to provide a diversion.

I

Decline and growth have no fixed time,
Everyone gets his share of both:
Master Shao of the melon patch
Used to be Lord of Tungling.
Cold weather alternated with hot   5
And so it is with human lives—
Intelligent men understand
And are beset no more with doubts.
When chance brings them a jug of wine
They take it gladly as night comes on.   10

III

The Way has declined almost a thousand years
And all men now hold back their impulses.
Give them wine, and they refuse to drink,

All they care for it their reputation
Whatever gives the body any value   5
Is it not just this one single life?
but how long is a lifetime after all?
It is brief as the startling lightening bolt.
Staid and stolid through their hundred years
What do they ever hope to get from this?   10

IV

Anxious, seeking, the bird lost from the flock—
The sun declines, and still he flies alone,
Back and forth without a place to rest;
From night to night, his cry becomes more sad,
A piercing sound of yearning for the dawn.   5
So far from home, with nothing for support
Until at last he finds the lonely pine
And folds his wings at this his journey's end.
In that harsh wind no tree can keep its leaves
This is the only shade that will not fail.   10
The bird has refuge here and resting place,
And in a thousand years will never leave.

V

I built my hut beside a traveled road
Yet hear no noise of passing carts and horses.
You would like to know how it is done?
With the mind detached, one's place becomes remote.
Picking chrysanthemums by the eastern hedge   5
I catch sight of the distant southern hills:
The mountain air is lovely as the sun sets
And flocks of flying birds return together.
In these things is a fundamental truth
I would like to tell, but lack the words.   10

VII

The fall chrysanthemums have lovely colors.
I pluck the petals that are wet with dew
And float them in this Care Dispelling Thing
To strengthen my resolve to leave the world.
I drink my solitary cup alone   5
And when it's empty, pour myself another.
The sun goes down, and all of nature rests
Homing birds fly chirping toward the grove.

(Tr. James Robert Hightower)

Passing Ch'ien-hsi as Military Adviser
in the Third Month of the Year Yi-ssu [405]

I don't travel much in these parts:
The months and years—how they've piled up.
Dawn to dusk, I see mountains and streams,
Everything just as they were before.
fine rain awash on tall groves,
Fresh wind riffling through cloud-feathers.
That's what I see: things as they are;
A fair wind doesn't cut everyone off,
And so, what about me?
Plodding along, tied down to this post: 10
A body, it seems, with no will of its own,
A simple soul that no one can change.
Fields and gardens daily haunt my dreams—
How long must one remain abroad?
My hope is forever in a boat bound for home,
And my happiness among the frost-nipped juniper.

(Tr. Eugene Eoyang)

Miscellaneous Poems, Six Selections

[1]

A man has no roots.
Blown about—like dust on the road,
In all directions, he tumbles with the wind:
Our lives are brief enough.
We come into this world as brothers and sisters:
But why must we be tied to flesh and blood?
Let's enjoy our happiness:
Here's a jug of wine, call in the neighbors.
The best times don't come often:
Each day dawns only once.   10
The seasons urge us on—
Time waits for no man.

[2]

Bright sun lights out over the western bank,
Pale moon comes out from behind the eastern ridge.
Far-reaching, this million-mile brilliance;
Transcendent, this scene in space.
A breeze comes through the window in my room.
At night the mat and pillow are cold.
The weather shifts: I sense the seasons change;
Unable to sleep, I know how long the night is.
I'd like to say something, but no one's around,
So I raise my cup, and toast my own shadow.   10
Days and months pass by—
One cannot keep pace with ambition.
Thinking these thoughts, I am depressed;
Right through till dawn, I find rest impossible.

[3]

Bright blossoms seldom last long;
Life's ups-and downs can't be charted.
What was a lotus flower in spring,
Is now the seed-husk of autumn.
Severe frost freezes the wild grass:
Decay has yet to finish it off.
Sun and moon come back once more,
But where I go, no sun will shine.
I look back longingly on times gone by—
Remembering the past wounds my soul.   10

[4]

A noble ambition spans the four seas;
Mine is simpler: not to grow old.
I'd like my family all in one place,
My sons and grandsons all caring for each other.
I want a goblet and a lute to greet each day,
And my wine casks never to run dry.
Belt loosened, I drink pleasure to the dregs:
I rise late, and retire early.
How can today be compared to yesterday?
My heart harbored both ice and coal.   10
In time, ashes return to ashes, dust to dust—
And vain is the way of fame and glory.

[5]

When I was young and in my prime,
If times were sad, I was happy on my own.
With brave plans that went beyond the sea,
I spread my wings, and dreamt of great flights.
But the course of time has run me down,
And my zest for life has begun to wane.
Enjoyment no longer makes me happy,
Each and every thing means more worry.

My strength is beginning to peter out,
I sense the change: one day's not like the last.   10
The hurrying barge can't wait for a moment:
It pulls me along and gives no rest.
The road ahead: how much farther?
I don't know where I will come to rest.
The ancients begrudged a shadow's inch-of-time:
Whin I think of this, it makes me shudder.

[6]

Years ago, when I heard the words of my elders,
I'd cover my ears, not liking what they said.
Now that I am fifty years old,
These things suddenly matter.
To recapture the joys of my youth—
Does not appeal to me in the slightest.
Going, going, it's very quickly gone.
Who ever lives this life twice?
Let's use the household money for entertainment,
Before the years catch up with us.   10
I have children, but no money left:
No use leaving post-mortem trusts.

(Tr. Eugene Eoyang)

Shen Yüeh (441-512)

"Four Recollections"[1]

I recall the times she came,
Radiantly treading up the steps,
Tenderly telling what it was to be parted,
Gravely protesting how she missed me,
How our visits were all too short,
How seeing me made her forget her hunger.

I recall the times she sat,
A tiny thing before the silk-gauze screen:
Now singing four or five refrains,
Or playing twice or thrice upon the strings.   10
When laughing she was quite beyond compare,
When vexed, more lovable than ever.

I recall the times she ate,
Above the dishes changing her expression,
Starting to sit and then too shy to sit,
Starting to eat and then too shy to eat,
Holding small morsels in her mouth as if not hungry,
Raising her cup like one who'd lost her strength.

And I recall the times she slept,
With others sleeping, forcing herself to stay awake: 20
Untying her gauze dress, not waiting to be coaxed,
But on the pillow once more needing to be led,
Distrustful lest the one beside her see,
Sweetly ashamed before the candlelight!

(Tr. Richard B. Mather)

1. The original title is "Six Recollections" (*Liu-yi-shih*), but with only four stanzas extant.

The Fishing Rod

My cassia boat, adrift and free,
Past verdant banks winds in and out.
Light silken line stirs tender water plants,
While muffled oars arouse a lone wild duck.
Tapping the gunwales heedless of the sunset
To my last years I will make this my pleasure!

(Tr. Richard B. Mather)

I Say Goodby to Fan An-ch'eng

In the usual way of the young
    we made appointments
and goodby was easy.
Now in our decay and fragility,
separation is difficult.

Don't say "One cup of wine."
Tomorrow will we hold this cup?
And if in dreams I can't find this road,
how, thinking of you,
    will I be comforted?

(Tr. Lenore Mayhew and William McNaughton)

Wang Fan-chih (590?-660?)

No One Lives Past a Hundred

No one lives past a hundred:
Why not write immortal rhymes.
Forge iron to fence off evil—
Demons just watch: clap hands and laugh.

I Saw Another Man Die

I saw another man die:
My stomach burned like fire.
Not that I felt sorry for him:
I was afraid I'd be next.

(Tr. Eugene Eoyang)

Han Shan (date uncertain)

Four Untitled Poems

[1]

Parrots dwell in the west country.
Foresters catch them with nets, to bring them to us.
Lovely women toy with them, morning and evening,
As they go to and from their courtyard pavilions.

They are given lordly gifts of golden cages—for their own storage!
Bolted in—their feathered coats are spoiled.
How unlike both swan and crane:
Wind-swirled and tossed, they fly off into the clouds!

[2]

Swine gobble dead men's flesh.
Men gobble dead pigs' guts.
Swine do not disdain the smell of men.
Men even talk about the scent of pork.

But—
Should a pig die—it is cast into the water.
Should a man die—the soil is dug to hide him.
Then—
Neither finds the one or the other to his taste.
Yet—
Lotus flowers wll live in boiling water!

(Tr. Edward H. Schafer)

[3]

Man lives his life in a dust bowl,
Just like vermin in the middle of a pot:
All day going round and round,
Never getting out from the inside.
Blessedness is not our lot:
Only nettlesomeness without end.
Time is like a flowing river—
One day, we wake up old men.

[4]

There is a poetaster named Wang
Who laughs at my much-flawed verse.
He says: "This line sounds waspish"[1]
And:"That line runs on knobby knees."[2]
"You have no command of versification,
But put words willy-nilly on the page."
I laugh and say: "The poetry *you* write
Is like a blind man faintly praising the sun!"

(Tr. Eugene Eoyang)

1. Literally, "wasps' waists," referring to one of the "eight blemishes" in the composition of poetry, in which the second and fourth words in the line have the same tone, according to Shen Yüeh's principles of prosody.
2. Literally, "stork's knees," referring to another of the "eight blemishes," in which the fifth and fifteenth words have the same tone.

Ch'ang Chien (fl.749)

A Visit to the Broken Hill Temple

At the break of day I come to an old temple,
As the first rays of the sun glow on the treetops.
A path in the bamboo grove leads to a quiet retreat—
A meditation hall hidden behind flowering boughs.
Here, mountain scenery delights the birds,
And the reflections in the pond empty a man's mind.
All murmurings are stilled in this presence,
But for the echoes of chimes and bells.

(Tr. Joseph J. Lee)

Li Po (701-762)

Calling on a Taoist Priest in Tai-t'ien Mountain
but Failing to See Him

A dog barks amid the sound of water;
Peach blossoms tinged by dew take on a deeper tone.
In the dense woods at times I see deer;
By the brook I hear no bells at noon.
Wild bamboos divide the blue haze;
Tumbling waterfalls hang from the green cliff.
No one can tell me where you are,
Saddened, I lean against the pines.

(Tr. Joseph J. Lee)

At Yellow Crane Tower Taking Leave of Meng Hao-jan as He Sets off for Kuang-ling

(The poet Meng Hao-jan [689-740] parted from Li Po at Yellow Crane Tower, overlooking the Yangtze at Wu-ch'ang in Hupei, to sail east down the river to Yang-chou in Kiangsu.)

My Old friend takes leave of the west at Yellow Crane Tower,
in misty third-month blossoms goes downstream to Yang-chou.
The far-off shape of his lone sail disappears in the blue-green
void, and all I see is the long river flowing to the edge of the sky.

(Tr. Burton Watson)

"They Fought South of the Walls"

Last year we fought
At the source of the Sang-kan River[1]:
this year we campaign
On the road to Ts'ung-ho.[2]
We wash our weapons in the waters of the T'iao-chih Sea[3]:
And graze our horses on the grass in T'ien Shan's[4] snow.
Fighting and more fighting for ten thousand miles,
Until the soldiers all grow weak and old.
The Tartars live on killing and slaughter;
Since of old there have been white bones in the yellow sands.   10
Where the Ch'in built a wall[5] to keep out the Tartars,
The Han still light a beacon fire.
Beacon fires are lit without cease,
And fighting goes on without end;
Men die in the wilds,
and horses of the vanquished wail mournfully towards the sky.

1. A major battle was fought in 742 on Sang-kan River south of Ta-t'ung, Shansi.
2. Ts'ung-ho, or Ts'ung-ling-ho, is a river in Sinkiang which a T'ang expedition crossed in 746.
3. T'iao-chih refers broadly to the region in modern Iran.
4. See Li Po's "Moon over Mountain Pass."
5. I.e., The Great Wall of China.

Vultures feed on human guts,
Carry them flying, then leave them hanging on withered
               mulberry branches.
Soldiers fall, their blood smearing grass and bushes;
The generals have striven in vain.   20
How well we know the curse of war;
May the wise rulers follow it only as the last recourse!

                                      (Tr. Joseph J. Lee)

Written in Behalf of My Wife

To cleave a running stream with a sword,
The water will never be severed.
My thoughts that follow you in your wanderings
Are as interminable as the stream.
Since we parted, the grass before our gate
In the autumn lane has turned green in spring.
I sweep it away but it grows back,
Densely it covers your footprints.
The singing phoenixes were happy together;
Startled, the male and the female each flies away.   10
On which mountaintop have the drifting clouds stayed?
Once gone, they never are seen to return.
From a merchant traveling to Ta-lou,
I learn you are there at Autumn Cove.
In the Liang Garden[1] I sleep in an empty embroidered bed;
On the Yang Terrace you dream of the drifting rain.[2]
Three times my family has produced a prime minister;
Then moved to west Ch'in since our decline.
We still have our old flutes and songs,
Their sad notes heard everywhere by neighbors.   20
When the music rises to the purple clouds,
I cry for the absence of my beloved.

1. A region in southeastern Honan.
2. Yang Terrace refers to the general area on the Yangtze. The line alludes not only to Li'Po's whereabouts, but also to Sung Yü's "Shen-nü Fu."

I am like a peach tree at the bottom of a well,
For whom will the blossoms smile?
You are like the moon high in the sky,
Unwilling to cast your light on me.
I cannot recognize myself when I look in the mirror,
I must have grown thin since you left home.
If only I could own the fabled parrot
To tell you of the feelings in my heart!

(Tr. Joseph J. Lee)

Tu Fu (712-770)

The Elegant Women

On the third day of the third month, in fresh weather,
The elegant women of the capital stroll on the riverbank—
Their manner regal and remote, their faces delicate,
their figures shapely and pleasing.
Wrapped in filmy silks bright with peacocks and silver unicorns,
They illumine the spring evening.
What do they wear in their hair?
The hummingbird headdress with jade leaves dangling
Past their lips.
What do you see upon their shoulders?
Capes with crushed pearls at their waists that cling
To their bodies.   10
One even glimpses from time to time,
Glittering beneath the canopies of the empresses' pavilion,
Those great ladies of the empire, Kuo and Ch'in.

Purple steak from the camel's hump broiled in a glistening pan
And the white flesh of fish are set out in rows of crystal dishes.
But the satiated ones stay their rhinoceros chopsticks,

And morsels minced by belled knives lie untouched.
Yet still the palace eunuchs arrive.
They rein in their horses without so much as stirring dust,
And set before the guests food rare as jewels
Brought from the eight corners of the earth.
The music of pipes and drums, strange enough to move the dead,
Accompanies the feast. A vast retinue blocks the main road.
Then in measured paces a saddled horse arrives;
The rider dismounts and enters on embroidered carpets.
Willow-down drifts like snow, masking white duckweed flowers;
And a bluebird flies off with a scarlet kerchief in his beak.
Be careful! So great is his power, his lightest touch can burn.
Do not approach the prime minister too close.
He may be angry.

(Tr. Mark Perlberg)

Moonlight Night

(Written in 756 when Tu Fu had been taken prisoner by the rebels and
was held captive in Ch'ang-an. His wife and family were at Fu-chou
to the north.)

From her room in Fu-chou tonight
all alone she watches the moon.
Far away, I grieve that her children
can't understand why she thinks of Ch'ang-an.
Fragrant mist in her cloud hair damp,
clear lucence on her jade arms cold —
when will we lean by chamber curtains
and let it light the two of us, our tear stains dried?

(Tr. Burton Watson)

Random Pleasures: Nine Quatrains

[1]

See a traveler in sorrow: deeper is his grief
As wanton spring steals into the river pavilion—
True, the flowers will rush to open,
Yet how the orioles will keep up their songs.

[2]

Those peach and plum trees planted by hand are not without
  a master:
The rude wall is low; still it's my home.
But 'tis just like the spring wind, that master bully:
Last night it blew so many blossomed branches down.

[3]

How well they know my study's low and small—
The swallows from the riverside find reason to visit me often:
Carrying mud to spot and spoil my lute and books,
And trailing a flight of gnats that strike my face.

[4]

March is gone, and April's come:
Old fellow, how many more chances to welcome the spring?
Don't think of the endless affairs beyond the hereafter;
Just drain your lifetime's few allotted cups.

[5]

Heartbroken—there springtime river trickles to its end:
Cane in hand, I slowly pace and stand on fragrant bank.
How impertinent the willow catkins to run off with the wind;
So fickle, the peach blossoms to drift with the stream!

[6]

I've grown so indolent I never leave the village;
At dusk I shout to the boy to shut the rustic gate.
Green moss, raw wine, calm in the grove;
Blue water, spring breeze, dusk on the land.

[7]

Path-strewn catkins spread out a white carpet;
Stream-dotting lotus leaves mound up green coins.
By the bamboo roots, a young pheasant unseen;
On the sandbank, ducklings by their mother, asleep.

[8]

West of my house, young mulberry leaves are ready for picking;
along the river, new wheat, so tender and soft.
How much more is left of life when spring has turned to
                                        summer?
Don't pass up good wine, sweeter than honey.

[9]

The willows by the gate are slender and graceful
Like the waist of a girl at fifteen.
Morning came, and who could fail to see
Mad wind had snapped the longest branch.

(Tr. Irving Y. Lo)

No Word

Haven't seen my friend Li Po for some time:
It's really too bad, his feigning madness.
The whole world would want him executed,
Save I who cherish his abilities.

A thousand fine and spirited poems he's written,
With a cup of wine, and wandering in solitude.
Here I am in K'uang Shan,[1] where he used to study:
He'd do worse than come back—now that his hair's turned white.

(Tr. Eugene Eoyang)

1. In the region of Shu, north of Mien-chou. Tu Fu had moved to
Ch'eng-tu in Szechwan at the very end of 759. William Hung
conjectures that this poem may have been written during the
farewell parties given in honor of his friend Yen Wu, who was
being summoned to the capital by the new emperor, Tai-tsung.

I Spend the Night in a Room by the River

Darkness still shadows the mountain road
As I gaze from my study above the water gate.
Streamers of cloud seem to rest upon the brow of a cliff,
While the lonely moon tumbles among the waves.
A line of cranes winds overhead in silent flight.
Below, a pack of wolves quarrels over food.
I am grieved by the war and have not slept.
Who has the strength to right heaven and earth?

(Tr. Mark Perlberg)

A Traveler at Night Writes His Thoughts

Delicate grasses, faint wind on the bank;
stark mast, a lone night boat:
stars hang down, over broad fields sweeping;
the moon boils up, on the great river flowing.
Fame—how can my writings win me that?
Office—age and sickness have brought it to an end.
Fluttering, fluttering—where is my likeness?
Sky and earth and one sandy gull.

(Tr. Burton Watson)

Ku K'uang (725?-ca. 814)

Upon a Brook

A girl gathering lotus upon a brook,
Timid in a tiny boat that shifts in the wind,
Startles a pair of mallards from their sleep;
Water clouds are splattered red.

(Tr. Irving Y. Lo)

Meng Chiao (751-814)

Lament for Lu Yin

Poets are usually pure, rugged,
Die from hunger, cling to desolate mountains.
Since this white cloud had no master,
When it flew off, its mind was free from care.
After long sickness, a corpse on a bed,
The servant boy too weak to manage the funeral.
Your old books, all gnawed by famished rats,
Lie strewn and scattered in your single room.
As you go off to the land of new ghosts,
I look on your features white as old jade.   10
I am ashamed that, when you enter the earth,
No one calls after you, to hold you back.
All the springs lament for you in vain.
As the day lengthens, murmuring waters mourn.

(Tr. Stephen Owen)

Han Yü (768-824)

Poem on Losing One's Teeth

Last year I lost an incisor
and this year a molar, and now
half a dozen more teeth fall out
all at once—and that's
not the end of it either.
The rest are all loose, and I know
there's no end till they're all gone.
The first one, I thought
what a shame for that obscene gap!

Two or three, and I thought
I was falling apart, almost
at death's door. Before, when one
loosened, I quaked and hoped
wildly it "wouldn't." The
gaps made it hard to chew
and with a loose tooth I'd
rinse my mouth gingerly.
Then when at last it fell out
it felt like a mountain collapsing.
But now I've got use to this
Nothing earthshaking. I've
still twenty left, though I know
one by one they'll all go.
But at one tooth per year it will
take me two decades, and gone,
all gone, will it matter
they went one by one
and not all at the same time?
People say when your teeth go
it's certain the end's near.
But seems to me life has
its limits, you die when you die
either with our without teeth.
They also say gaps scare
the people who see you. Well
two views to everything
as Chuang Tzu noted: A blasted
tree need not necessarily
be cut down, though geese
that don't hiss be slaughtered.[1]

1. Chuang Tzu saw a huge tree which the woodsman would not take because its wood was useless. Chuang Tzu said, "This tree is useless, thus it can live its natural life." Chuang Tzu then visited a friend and stayed at his house. The friend ordered a boy to slaughter a goose for the meal. One of the geese could sing and the other could not. The boy asked which goose to slaughter; the friend said, "Kill the one that cannot sing."

For the toothless who mumble
silence has its advantage, and
those who can't chew will find
soft food tastes better. This is a poem
I chanted and wrote
to startle my wife and children.

(Tr. Kenneth O. Hanson)

The Pond in a Bowl, Five Poems

[1]

In old age
I'm back
to childhood pleasures.

A bowl in the ground
Just add water—
it's a pool!

Throughout the night
frogs croaked
till it dawned,

as they did
when I fished
as a child at Feng-k'ou.

[2]

Who says
you can't make a pond
out of a bowl?

The lotus sprig
I planted not long ago
has already grown full size.

Don't forget,
if it rains
stop in for a visit.

Together we'll
listen to raindrops splash
on all the green leaves.

[3]

Come morning,
the water brightens
as if by magic.

One moment alive
with thousands of bugs
too small to have names,

Next moment
they're gone,
leaving no trace,

Only the small fish
this way and that
swim in formations.

[4]

Does the bowl
in the garden
mock nature

when night after night
green frogs gather
to prove it's a pool?

If you choose to come
and keep me company
need you fill

the dark with noise
and endless squabble
like husband and wife?

[5]

Say the bright pond
mirrors the sky
both blue.

If I pour
water, the pond
brims.

Let night
deepen
the moon go

how many stars
shine back
from the water!

(Tr. Kenneth O. Hanson)

Po Chü-yi (772-846)

The Old Man of Hsin-feng with the Broken Arm[1]

An old man from Hsin-feng, eighty-eight years old,
Hair on his temples and his eyebrows white as snow.
Leaning on his great-great-grandson, he walks to the front
       of the inn,
His left arm on the boy's shoulder, his right arm broken.
I ask the old man how long has his arm been broken,
and how it came about, how it happened.
The old man said he grew up in the Hsin-feng district.
He was born during blessed time, without war or strife,
And he used to listen to the singing and dancing in the
       Pear Garden,
Knew nothing of banner and spear, or bow and arrow.   10
Then, during the T'ien-pao period, a big army was recruited:
From each family, one was taken out of every three,
And of those chosen, where were they sent?
Five months, ten thousand miles away, to Yunnan,
where, it is said, the Lu River runs,
Where, when flowers fall from pepper trees, noxious fumes rise;
Where, when a great army fords the river, with its seething
       eddies,
Two or three out of ten never reach the other side.

The village, north and south, was full of the sound of wailing,
Sons leaving father and mother, husbands leaving wives.   20
They all said, of those who went out to fight the barbarians,
Not one out of a thousand lived to come back.
At the time, this old man was twenty-four,
And the army had his name on their roster.

---

1. Author's subtitle: To Warn Against Militarism: "New Music
Bureau Ballads" (Hsin Yüeh-fu), No. 9. Each poem in Po Chü-
yi's "New Music Bureau Ballads" carries a similar subtitle,
which states the moral implied.

"Then, late one night, not daring to let anyone know,
By stealth, I broke my arm, smashed it with a big stone.
Now I was unfit to draw the bow or carry the flag,
and I would be spared the fighting in Yunnan.
Bone shattered, muscles ached, it wasn't unpainful,
But I could count on being rejected and sent home.   30

"This arm has been broken now for over sixty years:
I've lost one limb, but the body's intact.
Even now, in cold nights, when the wind and rain blow,
Right up to daybreak, I hurt so much I cannot sleep,
But I have never had any regrets.
At least, now I alone have survived.
Or else, years ago at the River Lu,
I would have died, my spirit fled, and my bones left to rot:
I would have wandered, a ghost in Yunnan looking for home,
Mourning over the graves of ten thousands."   40

So the old man spoke: I ask you to listen.
Have you not heard the Prime Minister of the K'ai-yüan period,
    Sung K'ai-fu?
How he wouldn't reward frontier campaigns, not wanting to
            glorify war?
And, have you not heard of Yang Kuo-chung, the Prime Minister
            of the T'ien-pao period,
Wishing to seek favor, achieved military deeds at the frontier,
But, before he could pacify the frontier, the people became
            disgruntled:
Ask the old man of Hsin-feng with the broken arm!

                              (Tr. Eugene Eoyang)

Reading the Collected Works of Li Po and Tu Fu:
A Colophon

The time the Hanlin scholar was south of the River,[1]
The junior official made his home in Szechwan.[2]
You two never held any high rank or position,
Still you met with turmoil and hardship.
The remorse of a wanderer in the evening of his life;
The laments of a banished Muse in this floating world—
Both your songs and rhymes will last a thousand ages,
Your fame and renown will move the barbarians.
The learned world draws on your elegant lines,
The Music Bureau[3] awaits your new verses.   10
Heaven's wish you certainly have fulfilled:
For all people love great poetry.

(Tr. Irving Y. Lo)

1. Referring to the time when Li Po was on the staff of Prince Yung (Li Lin), whose rebellion against the throne implicated the poet.
2. Referring to the time Tu Fu was living in Szechwan after the An Lu-shan rebellion and served on the staff of Governor General Yen Wu.
3 *Yüeh-fu* ("Music Bureau") poetry, which generally contains social criticism, was always regarded by Po Chü-yi as in the mainstream of Chinese poetic tradition.

Li Shang-yin (813?-858)

For Lotus Flower[1]

Leaves and flowers are never rated the same:
Flowers put into pots of gold, leaves turn to dust.
Still there are the green foliage and the red blooms.
Folded, stretched out, open or closed: all naturally beautiful.
These flowers, these leaves, long mirror each other's glory:
When their greens pale, their reds fade—it's more than one can
bear.

(Tr. Eugene Eoyang and Irving Y. Lo)

Lu Kuei-meng (?-c. 881)

Fisherman on a Southern Stream

I'm naturally lazy, carefree;
A secluded spot is what I like.
River flows north of the village;
Heart craves for aimless wanderings.
My rustic house far away from others,
Lonely and isolated, myself given to loftiness:
Going out, I first grip a bamboo staff;
Meeting people, I do not bother with a hat.[1]

On the southern stream is a fisherman
Who frequently takes children to visit me.
I asked him how he fished.
He answered truly in words of wisdom:

10

1. Possibly intended for a woman.

1. Officials wore hats. Lu means that he is far from centers of
bureaucratic activity.

"From the start, I've speared fish and turtles,
Since I was a lad, right through to old age.
Their hideouts are second nature to me;
Thoroughly I know the secrets.
So I'd warn my people:
Heaven's gifts are not be be abused.
Reckon carefully: whether to spare or to kill the big or the small;
Wait for them to grow, multiply, and reap the reward.   20
All day I hunt fish for profit
And yet fish have never been exhausted."

We are housed together between sky and earth,
To abandon benevolence is to wrong heaven's bounties.
When I think of government officials,
I feel, this idea is hard for them to grasp.
People all die from extortion and fleecing,
None willing to show them pity or grief.
This year, rivers and marshes go dry;
Last season, mountain springs flooded.   30
Pleas and complaints fill the court:
Like the cawing of birds to my ears.
As (for instance) in the raising of chickens and ducks,
Surely you'll let them lay eggs and brood.
Mencius ridiculed the Man of Sun,[2]
Blaming him for hastiness in tugging rice sprouts.
I admire the fisherman's wise words,
In harmony with the teaching of the sages.
If I meet an official who collects poetry,
I'll dare to show him, in all sincerity, this little piece.   40

(Tr. Robin D. S. Yates)

2.Mencius, a late fourth-century B.C. Confucian philosopher,
tells a story about a man who pulled at his rich shoots because
he was worried at their slow growth. He states that one should
let all things take their natural course.

Ku Hsiung (fl. 928)

Tune: "Telling of Innermost Feelings"

In the endless night, having deserted me, where have you gone?
    No news of your coming!
    My perfumed chamber closed.
        My eyebrows knit—
    The moon is about to set.
How can you bear not to seek me?
    How lonely in my quilt!
Only if you bartered your heart for mine
    Would you know how much I miss you![1]

                 (Tr. James J. Y. Liu)

Li Yü (937-978)

Tune:"Crows Crying at Night" (*Wu yeh t'i*)

The spring scarlet of the forest blossoms fades and falls
    Too soon, too soon;
There is no escape from the cold rain of morning, the wind at
                     dusk.

    The tears on your rouged cheeks
    Keep us drinking together,
    For when shall we meet again?—
Thus the eternal sorrows of human life, like great rivers
    flowing ever east.

                 (Tr. Daniel Bryant)

1. The last two lines remind one of Sir Philip Sidney's famous poem "My true love hath my heart, and I have his," but while Sidney's poem rests on a rhetorical conceit intellectually worked out, the present poem is a passionate cry, moving in its simplicity and naiveté. Cf. Wang Kuo-wei, *Jen-chien Tz'u-hua* (with notes by Hsü Tiao-fu, Peking. 1955), p. 47.

Tune: "The Beautiful Lady Yü (*Yü Méi-jen*)

Spring blooms, autumn moon, when will they end?
How many yesterdays have passed?
Last night, at my little pavilion, the east wind again!
Oh, lost country, when moon is bright, I can't bear to
    look back.

Carved balustrades, marmorean stairs no doubt will stand;
Only the once bright faces have changed.
Ask the sum of grief there's to bear,
It's just a river in full spring flood flowing east to sea.

(Tr. Eugene Eoyang)

Wang Yü-ch'eng (954-1001)

Song of the Crow Pecking at My Scarred Donkey

Old crow of Shang Mountain, you are cruel!
Beak longer than a spike, sharper than an arrow.
Go gather bugs or peck at eggs—
Why must you harm this poor scarred beast of mine?
Since I was exiled to Shang-yu last year
There has only been this one lame donkey to move my things.
We climbed the Ch'in Mountains and the Ch'an to get here;
He carried a hundred volumes for me on his back.
The ropes cut his skin to the spine: the scar reached his belly;
Now with half a year's healing he's nearly well again.   10
But yesterday the crow suddenly swooped down
And pecked through his wound to get the living flesh.
The donkey brayed, my servant cried out and the crow flew
                        away!
Perched on the roof he preened his feathers and scraped his beak.
There was nothing my donkey and my servant could do

Without a crossbow to shoot or nets to spread.
But Shang Mountain has many birds of prey;
I'll ask your neighbor to lend me his autumn hawk:
With claws of iron and hooked talons
He'll snap the crow's neck and feed on this brain!
And this won't serve only to fill his empty gut;
No! It's revenge for my donkey's pain.

(Tr. Jonathan Chaves)

Mei Yao-ch'en (1002 -1060)

Elegy for a White Cock

White cock in my courtyard,
feathers white as white lard:
wild dogs were his daily fear;
malicious foxes never worried him.
Evenings, he'd roost in a nook in the eaves;
mornings, he'd peck by the foot of the stairs.
He crew before all the other birds,
even in wind and rain.
My granaries were running low
but I always gave him rice to eat.   10
Last night when the sky turned black,
a creature of darkness prowled and spied.
Stealthily it seized the cock—
I only heard the squawks of pain.
When I came to the rescue through the gate,
it was already past the eastern wall.
At the sound of my shouts, not daring to eat,
it dropped the cock and made its escape.
Throat covered with gushing blood,
the cock gasped for air on the brink of death.   20

Brilliant white breast stained deep vermilion,
frosty pinions broken and torn.
Compassionate, I wished him to live,
but his head was crushed and could not be healed.
I'll accept his fate and bury him;
who could bear to use cinnamon and ginger on him now?
Still I see his scattered feathers
floating, dancing with the breath of the wind.
I remember when he first came to this place,
how many favors he received: 30
he never had to fear the block,
and never passed his days in hunger.
Why did he meet this vicious beast?
Who ever thought he'd be destroyed!
Though this may be a trifling matter,
a deeper meaning may be discerned:
Mr. Teng[1] could coin a mountain of cash,
but starved to death in the end.
Such too, then, is the way of man—
I bow my head, full of sorrow.   40

(Tr. Jonathan Chaves)

1. Alluding to the story of Teng T'ung (fl. second century B.C.), an official of the Former Han dynasty and a favorite of Emperor Wen, who bestowed on him a mountain rich in copper ore in Szechwan, from which he could coin money. But Teng incurred the displeasure of the next emperor. His wealth was confiscated and he died of starvation.

Su Shun-ch'in (1008-1048)

Summertime

Behind secluded screens the hush of daytime scenes:
Breezes stir quietly at the bamboo weathercock,
In the lush green pond, fish lay golden roe,
In a shady yard a swallow guides her chicks.
Children squabble over dates fallen in the rain,
Under a clear sky my visitor helps me dry worm-eaten books:
Even this cozy nook is not free from dusty care;
To let things go, make do with a bowl of wine.

(Tr. Michael E Workman)

Wang An-shih (1021-1086)

Written on the Wall of Halfway Mountain Temple

Cold, we sit in the warmth,
hot, we walk in the cool:
everything is nothing but Buddha,
and Buddha is everything.

(Tr. Jan W. Walls)

Huang T'ing-chien (1045-1105)

Tune: "Pleasure of Returning to the Fields: A Prelude"
(*Kuei-t'ien-lo yin*)

Fine view, but I'm still getting thinner.
How I've been toyed with by this man.
    I too have a heart!
    He misses me and calls me;
    When he sees me, he scolds me:
Heavens, how can one put up with this!

We were lucky to have been so thick;
Now, before the winecups, I knit my brows again.
    This man wonders why!
He wronged me and made me give way to him.
    So let it go! I don't care!
    This time it's really all over!
But when we meet, it's just the same as before.

                    (Tr. James J. Y. Liu)

Li Ch'ing-chao (1084?-ca. 1151)

Tune: "Telling of Innermost Feelings"

Night found me so flushed with wine;
    I was slow to undo my hair.
The plum petals still stuck onto a dying branch.
Waking up, the scent of wine stirred me from spring sleep;
    my dream once broken, there was no going back.

    Now it's quiet,
    the moon hovers above,

the kingfisher blinds are drawn.
Still: I feel the fallen petals;
still: I touch their lingering scent;
still: I hold onto a moment of time.

(Tr. Eugene Eoyang)

Yang Wan-li (1124-1206)

Replying to a Poem by Li T'ien-lin

Writing poetry needs a mind that's nimble and free;
Thus even casual lines may appear sublime.
No cassock-and-bowl can be handed down for a thousand ages,[1]
Whether a hill or a feather it demands equal care.[2]
Sometimes as natural as a pond with spring grass[3];
Other words suggest dust-clouded eyes.[4]
How delicious is the taste of a good poem?
—Like that of a frosty crab, slightly wine-cured.

(Tr. Sherwin S. S. Fu)

1. According to the Buddhist tradition, the robe and the bowl were handed down generation after generation as insignia of the patriarch's authority.
2. I.e., an accomplished poet can handle everything with equal ease and felicity. To him a hill would seem just as light as a feather.
3. Alluding to Hsieh Ling-yün's celebrated line: "Spring grass grows by the pool," a verse much admired by critics for its freshness and spontaneity.
4. The image of dust-clouded eyes is derived from the Chuang-tzu, where the sages are described as having dust-clouded eyes when they gaze at and worry about the world.

Master Liu Painted a Portrait of Me in My Old Age and Asked me to Write a Poem About the Picture

Few hairs, made fewer by the comb;
short mustache, made shorter by the tweezers—
scratching my hair, and twisting my moustache,
when will I ever stop looking for poems!

(Tr. Jonathan Chaves)

Lu Yu (1125-1210)

In a Boat on a Summer Evening, I Heard the Cry of a Water Bird. It Was Very Sad and Seemed to Be Saying, "Madam Is Cruel! Moved, I Wrote This Poem.[1]

A girl grows up hidden in innermost rooms,
no glimpse of what may lie beyond her wall and hedge.
Then she climbs the carriage, moves to her new lord's home;
father and mother become strangers to her then.
"I was stupid, to be sure, yet I knew
that Madam, my mother-in-law, must be obeyed.
  Out of bed with the first cock's crowing ,
  I combed and bound my hair, put on blouse and skirt.
  I did my work, tidied the hall, sprinkling and sweeping,
  in the kitchen fixed their plates of food.   10
  Green green the mallows and goosefoot I gathered—

---

1. In this poem, written in 1183, Lu Yu employs a narrative framework—and the sound of the water bird's cry, *ku-wu* (which the poet transcribed by the two words meaning "Madam is cruel")—to recall a personal experience. Lu Yu married his first wife when he was about twenty and divorced her shortly thereafter, apparently because his mother found fault with the girl, whom he was very fond of; he wrote of her often in his poems.

too bad I couldn't make them taste like bear's paws.[2]
  When the least displeasure showed in madam's face,
  the sleeves of my robe were soon damp with tearstains.
  My wish was that I might bear a son,
  to see Madam dangle a grandson in her arms.
  But those hopes in the end failed and came to nothing;
ill-fated, they made me the butt of slander.
  Driven from the house, I didn't dare grumble,
  only grieved that I'd betrayed madam's kindness."   20
On the old road that runs along the edge of the swamp,
when fox fire glimmers through drizzling rain,
can you hear the voice crying "Madam is cruel!"
Surely it's the soul of the wife sent home.

(Tr. Burton Watson)

Hsin Ch'i-chi (1140-1207)

Tune: "Full River Red" (*Man-chiang hung*)

Parting sorrow shattered
Beyond the gauze window
Where the wind sweeps through bamboo.
    Her lover gone,
  The sound of the flute breaks off.
  Alone she leans against the railing.
Her eyes cannot stand late April's dusk;
Her head overwhelmed by the green of a thousand hills.
    She tries to read
  One page of a letter from him,   10
  Tries to read from the beginning.

---

2. Bear's paws are the epitome of delicious food.

Words of longing
Fill the page in vain;
Thoughts of longing
When would they suffice?
Upon her silken lapel tears fall, drop after drop;
Cascades of pearls brim her two hands.
Fragrant grass mustn't obscure a traveler's way home,
But hanging willow obstructs the eyes of someone left alone.
    Bitterest sorrow is   20
To stand and wait out the dusk moon
    Near a winding balustrade.

                      (Tr. Irving Y. Lo)

Kuan Han-ch'ing (ca. 1220-ca. 1300)

[Shuang-tiao] Tune:
"Song of Great Virtue" (*Ta-te ko*)

Spring

the cuckoo cries
go home, go home
but only spring returns
never my loved one.
how many more days of this languor?
willow fluff comes floating
fluttering, emptied, down.
all spring no word.
only a pair of swallows fly
mud in the beaks   10
to build a nest.

              (Tr. Jerome P. Seaton)

[Shuang-tiao] Tune: "Song of Great Virtue"
Winter, Two Songs

[1]

snow powder, flowery
dancing pear blossoms.
the misty hamlet's lost from view again.
thick falls fine rain: a picture.
evening crow caws in the distant grove.
yellow rushes screen the clear stream's glare.
there, in tangled halyards, a fishing boat.

[2]

toot once, strum once
give us a song
           to Great Virtue.
enjoy yourself, relax
stop setting snares.
how long can a man live, anyway?
be simple, plain
           and follow
where that leads you.
go find yourself a place to flop
and flop there.

(Tr. Jerome P. Seaton)

[Nan-lü] Tune: "A Sprig of Flowers" (Yi-chih hua)
Not Bowing to Old Age

[1]

I pluck the clustering flowers from the wall
snap off the greening roadside willow
the red unopened bud
the slimmest, the most supple green wand
I'm a dandy, and a rake I am
trusting this hand that plucks

the flower and the bough
that I can bear the willow's withering, the flower's fall
half a life I've picked as I pleased
half a life I've lain with flowers,   10
entwined in tender boughs

                                [2]

commander of the dandies' army
headman of the horde of rakes
when I'm red-faced old
I'll be the same
wasting my time with the flowers
losing my cares in wine
drinking and eating, carousing
punning and joking and playing with words
I'm smooth, I'm ripe
with the rhymes and the rules   10
there's no place in my heart
for mourning.
my companion's a girl with a silver guitar
she tunes it in front of a silver stand
and leans with a smile toward the silver screen;
my companion's an immortal of heavenly jade
I grasp her jade hand and shoulder
as we mount the tower of jade;
my companion's the "Gold Hairpin Guest"
she sings, "The Gold Lock of Hair"   20
offers the golden goblet up
fills the floating golden cup
you say I'm old, that I grow cold...

Don't think it.
I'm center stage, the boss
trimmer than ever
still slim and bold

I'm commander in chief of the brocade troupes
that throng this flowery encampment
and I travel the land
and wander the districts   30
for sport.

[3]

Now your modern-day wastrel is nothing but that
a pile of straw, or a hole in the sand
a newborn bunny set loose for the hunt
I'm the hoary blue pheasant
always slipping the noose
and dodging the net
I've known the tramp of cavalry horses
and survived the cold arrows of ambush
I'll never fall behind
Don't tell me, "with middle age, the game is up"   10
I won't go gently to my dotage.

[4]

I'm a bronze bean with a pure bell tone
steam me: I won't get tender
boil me: I'll never be cooked
pound me: I'll never be bean paste
roast me: I'll never pop
who told you dandies you could come in here
where the harlot weaves her brocade net
a thousand layers
which can be hacked, but not hacked out
which can be chopped, but not chopped down   10
which can be loosened, yet never quite undone
even discarded, but never for long?
my play's beneath a storied garden's moon
my drink is fabled Kai-feng wine
my current love's a Lo-yang flower
I only pick the willows of Chang Terrace

I can play go
and I can play football
I'm a hunter and a wag
I can dance and sing   20
play the flute
I spread a rare table
and chant a fine poem
I'm great at chess.
you can knock out my teeth
and break my jaw
you can cripple my legs
and rip off my arms
let heaven lay all these curses on me
I still won't stop   30

except old Yama calls on me himself
and brings his fiends to fetch me
when my soul returns to earth
and my animal self falls straight to Hell
then, and only then
I'll quit this flowered path
I ramble on

(Tr. Jerome P. Seaton)

Chang Yang-hao (1269-1329)

[Shuang-tiao] Tune: "Wild Geese Have Come Down; Song of Victory" (Yen-erh lo chien Te-sheng ling)

In the past I brought trouble upon myself when I sought rank and
  honor;
Now facing hills and streams, I forget fame and gain.
In the past I attended court at the crowing of cocks;
Now I'm still sound asleep at noontime.
In the past, I stood on vermilion steps in the palace, holding an official
  tablet;
Now I pluck chrysanthemums by the eastern hedge.
In the past I fawned upon the powerful and the mighty,
Now I have leisure to visit old friends.
In the past, I was wild and foolish,
An narrowly escaped flogging and banishment;   10
Now I'm taking it easy:
Have learned to write songs on wind and flowers, snow and moon.

(Tr. Sherwin S. S. Fu)

Sui Ching-ch'en (fl. 1300)

[Pan-she tiao] Tune: "Slow Chant"
[Han] Kao-tsu's[1] Homecoming

I

The village chief made the announcement from door to door:
"Whatever the assignment, there's no excuse to put it off."
This is no ordinary assignment—
On the one hand, we're ordered to provide fodder and food[2];
On the other, some of us are sent on errands.
Well, we have no choice but to comply.
Some say the royal chariot is coming;
All agree it's the imperial carriage—
Because the emperor is returning home today.
Wang, the village elder, holds an earthen plate;   10
Chao, the cowherd, grasps a wine gourd.
Wearing a newly brushed turban,
A silk gown just starched and ironed,
They jump at the chance to pose as village squires.

II

A bunch of fakers led by the blind musician Wang Liu
rush in headlong on horseback, playing flutes and beating drums.
Then a large crowd of men and horses arrive at the village gate,
Several flags fluttering at the very front:
One featuring a frosty rabbit enclosed within a white circle, [3]
One decorated with a three-legged crow inside a red curve,[4]

1. A posthumous title given t the first emperor of Han after his death. For humorous effect, it is translated literally as the "Great-Great-Grandfather" of Han in the last line of the poem.
2. The text reads *yeh kên,,* which has no specific meaning and is often thought to be padding words in a tune. But it has been suggested that *kên* may be a variant of *liang,* meaning "food."
3. The white circle represents the moon, where the jade rabbit was supposed to dwell.
4. Legend has it that there is a three-legged crow in the sun. Hence the expression "golden crow" (the sun).

One with a picture of hens learning how to dance,
One presenting a dog with two wings,
And another a gourd entwined by a snake.

III

Red-lacquered two-pronged pikes,
Silver-plated axes;
Some weapons like gilded sweet-melons and bitter-melons.
Shiny stirrups carried at the tip of spears;
Snow-white palace fans made of goose quill.
These fakers hold some implements never seen before;
They wear all kinds of bizarre clothes.

IV

Horses are hitched to the crossbars of the carriage,
Not a single donkey can be seen in harness.[5]
The handles of yellow-silk parasols are naturally curved.
In front of the carriage are eight officers, looking like judges in
    Heaven[6];
A lot of attendants follow the carriage.
There are also several lovely girls,[7]
Their dresses alike,
Their hairdos identical.

V

When that tall fellow[8] gets off the carriage,
Everyone salutes him,
But the tall fellow acts as if he didn't see them at all.

---

5. This is from the point of view of the villager who saw mules
and donkeys more often than horses.
6. Referring to mural paintings, sculptures, and the like seen in
most temples.
7. I.e., female musicians who served as attendants to an emperor
or a commander in chief.
8. According to his biography in the *Historical Records*, Liu Pang
was a tall fellow.

The village elders all bend their knees and lie prostrate before
                                            him,
But the tall fellow doesn't even bother to help them stand up.
All of a sudden I raise my head and look up;
By looking closely at him for some time I know who he is,
How my bosom almost bursts with anger!

VI

Your family name was originally Liu, wasn't it?
And your wife's was Lü.
I could trace the origin of your two families right from the
                                            beginning—
You used to be a village constable, fond of a few drinks[9];
Your father-in-law used to teach the kids of our village to read.
Once you lived to the east of our village,
Hired by me to feed cattle, cut grass,
Build dikes, and hoe the fields.

VII

In the spring you used to pick mulberry leaves:
In the winter you borrowed grain from me.
Bit by bit, you bought on credit a lot of rice and wheat.
By signing a new land contract, you made a profit of three
                                            steelyardfuls of hemp;
To repay wine debts, you once stole several bushels of beans.
These are not groundless accusations:
They are clearly recorded in ledgers and calendars;
I still have in my keeping all the documents.

9. The description of Liu Pang's humble origin and knavish
personality is based on historical facts.

VII

The money you owe me you can pay me back with the bribes you
      collected,
The grain you owe me you can repay by reducing my taxes. [10]
Nobody would arrest you, Number Three Liu[11]—
Why did you bother to change your name to "Great-Great-
      Grandfather of Han"?

(Tr. Sherwin S. S. Fu)

10. The implication is clearly that there is no difference between
the taxes imposed by the emperor and the money he once stole.
11. Originally Liu Pang had no name and was known as
Number Three Liu because he was the third son of the family.
After he became the emperor he named himself *Pang*.

Kao Ch'i (1336-1374)

"Lament of a Soldier's Wife"

My husband never desired the official seal of a marquis,
But a tiger's tally[1] sent him to join the ranks in a foreign land.
For many nights I was visited in my bedroom by bad dreams,
Now I hear from the general's headquarters of the army's defeat.
His body perished, yet his faded soldier's cloak remains;
His old comrade-in-arms has brought it home for me.
A woman, I'd never find the road to the border—
How could I get to far Wu-wei[2] to find his unburied bones?
I can only cut out paper pennants to summon back his soul;
And turn them toward that place where we once parted.   10

(Tr. Irving Y. Lo)

Sunflower[1]

Its radiance bursts forth in summer's bright light,
In clusters nestling along the dense green shade.
Evenings, it droops like the common hibiscus,
But blazes at noon with the pomegranate flowers.
A subtle scent spreads across our mat,
A fresh splendor shines upon our feast.
When all the other flowers have bid us farewell,
This last survivor now rouses our pity.

(Tr. Irving Y. Lo)

1. I.e., wartime dispatch. The term is derived from the ancient custom of employing messengers to carry important messages carved on tallies of bamboo or metal.
2. Wu-wei, also known as Liang-chou, is a district in modern Kansu province.

1. From a series entitled "Three Songs Written by the Pond of Western Studio."

Indian

Literature

A NOTE ON SANSKRIT PRONUNCIATION

Indic words are rendered in Roman script, using international conventions for transliteration. In reading Sanskrit words, the accent may be placed on a syllable when this is heavy. A syllable is heavy if it contains a long simple vowel (*ā, ī, ū, ṛ*), a dipthong (*e, o, ai, au*), or a short vowel followed by more than one consonant. It should be noted that the aspirated consonants *kh, gh, ch, jh, ṭh, ḍh, th, dh, ph,* and *bh,* are considered single consonants in the Sanskrit alphabet.

Vowels, except *a,* are given their full value as in Italian or German:

a	as *u* in c*u*t
ā	as *a* in *fa*ther
i	as *i* in p*i*t
ī	as *i* in mach*i*ne
u	as *u* in p*u*t
ū	as *u* in r*u*le
ṛ	a short vowel; as *ir* in b*ir*d, but often rendered *ri* in Anglicized words
e	as *ay* in s*ay*
ai	as *ai* in *ai*sle
o	as *o* in g*o*
au	as *ow* in c*ow*
ṁ	nasalizes the preceding vowel and makes the syllable heavy
ḥ	a rough breathing vowel, replacing an original *s* or *r*; occurs only at the end of a syllable or word and makes the syllable heavy

Most consonants are analogous to the English, if the distinction between aspirated and nonaspirated consonants is observed; for example, the aspirated consonants *th* and *ph* must never be pronounced as in English *th*in and *ph*ial, but as in ho*th*ouse and she*ph*erd (similarly, *kh, gh, ch, jh, dh, bh*). The differences between the Sanskrit "cerebral" *ṭ, ṭh, ḍ, ḍh, ṇ, ṣ* and "dental" *t, th, d, dh, n, s* are another distinctive feature of the language. The dentals are formed with the tongue against the teeth, the cerebrals with the tongue flexed back along the palate. Note also:

g	as *g* in *g*oat
ṅ	as *n* in i*n*k, or si*n*g
c	as *ch* in *ch*urch
ñ	as *ñ* in Spanish se*ñ*or
ś	as *s* in *s*ugar

KĀLIDĀSA'S WORLD AND HIS PLAYS

BARBARA STOLER MILLER

Kālidāsa: Servant of the Goddess and Devotee of Śiva

Although Kālidāsa is the acknowledged master-poet of Sanskrit, we lack any historical evidence of his life. Throughout the centuries the quality of his poetry attracted many legends to his name. These are known from sources in Sanskrit and other languages. When the Tibetan Lama Tāranātha wrote his *History of Buddhism in India* in the seventeenth century, the legendary Kālidāsa was included among the spiritual adepts of India. Tāranātha recounts the tale of Kālidāsa's transformation from fool to poet through a series of events that bring him the grace of the goddess Kālī. It is a parable filled with magic, paradox, and allusions to the power of speech.

That Kālidāsa was a devotee of Śiva and the Goddess is evident from his work as well as from his legends. The powerful images of nature that dominate his poetry and drama are ultimately determined by his conception of Śiva's creative mystery. This is implicit in the doctrine of Śiva's eight manifest forms (*aṣṭamūrti*), which he states in the benediction of the *Śākuntala*.

> The water that was first created,
> the sacrifice-bearing fire, the priest,
> the time-setting sun and moon,
> audible space that fills the universe,
> what men call nature, the source of all seeds,
> the air that living creatures breathe—
> through his eight embodied forms,
> may Lord Śiva come to bless you!

The natural world of Kālidāsa's poetry is never a static landscape; it reverberates with Śiva's presence. Nature functions not as a setting or allegorical landscape but as a dynamic surface on which the unmanifest cosmic unity plays. This unity is Śiva; his creative nature is expressed through the eight essential principles of empirical existence: the elements, (water, fire, ether, earth, air) the sun and the moon, and the ritual sacrificer, who is integrated into this cosmic system. In the sustained interplay of these basic constituents of nature, the creation and destruction of life occur. Śiva is present in each aspect of life and fulfills all the functions that the eight forms collectively perform.

The conception of Śiva's eight manifest forms has inherent in it the identification of Śiva himself with Nature (*prakṛti*), the female half of his cosmic totality. Śiva is called "The God Who Is Half Female" (*ardhanārīśvara*). The male and female aspects of existence, *puruṣa* and *prakṛti*, separately personified as Śiva and the goddess Umā, are bound into a single androgynous figure. These concepts are fundamental to the meaning of Kālidāsa'a poetry; in his dramas they set the romantic relationship between the hero and heroine in a definite religious context.

The King as Hero and Patron

The hero in each play is a king whose character is shaped by the poet's view of kingship and its relation to cosmic order. Kālidāsa shared with the ancient priesthood of Vedic brahmans a belief that nature's structure is constantly recreated by ritual sacrifice. In the Vedic rites of royal consecration (*rājasūya*), the symbols of the ritual link all the elements of the world to the king, so that he stands at the center of the universe. It is through the king that the natural, social, and divine worlds have unity and order. The king's supernatural nature is indicated by his intimate associations with the Vedic gods. According to Manu, an ancient authority on Hindu law, a king is composed of eternal particles of eight divine powers, and because of them he surpasses all other created beings. He is the human counterpart of Indra, king of the gods, and is his equal in many ways.

The high qualities of kingship that Kālidāsa's heroes possess qualify them to be called royal sages. The epithet "royal sage" (*rājarṣi*) signifies that the king's spiritual power is equal to his martial strength and moral superiority. He is a sage (*ṛṣi*) by virtue of his discipline (*yoga*), austerity (*tapas*), and knowledge of sacred law (*dharma*). It is his religious duty to keep order in the cosmos by guarding his kingdom; in this he is like a sage guarding the realm of holy sacrifice. His responsibility to guide and protect those beneath him involves him in acts of penance that place him in the highest position of the temporal and spiritual hierarchy.

The ideal royal sage is a figure of enormous physical strength and energy who also has the power to control his senses. The conflict between desire (*kāma*) and duty (*dharma*) that is enacted in each of Kālidāsa's dramas involves a tension between the energy of physical passion and the constraints of self-control. In two of the plays, the *Vikramorvaśīya* and the *Śākuntala,* the tension is resolved in the king's recognition of his son and heir. Each boy is portrayed as a natural warrior despite his birth in a hermitage and his education in religious practice. Royal power combined with religious discipline makes the prince destined to be "a king who turns the wheel of empire" (*cakravartin*), a universal emperor whose great spiritual and temporal conquests mark him with divinity ...

Classical Culture and Kālidāsa's Dramas

... Indian heroic romances represent human emotions in a theatrical universe of symbolically charged characters and events in order to lead the audience into a state of extraordinary pleasure and insight. The goal of a Sanskrit drama is to re-establish emotional harmony in the microcosm of the audience by exploring the deeper relations that bind apparent conflicts of existence. The manifestation of these relations produces the intense aesthetic experience called *rasa*. All Kālidāsa's plays focus on the critical tension between desire and duty that is aesthetically manifest in the relation of the erotic sentiment (*śṛṅgārarasa*) to the heroic (*vīrarasa*).

The production of *rasa* is basic to classical Indian theater. The concept is difficult to translate in a single word. Though "sentiment" and "mood," the conventional translations, approximate its meaning, *rasa* more literally means the "flavor" or "taste" of something. The *rasa* is essentially the flavor that the poet distills from a given emotional situation in order to present it for aesthetic appreciation. In Indian aesthetic theory human emotion (*bhāva*) is thought to exist in the heart as latent impressions left by past experiences. Early theorists divide emotion into eight categories, each of which has the potential to become a *rasa,* a state of emotional integration. The eight *rasas* are the erotic, the heroic, the comic, the pathetic, the furious, the horrible, the marvelous, and the disgusting.   Every drama or dramatic episode has a dominant *rasa;* of these the erotic and the heroic are of central importance throughout Sanskrit drama ...

It is through stylized enactment, including gesture, verbal delivery, costume, makeup, and conventional signs of emotion, that the special atmosphere of traditional Indian theater is created. The word for acting in Sanskrit is *abhinaya*.   It comes from the root *nī,* which means "to lead," the same root from which are derived the words for the protagonists, the dramatic hero (*nāyaka*) and heroine (*nāyikā*). *Abhinaya* effectively leads the play toward the audience. The term refers to every means by which this object is achieved and to the synthesis resulting from the combination of its aspects. Bharata analyzes acting into four components.

1. Acting through the body (*āṅgika*), relating to gestures and movements of the body, hands, and eyes.

2. Acting through speech (*vācika*), relating to voice intonation, recitation, and singing.

3. Acting through accessories (*āhārya*), which include makeup, costume, and jewelry—scenery and props are little used, since suggestive gestures and descriptive verses function to evoke scenes and objects for the audience.

4. Acting through signs of emotion (*sāttvika*), relating to the physical manifestations of emotional states, such as tears, change of color, voice trembling, and fainting.

A language of gesture developed as a distinctive feature of the Indian stage from the earliest times. Particular importance was given to the use of hands and eyes for translating ideas, objects, and emotions into aesthetic statements.

Kālidāsa's plays, so rich in verbal images, depend on gesture for the full expression of their texts. In the first meeting of Śakuntalā and Duṣyanta, the heroine barely speaks. The king recites verse after verse, set against the rhythms of the Prakrit dialogue of her two friends. While this verbal poetry is being presented, the heroine represents her responses through gesture and dance, visually expressing the text through her movements. At one point, the stage direction specifies that she is to show the bee's "attack" while the king addresses the bee:

> Bee, you touch the quivering
> corners of her frightened eyes;
> you hover softly near
> to whisper secrets in her ear;
> a hand brushes you away,
> but you drink her lips' treasure—
> while the truth we seek defeats us,
> you are truly blessed.

Like the verse, which portrays the bee by means of a few essential traits, quivering and fluttering gestures of fingers and eyes would be used to represent the erratic movements of the bee ...

Gestures thus learned are not intended to imitate nature realistically, but rather to recreate the experience of it. Gestures function not only to make vivid pictures, but also to communicate abstract ideas and to suggest nuances of emotion. An actor would have to control a whole range of gestures to communicate the motions and emotions that are fundamental to the production of *rasa* in each of Kālidāsa's plays.

Classical Language and the Languages of Drama

The techniques of performance used in the classical Indian theater were appropriate to the complicated verbal texts of Kālidāsa's dramas. These multilingual poetic dramas reflect an ancient Indian preoccupation with the nature of language ...

Sanskrit was the hieratic language of the brahman priests from ancient times. Under various rulers, it was also the status language of royal administration and poetry ...

Sanskrit was dominant in the classical tradition, this should not blind us to the dynamism that always characterized Indian culture beneath the surface of seeming linguistic and cultural uniformity. Sanskrit never really supplanted other languages. Various other post-Vedic dialects continued to develop independently of Sanskrit; the grammarians referred to them by the collective term Prakrit (*prākṛta,* a derivative of the noun *prakṛti,* from the root *kṛ* "to make," with the prefix *pra* "before"), which means "original" or "natural ...".

Kālidāsa is the only early Sanskrit author besides Aśvaghoṣa known to have composed both poems and plays. Kālidāsa's poems, like the Gupta inscriptions, are in courtly Sanskrit. The high tone of the poetry prevails and excursions into humor or lower registers of language and thought are rare. In their digressive elegance, the poems were for a select audience of men who could concentrate on the sustained subtleties of a refined literary language ...

The demands of the theater generated conventions of composition that were distinct from those of classical poetry. The art of Kālidāsa's plays is deliberately more eclectic than that of his poems. Languages, characters, and plots from the idealized epic universe are juxtaposed with elements from popular literature and everyday life. A fundamental clue to this is the language of his dramas.

An acute sensitivity to spoken language enabled Kālidāsa to effectively use the linguistic conventions that defined dramatic character. In most classical drama the Sanskrit language was deliberately mixed with several stylized forms of "natural" language, the dramatic Prakrits. Linguistic diversity was conventionalized in the plays and formalized in the *Nāṭyaśāstra.* Sanskrit was the language spoken by twice-born men: the king, his advisers, and others of high status in religious or political spheres. It was occasionally spoken by a woman of learning, such as the nun in the *Mālavikāgnimitra.* The brahman buffoon (*vidūṣaka*), the women of the court, city, and hermitage, as well as various minor characters, spoke different Prakrits. This mixture represents the multilingual nature of Indian society, where contrasting languages have served to define layers of the social hierarchy. The languages and the value systems encoded in them were woven into the intricate patterns of the classical drama ...

The Heroine and the King

The hero and heroine, as well as the clusters of characters that surround them, appear as symbolic personalities, defined by language and gender. Males are kings, princes, sages, buffoons, ministers, priests, generals, chamberlains, dancing masters, students, policemen, and fishermen. Females are nymphs, queens, princesses, nuns, ascetics, doorkeepers, bow-bearers, and serving maids. With the exception of the buffoon and other comic characters, like the policemen, the male characters in Kālidāsa's plays generally speak Sanskrit. With the exception of the nun in *Mālavikāgnimitra,* the female characters speak Prakrit.

In the microcosm of the Indian theater, the resolution of psychological, social, and religious disharmonies is enacted by characters who represent generic types. They are not unique individuals with personal destinies, like Shakespeare's Hamlet or Lear. Indian characters live within stylized social contexts that reflect the hierarchical nature of traditional Indian society. The hierarchies are equally strict in the hermitages of Kanva and Mārīca or at the courts of Duṣyanta and his divine counterpart Indra.

Kālidāsa's dramas achieve their aesthetic and moral impact not through the conflicts of individuals but through the perennial human conflict between duty (*dharma*) and desire (*kāma*). His dramatic expositions are rooted in an ancient Indian scheme for reconciling life's multiple possibilities. The scheme is called the "four human pursuits" (*puruṣārtha*) and is divided into a wordly triad of duty (*dharma*), material gain (*artha*), and pleasure (*kāma*), plus a supermundane concern for liberation from worldly existence (*mokṣa*).

The conflict is transformed into aesthetic experience by the poet's skillful presentation of his characters' emotional reactions to various situations. When a poet explores the emotional reactions of a king or other exalted person through the medium of a traditional story, the drama is known as a *nāṭaka*. Insofar as this type of drama combines two major *rasas*, the heroic and the erotic, it is reasonably termed "heroic romance." Dramatic romance in Western literature, represented by examples such as Aeschylus' *Oresteia*, Euripides' *Alcestis*, or Shakespeare's *The Tempest* is comparable in many ways, though the mode of these plays may not be heroic. The *Śākuntala* is the model of this genre. ···

In each of Kālidāsa's plays the hero and heroine are the focal dramatic vehicles for exposing the states of mind of the poet and his audience. The heroes of the plays are royal sages whose character is expressed according to the norms of classical society and dramatic theory. The nature of Kālidāsa's heroines is more enigmatic. They are goddess-like, but sexually and emotionally vulnerable. Śakuntalā is the daughter of a nymph and a royal sage, inappropriately living in an ascetics' grove. When the play begins, her adoptive father has gone on a pilgrimage to avert some threat to her. In his absence, she meets Duṣyanta and agrees to a secret love-wedding ···

In some measure each of the heroines embodies both the goddess of beauty and fortune, Lakṣmī, and goddess of speech, Vāk. Kālidāsa, like the ancient singers of the *Ṛg Veda*, identifies himself with the sacred power of language. In their hymns the Vedic poets stress that their language does not serve the function of separating elements of the cosmos. Instead it is a unifying force, personified as Vāk. She is seen by the poets as a manifestation of their own power to communicate with the divine, to unify men with nature and the cosmos ···

As she continues to manifest herself in the imaginations of Indian poets, Vāk is not a fixed idea or image. Rather, her attributes are found in various forms, and her powerful cosmic energy (*śakti*) works in diverse ways to arouse men and to bear the fruit of their inspiration. This goddess can readily transfer her energy to the male who consorts with her.

In Indian dramatic theory each performance is conceived as a conflict between opposing forces of existence.[66] The dramatic union of the hero with the heroine is a substitute for the Vedic sacrificial union of Indra, king of the gods, with Vāk. The heroine appears as a beautiful nymph whose spontaneous love embraces the hero and leads him beyond the world of everyday experience into the imaginative universe where dichotomies of sensual desire (*kāma*) and sacred duty (*dharma*) are reintegrated. The heroine's presence, through her various forms and transformations, reassures the audience that the energy of nature is always available to reintegrate conflicting aspects of life.

Śakuntalā is known from Vedic literature as a nymph who conceived her superhuman son Bharata at a sacred place called Nādapit. In the *Mahābhārata* episode on which Kālidāsa based his drama, Śakuntalā is identified as the daughter born of a union between the nymph Menakā and the royal sage Viśvāmitra. Menakā, meaning "woman," is a paradigmatic figure of feminine beauty. It is noteworthy that the wife of the mountain-king Himālaya, and the mother of Pārvatī, has a variant of this name, Menā. Menakā is sent to seduce Viśvāmitra when his ascetic powers threaten the gods. She succeeds and becomes pregnant with a daughter whom she bears and abandons to birds of prey near a river. The birds worship and protect her until another great sage, the ascetic Kaṇva, finds her and brings her to live in his forest hermitage as his daughter. Having found her among the śakunta birds, he names her Śakuntalā.

Kālidāsa shapes the epic story to focus attention on details of Śakuntalā's semidivine origin and her role within the universe of Śiva. The epic story begins with the scene of a tumultuous hunt in which Duṣyanta kills numerous forest animals. The play begins with the benediction to Śiva and the prologue, followed by a scene in which the king enters with his charioteer, armed with a bow and arrow, like "the wild bowman Śiva, hunting the dark antelope." The intensity of the hunt is interrupted by two ascetics, who identify the antelope as a creature of sage Kaṇva's hermitage.

The entire scene is set with great economy and magical speed by the black buck as he penetrates the forest and charges the atmosphere with danger. Kālidāsa portrays the elegant animal altered by the violence of the hunt (1.7):

> The graceful turn of his neck
> as he glances back at our speeding car,
> his haunches folded into his chest
> in fear of my speeding arrow;
> the open mouth dropping
> half-chewed grass on our path—
> watch how he leaps, bounding on air,
> barely touching the earth!

The antelope is Śakuntalā's "son," adopted by her when it was orphaned as a fawn. This scene shows the king captivated by the graceful creature of nature he is bent on killing. His passion threatens the calm of the forest and the animal it is his duty to protect. This is the prelude to Duṣyanta's discovery of Śakuntalā. As the buffoon aptly jests to the king "you've turned that ascetics' grove into a pleasure garden."

It is summertime as the drama begins. Śakuntalā is in the dangerous state of being a nubile virgin. The king's physical presence arouses the whole world of nature. When he enters the hermitage, he hides behind a tree to watch Śakuntalā and her friends watering the trees of the ascetics' grove. While they are watering the trees and plants, the friends notice that the spring Mādhavī vine she loves like a sister is blossoming unseasonably, clinging to the male mango tree. A bee in the grove lustily attacks Śakuntalā, giving the king a chance to reveal himself as her protector. As her apparent inaccessibility to him vanishes with the revelation that she is not the child of a brahman hermit, but of a warrior sage, he pursues her insistently, controlled only by her weak resistance. Finally passion overwhelms them both and they consummate their love in a secret *gāndharva* marriage of mutual consent. Śakuntalā transfers her creative energy from the forest animals and plants she nurtured by her touch to her human lover, she herself becoming pregnant in the process. Soon after their union, the king is recalled to his capital and leaves Śakuntalā behind. He gives her his signet ring as a sign of their marriage and promises to send for her.

Act Four, which critics consider to be the core, or womb (*garbha*) of the drama, begins with Śakuntalā distracted by her lover's parting and negligent of her religious duties in the hermitage. She ignores the approach of the irascible sage Durvāsas, arouses his wrath, and incurs his curse. The wrath has its fulfillment in Śakuntalā herself, who rises to anger when she is later rejected by the king. The curse makes the king forget her, until he sees the ring again. Kaṇva learns from the voice of the forest, Vāk herself, that Śakuntalā is pregnant. He presides over the ceremonies that sanctify her marriage and poignantly arranges for her departure from the hermitage. The ascetic women come to worship her, and two hermit boys who had been sent to gather flowers from the trees in the woods enter with offerings of jewels and garments produced by the forest trees. The scene of her last moments in the hermitage is an emotional ritual of breaking her bonds with it. On the way to the king's capital, Śakuntalā and her escorts stop to worship at the river shrine of Indra's consort, Śacī. There she loses the ring and brings Durvāsas' curse into effect, so that the king does not remember her. When she is rejected by the king and abandoned by the ascetics, Śakuntalā, in her anger, invokes the earth to open and receive her. Before the eyes of the king's astonished priest, a light in the shape of a woman appears and carries her off. Eventually the ring is retrieved by a fisherman and when the king sees it, the curse is broken.

But Dusyanta transgressed his duty in the hermitage, and he too has to undergo a trial of separation before he is ready to be reunited with Śakuntalā. The fire of parted love that the king experiences as he worships her in his memory consecrates him for the sacred work of destroying cosmic demons that threaten the gods. After he has done this, he is transported by Indra's charioteer to the hermitage of the divine ascetic Mārīca on the celestial mountain called Golden Peak. The scene of their descent in Indra's aerial chariot recalls and

parallels the earlier entry of Duṣyanta and his earthly charioteer into the forest near Kaṇva's hermitage, where he first
encountered Śakuntalā.

In this enchanted grove of coral trees, the king observes a
child. As he analyzes his attraction to the boy, the king's
Sanskrit is set in contrast with the Prakrit speeches of two
female ascetics and the hermit boy whom Duṣyanta begins to
suspect is his own son. The scene recalls and parallels the
scene in the first act, when Duṣyanta discovers Śakuntalā in
the company of her two friends in the hermitage of Kaṇva.
One notes the formality of his language and the directness of
the women's speech, as well as the legalism of his conceptions
in contrast with the spontaneity of the women's thought and
judgment. The scene culminates in a Prakrit pun on Śakuntalā's name, followed by her appearance before the contrite
king. The fugue-like interplay of Sanskrit prose and verse
with Prakrit prose emphasizes the tension between emotional
responses and socially ordained behavior, which is Kālidāsa's
major theme. He is not advocating unrestrained passion, but
passion tempered by duty and duty brought alive by passion.
Once the balance of these vital forces is restored, the king can
recognize Śakuntalā as his wife and the great mother of a son
who will turn the wheel of empire. Duṣyanta's victory over
the demons, unlike his wanton pursuit of the antelope, is an
act of heroism that entitles him to love.

Although the more austere aspects of suffering are focused
on in Greek tragedy, the end of Oedipus in *Oedipus at Colonus*
is not so different. The world view of Greek tragedy seems to
presume the irreconcilability of forces such as passion and
duty; their clash is violent, but neither passion nor duty is
inevitably crushed. Within Greek tragedies, the conservative
community often appears as the chorus, articulating traditional morality in a grieving, ominous voice. The chorus'
relationship to the other actors may be one of fugue-like tension, or it may sound a single key that is stubbornly sustained, defeating attempts to modulate it. Victory may mean
the triumph of the social order, but heroic efforts can trans-

form it, as in the *Oresteia*. In spite of necessity (*ananke*), there is in some tragedies a transcendence that parallels the kind of integration inherent in the creative forces that dominate Indian romance.

Kālidāsa's Aesthetic of Memory

In the prologue of the *Śākuntala*, the director and the audience are so enchanted by the actress's song of summer that they are transported beyond mundane concerns. On awakening, the director recognizes its effect:

> The mood of your song's melody
> carried me off by force,
> just as the swift dark antelope
> enchanted King Duṣyanta.

The actress' singing, like the beautiful movements of the magical antelope, or the art of poetry, makes the audience "forget" the everyday world (*laukika*) and enter the fantastic (*alaukika*) realm of imagination that is latent within them.

The entire play is a reenactment of this idea. The mind of the poet, the hero, and the audience is symbolized here by the director, who holds together the various strands of the theater so that the *rasa* of the play can be realized and savored.

In religious and literary texts there is a recurrent association between memory and love; one of the Sanskrit words for memory (*smara*) is a common epithet of the god of love. Memory is crucial to the production of romantic sentiment throughout Sanskrit literature. Forgetfulness and memory function prominently in several works: the epic *Rāmāyaṇa*, the play *Avimāraka* attributed to Bhāsa; Bhavabhūti's drama the *Uttararāmacarita;* the collection of love-thief poems called the *Caurapañcāśikā*, attributed to Bilhaṇa; and Jayadeva's dramatic lyrical poem, the *Gītagovinda*.

In this Sanskrit literature, an act of remembering is a conventional technique for relating the antithetical modes of love-in-separation (*vipralambha-śṛṅgāra*) and love-in-union (*saṁbhoga-śṛṅgāra*). In the *Caurapañcāśika*, for example, each of the verses is a miniature painting of the princess with whom the poet enjoyed an illicit love. For his recklessness in this love he is condemned to death. The love-thief's final thoughts are details of his mistress' beauty:

> Even now,
> I remember her eyes
> restlessly closed after love,
> her slender body limp,
> fine cloths and heavy hair loose—
> a wild goose in a thicket of lotuses of passion.
> I shall recall her in my next life
> and even at the end of time.

By remembering the exquisite details of her physical beauty and her behavior in love, he brings her into his presence and the lovers are reunited in his mind. Even as a literary convention of intense love, memory has the power to break through the logic of everyday experience—it makes visible what is invisible, obliterates distances, reverses chronologies, and fuses what is ordinarily separate.

We find both this vivid form of remembering and memory of a deeper metaphysical kind working throughout Kālidāsa's plays, most explicitly in the fifth, sixth, and seventh acts of the *Śākuntala*. When he emphasizes the role of memory in aesthetic experience, Kālidāsa seems to be basing his conception on established philosophical notions. Later theorists of *rasa* take this analysis further. Indian epistemologists hold that whatever we perceive by means of the sense organs leaves an impression on the mind. Memory occurs when a latent impression is awakened. Indian literary theorists define memory as a recollection of a condition of happiness or misery, whether it was conceived in the mind or actually occurred. In what is considered one of the key passages of Sanskrit aesthetics, the tenth-century Kashmiri philosopher Abhinavagupta explains what Kālidāsa means by "memory." It is not discursive recollection of past events, but rather an intuitive insight into the past that transcends personal experience, into the imaginative universe that beauty evokes.

To illustrate this Abhinavagupta cites the final verse from the opening scene of Act Five of the *Śākuntala*. The king and the buffoon are listening to a song being sung by Lady Haṁsapadikā, whom the king once loved and forgot. The king muses to himself: "Why did hearing the song's words fill me with such strong desire? I'm not parted from anyone I love . . ."

> Seeing rare beauty,
> hearing lovely sounds,
> even a happy man
> becomes strangely uneasy . . .
> perhaps he remembers,
> without knowing why,
> loves of another life
> buried deep in his being.

When the king looks at Śakuntalā at the end of Act Five, his clouded memory struggles to clarify what he feels intuitively, increasing the intensity of their "separation" for the audience. When his vivid memory is restored by seeing the ring, the image of the bee in Haṁsapadikā's song becomes visible in the picture he paints of Śakuntalā and her friends as he first saw them in the hermitage. He uses the painting to represent his experience, but love makes him create a picture of such perfection that he rises in anger to chastise the painted bee who attacks Śakuntalā. When the buffoon "reminds" him that he is raving at a picture, he awakens from tasting the joy of love and returns to the painful reality of separation (6.21):

> My heart's affection made me feel
> the joy of seeing her—
> but you reminded me again
> that my love is only a picture.

This episode evokes for the audience the first meeting of the king and Śakuntalā, that unique moment of sensory and emotional awareness in which their mutual passion sowed the seed of separation, various levels of memory experience, and then reconciliation. The richly developed counterpoint of the final act is built from latent impressions of images and events that accumulate throughout the play. By sharing these with Duṣyanta as he moves through the enchanted celestial grove to find his son and Śakuntalā, the audience participates in the celebration of their reunion.

⊛

Śakuntalā and the Ring of Recollection

TRANSLATED BY BARBARA STOLER MILLER

CHARACTERS

Players in the prologue:
DIRECTOR: Director of the players and manager of the theater (*sūtradhāra*).
ACTRESS: The lead actress (*naṭī*).

Principal roles:
KING: Duṣyanta, the hero (*nāyaka*); ruler of Hastināpura; a royal sage of the lunar dynasty of Puru.
ŚAKUNTALĀ: The heroine (*nāyikā*); daughter of the royal sage Viśvāmitra and the celestial nymph Menakā; adoptive daughter of the ascetic Kaṇva.
BUFFOON: Mādhavya, the king's comical brahman companion (*vidūṣaka*).

Members of Kaṇva's hermitage:
ANASŪYĀ and PRIYAṀVADĀ: Two young female ascetics; friends of Śakuntalā.
KAṆVA: Foster father of Śakuntalā and master of the hermitage; a sage belonging to the lineage of the divine creator Marīci, and thus related to Mārīca.
GAUTAMĪ: The senior female ascetic.
ŚĀRṄGARAVA and ŚĀRADVATA: Kaṇva's disciples.

Various inhabitants of the hermitage: a monk with his two

pupils, two boy ascetics (named Gautama and Nārada), a young disciple of Kaṇva, a trio of female ascetics.

Members of the king's forest retinue:
CHARIOTEER: Driver of the king's chariot (*sūta*).
GUARD: Raivataka, guardian of the entrance to the king's quarters (*dauvārika*).
GENERAL: Commander of the king's army (*senāpati*).
KARABHAKA: Royal messenger.

Various attendants, including Greco-Bactrian bow-bearers (*yavanyaḥ*).

Members of the king's palace retinue:
CHAMBERLAIN: Vātāyana, chief officer of the king's household (*kañcukī*).
PRIEST: Somarāta, the king's religious preceptor and household priest (*purohita*).
DOORKEEPER: Vetravatī, the female attendant who ushers in visitors and presents messages (*pratīhārī*).
PARABHṚTIKĀ and MADHUKARIKĀ: Two maids assigned to the king's garden.
CATURIKĀ: A maidservant.

City dwellers:
MAGISTRATE: The king's low-caste brother-in-law (*śyāla*); chief of the city's policemen.
POLICEMEN: Sūcaka and Jānuka.
FISHERMAN: An outcaste.

Celestials:
MĀRĪCA: A divine sage; master of the celestial hermitage in which Śakuntalā gives birth to her son; father of Indra, king of the gods, whose armies Duṣyanta leads.
ADITI: Wife of Mārīca.
MĀTALI: Indra's charioteer.
SĀNUMATĪ: A nymph; friend of Śakuntalā's mother Menakā.

Various members of Mārīca's hermitage: two female ascetics, Mārīca's disciple Gālava.

BOY: Sarvadamana, son of Śakuntalā and Dusyanta; later known as Bharata.

Offstage voices:
VOICE OFFSTAGE: From the backstage area or dressing room (*nepathye*); behind the curtain, out of view of the audience. The voice belongs to various players before they enter the stage, such as the monk, Śakuntalā's friends, the buffoon, Mātali; also to figures who never enter the stage, such as the angry sage Durvāsas, the two bards who chant royal panegyrics (*vaitālikau*).
VOICE IN THE AIR: A voice chanting in the air (*ākāśe*) from somewhere offstage: the bodiless voice of Speech quoted in Sanskrit by Priyaṁvadā (4.4); the voice of a cuckoo who represents the trees of the forest blessing Śakuntalā in Sanskrit (4.11); the voice of Haṁsapadikā singing a Prakrit love song (5.1).

Aside from Dusyanta, Śakuntalā, and the buffoon, most of the characters represent types that reappear in different contexts within the play itself, an aspect of the circular structure of the play in which complementary relations are repeated. In terms of their appearance, the following roles might be played by the same actor or actress:
Kaṇva—Mārīca
Gautamī—Aditi
Anasūyā and Priyaṁvadā—
    Sānumatī and Caturikā—
    Two Ascetic Women in the hermitage of Mārīca
Charioteer—Mātali
Monk—Sārṅgarava
General—Chamberlain
Karabhaka—Priest

The setting of the play shifts from the forest hermitage (Acts 1–4) to the palace (Acts 5–6) to the celestial hermitage (Act 7). The season is early summer when the play begins and spring during the sixth act; the passage of time is otherwise indicated by the birth and boyhood of Śakuntalā's son.

ACT ONE

The water that was first created,
the sacrifice-bearing fire, the priest,
the time-setting sun and moon,
audible space that fills the universe,
what men call nature, the source of all seeds,
the air that living creatures breathe—
through his eight embodied forms,
may Lord Śiva come to bless you!   (1)

PROLOGUE

DIRECTOR (*looking backstage*): If you are in costume now,
madam, please come on stage!
ACTRESS: I'm here, sir.
DIRECTOR: Our audience is learned. We shall play Kālidāsa's
new drama called *Śakuntalā and the Ring of Recollection*. Let the
players take their parts to heart!
ACTRESS: With you directing, sir, nothing will be lost.
DIRECTOR: Madam, the truth is:

I find no performance perfect
until the critics are pleased;
the better trained we are
the more we doubt ourselves.   (2)

ACTRESS: So true . . . now tell me what to do first!
DIRECTOR: What captures an audience better than a song?

Sing about the new summer season and its pleasures:

> To plunge in fresh waters
> swept by scented forest winds
> and dream in soft shadows
> of the day's ripened charms. (3)

ACTRESS (*singing*):

> Sensuous women
> in summer love
> weave
> flower earrings
> from fragile petals
> of mimosa
> while wild bees
> kiss them gently. (4)

DIRECTOR: Well sung, madam! Your melody enchants the audience. The silent theater is like a painting. What drama should we play to please it?

ACTRESS: But didn't you just direct us to perform a new play called *Śakuntalā and the Ring of Recollection*?

DIRECTOR: Madam, I'm conscious again! For a moment I forgot.

> The mood of your song's melody
> carried me off by force,
> just as the swift dark antelope
> enchanted King Duṣyanta. (5)

(*They both exit; the prologue ends. Then the king enters with his charioteer, in a chariot, a bow and arrow in his hand, hunting an antelope.*)

CHARIOTEER (*watching the king and the antelope*):

> I see this black buck move
> as you draw your bow
> and I see the wild bowman Śiva,
> hunting the dark antelope. (6)

KING: Driver, this antelope has drawn us far into the forest. There he is again:

> The graceful turn of his neck
> as he glances back at our speeding car,
> the haunches folded into his chest
> in fear of my speeding arrow,
> the open mouth dropping
> half-chewed grass on our path—
> watch how he leaps, bounding on air,
> barely touching the earth.   (7)

(*He shows surprise.*)
Why is it so hard to keep him in sight?
CHARIOTEER: Sir, the ground was rough. I tightened the reins to slow the chariot and the buck raced ahead. Now that the path is smooth, he won't be hard to catch.
KING: Slacken the reins!
CHARIOTEER: As you command, sir.
(*He mimes the speeding chariot.*)
Look! ˙

> Their legs extend as I slacken the reins,
> plumes and manes set in the wind, ears angle back;
> our horses outrun their own clouds of dust,
> straining to match the antelope's speed.   (8)

KING: These horses would outrace the steeds of the sun.

> What is small suddenly looms large,
> split forms seem to reunite,
> bent shapes straighten before my eyes—
> from the chariot's speed
> nothing ever stays distant or near.   (9)

CHARIOTEER: The antelope is an easy target now.
(*He mimes the fixing of an arrow.*)
VOICE OFFSTAGE: Stop! Stop, king! This antelope belongs to our hermitage! Don't kill him!
CHARIOTEER (*listening and watching*): Sir, two ascetics are protecting the black buck from your arrow's deadly aim.

KING (*showing confusion*): Rein in the horses!
CHARIOTEER: It is done!
(*He mimes the chariot's halt. Then a monk enters with two pupils, his hand raised.*)
MONK: King, this antelope belongs to our hermitage.

> Withdraw your well-aimed arrow! Your weapon
> should rescue victims, not destroy the innocent!   (10)

KING: I withdraw it.
(*He does as he says.*)
MONK: An act worthy of the Puru dynasty's shining light!

> Your birth honors
> the dynasty of the moon!
> May you beget a son
> to turn the wheel of your empire!   (11)

THE TWO PUPILS (*raising their arms*): May you beget a son to turn the wheel of your empire!
KING (*bowing*): I welcome your blessing.
MONK: King, we were going to gather firewood. From here you can see the hermitage of our master Kaṇva on the bank of the Mālinī river. If your work permits, enter and accept our hospitality.

> When you see the peaceful rites of devoted ascetics,
> you will know how well your scarred arm protects us. (12)

KING: Is the master of the community there now?
MONK: He went to Somatīrtha, the holy shrine of the moon, and put his daughter Śakuntalā in charge of receiving guests. Some evil threatens her, it seems.
KING: Then I shall see her. She will know my devotion and commend me to the great sage.
MONK: We shall leave you now.
(*He exits with his pupils.*)
KING: Driver, urge the horses on! The sight of this holy hermitage will purify us.

CHARIOTEER: As you command, sir.

(*He mimes the chariot's speed.*)

KING (*looking around*): Without being told one can see that this is a grove where ascetics live.

CHARIOTEER: How?

KING: Don't you see—

> Wild rice grains under trees
> where parrots nest in hollow trunks,
> stones stained by the dark oil
> of crushed iṅgudī nuts,
> trusting deer who hear human voices
> yet don't break their gait,
> and paths from ponds streaked
> by water from wet bark cloth. (13)

CHARIOTEER: It is perfect.

KING (*having gone a little inside*): We should not disturb the grove! Stop the chariot and let me get down!

CHARIOTEER: I'm holding the reins. You can dismount now, sir.

KING (*dismounting*): One should not enter an ascetics' grove in hunting gear. Take these!

(*He gives up his ornaments and his bow.*)

Driver, rub down the horses while I pay my respects to the residents of the hermitage!

CHARIOTEER: Yes, sir!

(*He exits.*)

KING: This gateway marks the sacred ground. I will enter.

(*He enters, indicating he feels an omen.*)

> The hermitage is a tranquil place,
> yet my arm is quivering . . .
> do I feel a false omen of love
> or does fate have doors everywhere? (14)

VOICE OFFSTAGE: This way, friends!

KING (*straining to listen*): I think I hear voices to the right of the grove. I'll find out.

(*Walking around and looking.*)
Young female ascetics with watering pots cradled on their
hips are coming to water the saplings.
(*He mimes it in precise detail.*)
This view of them is sweet.

> These forest women have beauty
> rarely seen inside royal palaces—
> the wild forest vines far surpass
> creepers in my pleasure garden. (15)

I'll hide in the shadows and wait.
(*Śakuntalā and her two friends enter, acting as described.*)
ŚAKUNTALĀ: This way, friends!
ANASŪYĀ: I think Father Kaṇva cares more about the trees in
the hermitage than he cares about you. You're as delicate as a
jasmine, yet he orders you to water the trees.
ŚAKUNTALĀ: Anasūyā, it's more than Father Kaṇva's order. I
feel a sister's love for them.
(*She mimes the watering of trees.*)
KING (*to himself*): Is this Kaṇva's daughter? The sage does
show poor judgment in imposing the rules of the hermitage on
her.

> The sage who hopes to subdue
> her sensuous body by penances
> is trying to cut firewood
> with a blade of blue-lotus leaf. (16)

Let it be! I can watch her closely from here in the trees.
(*He does so.*)
ŚAKUNTALĀ: Anasūyā, I can't breathe! Our friend Pri-
yaṁvadā tied my bark dress too tightly! Loosen it a bit!
ANASŪYĀ: As you say.
(*She loosens it.*)
PRIYAṀVADĀ: (*laughing*): Blame your youth for swelling your
breasts. Why blame me?
KING: This bark dress fits her body badly, but it ornaments
her beauty . . .

A tangle of duckweed adorns a lotus,
a dark spot heightens the moon's glow,
the bark dress increases her charm—
beauty finds its ornaments anywhere.   (17)

ŚAKUNTALĀ (*looking in front of her*): The new branches on this mimosa tree are like fingers moving in the wind, calling to me. I must go to it!
(*Saying this, she walks around.*)
PRIYAṀVADĀ: Wait, Śakuntalā! Stay there a minute! When you stand by this mimosa tree, it seems to be guarding a creeper.
ŚAKUNTALĀ: That's why your name means "Sweet-talk."
KING: "Sweet-talk" yes, but Priyaṁvadā speaks the truth about Śakuntalā:

Her lips are fresh red buds,
her arms are tendrils,
impatient youth is poised
to blossom in her limbs.   (18)

ANASŪYĀ: Śakuntalā, this is the jasmine creeper who chose the mango tree in marriage, the one you named "Forest-light." Have you forgotten her?
ŚAKUNTALĀ: I would be forgetting myself!
(*She approaches the creeper and examines it.*)
The creeper and the tree are twined together in perfect harmony. Forestlight has just flowered and the new mango shoots are made for her pleasure.
PRIYAṀVADĀ (*smiling*): Anasūyā, don't you know why Śakuntalā looks so lovingly at Forestlight?
ANASŪYĀ: I can't guess.
PRIYAṀVADĀ: The marriage of Forestlight to her tree makes her long to have a husband too.
ŚAKUNTALĀ: You're just speaking your own secret wish.
(*Saying this, she pours water from the jar.*)
KING: Could her social class be different from her father's? There's no doubt!

She was born to be a warrior's bride,
for my noble heart desires her—
when good men face doubt,
inner feelings are truth's only measure. (19)

Still, I must learn everything about her.

ŚAKUNTALĀ (*flustered*): The splashing water has alarmed a bee. He is flying from the jasmine to my face.

(*She dances to show the bee's attack.*)

KING (*looking longingly*):

Bee, you touch the quivering
corners of her frightened eyes,
you hover softly near
to whisper secrets in her ear;
a hand brushes you away,
but you drink her lips' treasure—
while the truth we seek defeats us,
you are truly blessed. (20)

ŚAKUNTALĀ: This dreadful bee won't stop. I must escape.

(*She steps to one side, glancing about.*)

Oh! He's pursuing me . . . Save me! Please save me! This mad bee is chasing me!

BOTH FRIENDS (*laughing*): How can we save you? Call King Duṣyanta. The grove is under his protection.

KING: Here's my chance. Have no fear . . .

(*With this half-spoken, he stops and speaks to himself.*)

Then she will know that I am the king . . . Still, I shall speak.

ŚAKUNTALĀ (*stopping after a few steps*): Why is he still following me?

KING (*approaching quickly*):

While a Puru king rules the earth
to punish evildoers,
who dares to molest
these innocent young ascetics? (21)

(*Seeing the king, all act flustered.*)

ANASŪYĀ: Sir, there's no real danger. Our friend was frightened when a bee attacked her.

(*She points to Śakuntalā.*)

KING (*approaching Śakuntalā*): Does your ascetic practice go well?

(*Śakuntalā stands speechless.*)

ANASŪYĀ: It does now that we have a special guest. Śakuntalā, go to our hut and bring the ripe fruits. We'll use this water to bathe his feet.

KING: Your kind speech is hospitality enough.

PRIYAṀVADĀ: Please sit in the cool shadows of this shade tree and rest, sir.

KING: You must also be tired from your work.

ANASŪYĀ: Śakuntalā, we should respect our guest. Let's sit down.

(*All sit.*)

ŚAKUNTALĀ (*to herself*): When I see him, why do I feel an emotion that the forest seems to forbid?

KING (*looking at each of the girls*): Youth and beauty complement your friendship.

PRIYAṀVADĀ (*in a stage whisper*): Anasūyā, who is he? He's so polite, fine looking, and pleasing to hear. He has the marks of royalty.

ANAYSŪYĀ: I'm curious too, friend. I'll just ask him.

(*Aloud.*)

Sir, your kind speech inspires trust. What family of royal sages do you adorn? What country mourns your absence? Why does a man of refinement subject himself to the discomfort of visiting an ascetics' grove?

ŚAKUNTALĀ: (*to herself*): Heart, don't faint! Anasūyā speaks your thoughts.

KING (*to himself*): Should I reveal myself now or conceal who I am? I'll say it this way:

(*Aloud.*)

Lady, I have been appointed by the Puru king as the officer in charge of religious matters. I have come to this sacred forest to assure that your holy rites proceed unhindered.

ANASŪYĀ: Our religious life has a guardian now.

(*Śakuntalā mimes the embarrassment of erotic emotion.*)

BOTH FRIENDS (*observing the behavior of Śakuntalā and the king; in a stage whisper*): Śakuntalā, if only your father were here now!

ŚAKUNTALĀ (*angrily*): What if he were?

BOTH FRIENDS: He would honor this distinguished guest with what he values most in life.

ŚAKUNTALĀ: Quiet! Such words hint at your hearts' conspiracy. I won't listen.

KING: Ladies, I want to ask about your friend.

BOTH FRIENDS: Your request honors us, sir.

KING: Sage Kaṇva has always been celibate, but you call your friend his daughter. How can this be?

ANASŪYĀ: Please listen, sir. There was a powerful royal sage of the Kauśika clan . . .

KING: I am listening.

ANASŪYĀ: He begot our friend, but Kaṇva is her father because he cared for her when she was abandoned.

KING: "Abandoned"? The word makes me curious. I want to hear her story from the beginning.

ANASŪYĀ: Please listen, sir. Once when this great sage was practicing terrible austerities on the bank of the Gautamī river, he became so powerful that the jealous gods sent a nymph named Menakā to break his self-control.

KING: The gods dread men who meditate.

ANASŪYĀ: When springtime came to the forest with all its charm, the sage saw her intoxicating beauty . . .

KING: I understand what happened then. She is the nymph's daughter.

ANASŪYĀ: Yes.

KING: It had to be!

> No mortal woman could give birth to such beauty—
> lightning does not flash out of the earth.   (22)

(*Śakuntalā stands with her face bowed. The king continues speaking to himself.*)

My desire is not hopeless. Yet, when I hear her friends teasing her about a bridegroom, a new fear divides my heart.

PRIYAMVADĀ (*smiling, looking at Śakuntalā, then turning to the king*): Sir, you seem to want to say more.

(*Śakuntalā makes a threatening gesture with her finger.*)

KING: You judge correctly. In my eagerness to learn more about your pious lives, I have another question.

PRIYAMVADĀ: Don't hesitate! Ascetics can be questioned frankly.

KING: I want to know this about your friend:

> Will she keep the vow of hermit life
> only until she marries . . .
> or will she always exchange
> loving looks with deer in the forest? (23)

PRIYAMVADĀ: Sir, even in her religious life, she is subject to her father, but he does intend to give her to a suitable husband.

KING (*to himself*): His wish is not hard to fulfill.

> Heart, indulge your desire—
> now that doubt is dispelled,
> the fire you feared to touch
> is a jewel in your hands. (24)

ŚAKUNTALĀ (*showing anger*): Anasūyā, I'm leaving!

ANASŪYĀ: Why?

ŚAKUNTALĀ: I'm going to tell Mother Gautamī that Priyaṁvadā is talking nonsense.

ANASŪYĀ: Friend, it's wrong to neglect a distinguished guest and leave as you like.

(*Śakuntalā starts to go without answering.*)

KING (*wanting to seize her, but holding back, he speaks to himself*): A lover dare not act on his impulsive thoughts!

> I wanted to follow the sage's daughter,
> but decorum abruptly pulled me back;
> I set out and returned again
> without moving my feet from this spot. (25)

PRIYAMVADĀ (*stopping Śakuntalā*): It's wrong of you to go!
ŚAKUNTALĀ (*bending her brow into a frown*): Give me a reason why!
PRIYAMVADĀ: You promised to water two trees for me. Come here and pay your debt before you go!
(*She stops her by force.*)
KING: But she seems exhausted from watering the trees:

> Her shoulders droop, her palms
> are red from the watering pot—
> even now, breathless sighs
> make her breasts shake;
> beads of sweat on her face
> wilt the flower at her ear;
> her hand holds back
> disheveled locks of hair.   (26)

Here, I'll pay her debt!
(*He offers his ring. Both friends recite the syllables of the name on the seal and stare at each other.*)
Don't mistake me for what I am not! This is a gift from the king to identify me as his royal official.
PRIYAMVADĀ: Then the ring should never leave your finger. Your word has already paid her debt.
(*She laughs a little.*)
Śakuntalā, you are freed by this kind man . . . or perhaps by the king. Go now!
ŚAKUNTALĀ (*to herself*): If I am able to . . .
(*Aloud.*)
Who are you to keep me or release me?
KING (*watching Śakuntalā*): Can she feel toward me what I feel toward her? Or is my desire fulfilled?

> She won't respond directly to my words,
> but she listens when I speak;
> she won't turn to look at me,
> but her eyes can't rest anywhere else.   (27)

VOICE OFFSTAGE: Ascetics, be prepared to protect the creatures of our forest grove! King Duṣyanta is hunting nearby!

Dust raised by his horses' hooves
falls like a cloud of locusts swarming
at sunset over branches of trees
where wet bark garments hang.   (28)

In terror of the chariots, an elephant
charged into the hermitage
and scattered the herd of black antelope,
like a demon foe of our penances—
his tusks garlanded with branches
from a tree crushed by his weight,
his feet tangled in vines
that tether him like chains.   (29)

(*Hearing this, all the girls are agitated.*)
KING (*to himself*): Oh! My palace men are searching for me
and wrecking the grove. I'll have to go back.
BOTH FRIENDS: Sir, we're all upset by this news. Please let us
go to our hut.
KING (*showing confusion*): Go, please. We will try to protect
the hermitage.
(*They all stand to go.*)
BOTH FRIENDS: Sir, we're ashamed that our bad hospitality is
our only excuse to invite you back.
KING: Not at all. I am honored to have seen you.
(*Śakuntalā exits with her two friends, looking back at the king,
lingering artfully.*)
I have little desire to return to the city. I'll join my men and
have them camp near the grove. I can't control my feelings
for Śakuntalā.

My body turns to go,
my heart pulls me back,
like a silk banner
buffeted by the wind.   (30)

(*All exit.*)

END OF ACT ONE

ACT TWO

(The buffoon enters, despondent.)

BUFFOON *(sighing)*: My bad luck! I'm tired of playing side-kick to a king who's hooked on hunting. "There's a deer!" "There's a boar!" "There's a tiger!" Even in the summer mid-day heat we chase from jungle to jungle on paths where trees give barely any shade. We drink stinking water from mountain streams foul with rusty leaves. At odd hours we eat nasty meals of spit-roasted meat. Even at night I can't sleep. My joints ache from galloping on that horse. Then at the crack of dawn, I'm woken rudely by a noise piercing the forest. Those sons of bitches hunt their birds then. The torture doesn't end—now I have sores on top of my bruises. Yesterday, we lagged behind. The king chased a buck into the hermitage. As luck would have it, an ascetic's daughter called Śakuntalā caught his eye. Now he isn't even thinking of going back to the city. This very dawn I found him wide-eyed, mooning about her. What a fate! I must see him after his bath.
(He walks around, looking.)
Here comes my friend now, wearing garlands of wild flowers. Greek women carry his bow in their hands. Good! I'll stand here pretending my arms and legs are broken. Maybe then I'll get some rest.
(He stands leaning on his staff. The king enters with his retinue, as described.)
KING *(to himself)*:

> My beloved will not be easy to win,
> but signs of emotion revealed her heart—
> even when love seems hopeless,
> mutual longing keeps passion alive.   (1)

(*He smiles.*)
A suitor who measures his beloved's state of mind by his own desire is a fool.

> She threw tender glances
> though her eyes were cast down,
> her heavy hips swayed
> in slow seductive movements,
> she answered in anger
> when her friend said, "Don't go!"
> and I felt it was all for my sake . . .
> but a lover sees in his own way. (2)

BUFFOON (*still in the same position*): Dear friend, since my hands can't move to greet you, I have to salute you with my voice.

KING: How did you cripple your limbs?

BUFFOON: Why do you ask why I cry after throwing dust in my eyes yourself?

KING: I don't understand.

BUFFOON: Dear friend, when a straight reed is twisted into a crooked reed, is it by its own power, or is it the river current?

KING: The river current is the cause.

BUFFOON: And so it is with me.

KING: How so?

BUFFOON: You neglect the business of being a king and live like a woodsman in this awful camp. Chasing after wild beasts every day jolts my joints and muscles till I can't control my own limbs anymore. I beg you to let me rest for just one day!

KING: (*to himself*): He says what I also feel. When I remember Kanva's daughter, the thought of hunting disgusts me.

> I can't draw my bowstring
> to shoot arrows at deer
> who live with my love
> and teach her tender glances. (3)

BUFFOON: Sir, you have something on your mind. I'm crying in a wilderness.

KING (*smiling*): Yes, it is wrong to ignore my friend's plea.
BUFFOON: Live long!
(*He starts to go.*)
KING: Dear friend, stay! Hear what I have to say!
BUFFOON: At your command, sir!
KING: When you have rested, I need your help in some work that you will enjoy.
BUFFOON: Is it eating sweets? I'm game!
KING: I shall tell you. Who stands guard?
GUARD (*entering*): At your command, sir!
KING: Raivataka! Summon the general!
(*The guard exits and reenters with the general.*)
GUARD: The king is looking this way, waiting to give you his orders. Approach him, sir!
GENERAL (*looking at the king*): Hunting is said to be a vice, but our king prospers:

> Drawing the bow only hardens his chest,
> he suffers the sun's scorching rays unburned,
> hard muscles mask his body's lean state—
> like a wild elephant, his energy sustains him. (4)

(*He approaches the king.*)
Victory, my lord! We've already tracked some wild beasts. Why the delay?
KING: Mādhavya's censure of hunting has dampened my spirit.
GENERAL (*in a stage whisper, to the buffoon*): Friend, you stick to your opposition! I'll try to restore our king's good sense.
(*Aloud.*)
This fool is talking nonsense. Here is the king as proof:

> A hunter's belly is taut and lean,
> his slender body craves exertion;
> he penetrates the spirit of creatures
> overcome by fear and rage;
> his bowmanship is proved
> by arrows striking a moving target—
> hunting is falsely called a vice.
> What sport can rival it? (5)

BUFFOON (*angrily*): The king has come to his senses. If you keep chasing from forest to forest, you'll fall into the jaws of an old bear hungry for a human nose . . .

KING: My noble general, we are near a hermitage; your words cannot please me now.

> Let horned buffaloes plunge into muddy pools!
> Let herds of deer huddle in the shade to eat grass!
> Let fearless wild boars crush fragrant swamp grass!
> Let my bowstring lie slack and my bow at rest!   (6)

GENERAL: Whatever gives the king pleasure.

KING: Withdraw the men who are in the forest now and forbid my soldiers to disturb the grove!

> Ascetics devoted to peace
> possess a fiery hidden power,
> like smooth crystal sunstones
> that reflect the sun's scorching rays.   (7)

GENERAL: Whatever you command, sir!

BUFFOON: Your arguments for keeping up the hunt fall on deaf ears!

(*The general exits.*)

KING (*looking at his retinue*): You women, take away my hunting gear! Raivataka, don't neglect your duty!

RETINUE: As the king commands!

(*They exit.*)

BUFFOON: Sir, now that the flies are cleared out, sit on a stone bench under this shady canopy. Then I'll find a comfortable seat too.

KING: Go ahead!

BUFFOON: You first, sir!

(*Both walk about, then sit down.*)

KING: Mādhavya, you haven't really used your eyes because you haven't seen true beauty.

BUFFOON: But you're right in front of me, sir!

KING: Everyone is partial to what he knows well, but I'm speaking about Śakuntalā, the jewel of the hermitage.

BUFFOON (*to himself*): I won't give him a chance!
(*Aloud.*)
Dear friend, it seems that you're pursuing an ascetic's daughter.
KING: Friend, the heart of a Puru king wouldn't crave a forbidden fruit . . .

> The sage's child is a nymph's daughter,
> rescued by him after she was abandoned,
> like a fragile jasmine blossom
> broken and caught on a sunflower pod. (8)

BUFFOON (*laughing*): You're like the man who loses his taste for dates and prefers sour tamarind! How can you abandon the gorgeous gems of your palace?
KING: You speak this way because you haven't seen her.
BUFFOON: She must be delectable if you're so enticed!
KING: Friend, what is the use of all this talk?

> The divine creator imagined perfection
> and shaped her ideal form in his mind—
> when I recall the beauty his power wrought,
> she shines like a gemstone among my jewels. (9)

BUFFOON: So she's the reason you reject the other beauties!
KING: She stays in my mind:

> A flower no one has smelled,
> a bud no fingers have plucked,
> an uncut jewel, honey untasted,
> unbroken fruit of holy deeds—
> I don't know who is destined
> to enjoy her flawless beauty. (10)

BUFFOON: Then you should rescue her quickly! Don't let her fall into the arms of some ascetic who greases his head with iṅgudī oil!
KING: She is someone else's ward and her guardian is away.
BUFFOON: What kind of passion did her eyes betray?

KING: Ascetics are timid by nature:

> Her eyes were cast down in my presence,
> but she found an excuse to smile—
> modesty barely contained the love
> she could neither reveal nor conceal. (11)

BUFFOON: Did you expect her to climb into your lap when she'd barely seen you?

KING: When we parted her feelings for me showed despite her modesty.

> "A blade of kuśa grass
> pricked my foot,"
> the girl said for no reason
> after walking a few steps away;
> then she pretended to free
> her bark dress from branches
> where it was not caught
> and shyly glanced at me. (12)

BUFFOON: Stock up on food for a long trip! I can see you've turned that ascetics' grove into a pleasure garden.

KING: Friend, some of the ascetics recognize me. What excuse can we find to return to the hermitage?

BUFFOON: What excuse? Aren't you the king? Collect a sixth of their wild rice as tax!

KING: Fool! These ascetics pay tribute that pleases me more than mounds of jewels.

> Tribute that kings collect
> from members of society decays,
> but the share of austerity
> that ascetics give lasts forever. (13)

VOICE OFFSTAGE: Good, we have succeeded!

KING (*listening*): These are the steady, calm voices of ascetics.

GUARD (*entering*): Victory, sir! Two boy ascetics are waiting near the gate.

KING: Let them enter without delay!

GUARD: I'll show them in.
(*He exits; reenters with the boys.*)
Here you are!
FIRST BOY: His majestic body inspires trust. It is natural when a king is virtually a sage.

> His palace is a hermitage
> with its infinite pleasures,
> the discipline of protecting men
> imposes austerities every day—
> pairs of celestial bards praise
> his perfect self-control,
> adding the royal word "king"
> to "sage," his sacred title. (14)

SECOND BOY: Gautama, is this Duṣyanta, the friend of Indra?
FIRST BOY: Of course!
SECOND BOY:

> It is no surprise that this arm of iron
> rules the whole earth bounded by dark seas—
> when demons harass the gods, victory's hope
> rests on his bow and Indra's thunderbolt. (15)

BOTH BOYS (*coming near*): Victory to you, king!
KING (*rising from his seat*): I salute you both!
BOTH BOYS: To your success, sir!
(*They offer fruits.*)
KING (*accepting their offering*): I am ready to listen.
BOTH BOYS: The ascetics know that you are camped nearby and send a petition to you.
KING: What do they request?
BOTH BOYS: Demons are taking advantage of Sage Kaṇva's absence to harass us. You must come with your charioteer to protect the hermitage for a few days!
KING: I am honored to oblige.
BUFFOON (*in a stage whisper*): Your wish is fulfilled!
KING (*smiling*): Raivataka, call my charioteer! Tell him to bring the chariot and my bow!
GUARD: As the king commands!

(*He exits.*)
BOTH BOYS (*showing delight*):

> Following your ancestral duties
> suits your noble form—
> the Puru kings are ordained
> to dispel their subjects' fear.   (16)

KING (*bowing*): You two return! I shall follow.
BOTH BOYS: Be victorious!
(*They exit.*)
KING: Mādhavya, are you curious to see Śakuntalā?
BUFFOON: At first there was a flood, but now with this news of demons, not a drop is left.
KING: Don't be afraid! Won't you be with me?
BUFFOON: Then I'll be safe from any demon . . .
GUARD (*entering*): The chariot is ready to take you to victory . . . but Karabhaka has just come from the city with a message from the queen.
KING: Did my mother send him?
GUARD: She did.
KING: Have him enter then.
GUARD: Yes.
(*He exits; reenters with Karabhaka.*)
Here is the king. Approach!
KARABHAKA: Victory, sir! Victory! The queen has ordered a ceremony four days from now to mark the end of her fast. Your Majesty will surely give us the honor of his presence.
KING: The ascetics' business keeps me here and my mother's command calls me there. I must find a way to avoid neglecting either!
BUFFOON: Hang yourself between them the way Triśaṅku hung between heaven and earth.
KING: I'm really confused . . .

> My mind is split in two
> by these conflicting duties,
> like a river current split
> by boulders in its course.   (17)

(*Thinking*.)

Friend, my mother has treated you like a son. You must go back and report that I've set my heart on fulfilling my duty to the ascetics. You fulfill my filial duty to the queen.

BUFFOON: You don't really think I'm afraid of demons?

KING (*smiling*): My brave brahman, how could you be?

BUFFOON: Then I can travel like the king's younger brother.

KING: We really should not disturb the grove! Take my whole entourage with you!

BUFFOON: Now I've turned into the crown prince!

KING (*to himself*): This fellow is absent-minded. At any time he may tell the palace women about my passion. I'll tell him this:

(*Taking the buffoon by the hand, he speaks aloud.*)

Dear friend, I'm going to the hermitage out of reverence for the sages. I really feel no desire for the young ascetic Śakuntalā.

> What do I share with a rustic girl
> reared among fawns, unskilled in love?
> Don't mistake what I muttered
> in jest for the real truth, friend!   (18)

(*All exit.*)

END OF ACT TWO

ACT THREE

(*A disciple of Kaṇva enters, carrying kuśa grass for a sacrificial rite.*)

DISCIPLE: King Duṣyanta is certainly powerful. Since he entered the hermitage, our rites have not been hindered.

> Why talk of fixing arrows?
> The mere twang of his bowstring
> clears away menacing demons
> as if his bow roared with death. (1)

I'll gather some more grass for the priests to spread on the sacrificial altar.
(*Walking around and looking, he calls aloud.*)
Priyaṁvadā, for whom are you bringing the ointment of fragrant lotus root fibers and leaves?
(*Listening.*)
What are you saying? Śakuntalā is suffering from heat exhaustion? They're for rubbing on her body? Priyaṁvadā, take care of her! She is the breath of Father Kanva's life. I'll give Gautamī this water from the sacrifice to use for soothing her.
(*He exits; the interlude ends. Then the king enters, suffering from love, deep in thought, sighing.*)
KING:

> I know the power ascetics have
> and the rules that bind her,
> but I cannot abandon my heart
> now that she has taken it. (2)

(*Showing the pain of love.*)

Love, why do you and the moon both contrive to deceive lovers by first gaining our trust?

> Arrows of flowers and cool moon rays
> are both deadly for men like me—
> the moon shoots fire through icy rays
> and you hurl thunderbolts of flowers.   (3)

(*Walking around.*)
Now that the rites are concluded and the priests have dismissed me, where can I rest from the weariness of this work?
(*Sighing.*)
There is no refuge but the sight of my love. I must find her.
(*Looking up at the sun.*)
Śakuntalā usually spends the heat of the day with her friends in a bower of vines on the Mālinī riverbank. I shall go there.
(*Walking around, miming the touch of breeze.*)
This place is enchanted by the wind.

> A breeze fragrant with lotus pollen
> and moist from the Mālinī waves
> can be held in soothing embrace
> by my love-scorched arms.   (4)

(*Walking around and looking.*)

> I see fresh footprints
> on white sand in the clearing,
> deeply pressed at the heel
> by the sway of full hips.   (5)

I'll just look through the branches.
(*Walking around, looking, he becomes joyous.*)
My eyes have found bliss! The girl I desire is lying on a stone couch strewn with flowers, attended by her two friends. I'll eavesdrop as they confide in one another.
(*He stands watching. Śakuntalā appears as described, with her two friends.*)
BOTH FRIENDS (*fanning her affectionately*): Śakuntalā, does the breeze from this lotus leaf please you?

ŚAKUNTALĀ: Are you fanning me?

(*The friends trade looks, miming dismay.*)

KING (*deliberating*): Śakuntalā seems to be in great physical pain. Is it the heat or is it what is in my own heart?

(*Miming ardent desire.*)

My doubts are unfounded!

> Her breasts are smeared with lotus balm,
> her lotus-fiber bracelet hangs limp,
> her beautiful body glows in pain—
> love burns young women like summer heat,
> but its guilt makes them more charming.   (6)

PRIYAMVADĀ (*in a stage whisper*): Anasūyā, Śakuntalā has been pining since she first saw the king. Could he be the cause of her sickness?

ANASŪYĀ: She must be suffering from lovesickness. I'll ask her . . .

(*Aloud.*)

Friend, I have something to ask you. Your pain seems so deep . . .

ŚAKUNTALĀ (*raising herself halfway*): What do you want to say?

ANASŪYĀ: Śakuntalā, though we don't know what it is to be in love, your condition reminds us of lovers we have heard about in stories. Can you tell us the cause of your pain? Unless we understand your illness, we can't begin to find a cure.

KING: Anasūyā expresses my own thoughts.

ŚAKUNTALĀ: Even though I want to, suddenly I can't make myself tell you.

PRIYAMVADĀ: Śakuntalā, my friend Anasūyā means well. Don't you see how sick you are? Your limbs are wasting away. Only the shadow of your beauty remains . . .

KING: What Priyaṁvadā says is true:

> Her cheeks are deeply sunken,
> her breasts' full shape is gone,
> her waist is thin, her shoulders bent,
> and the color has left her skin—

tormented by love,
she is sad but beautiful to see,
like a jasmine creeper
when hot wind shrivels its leaves.   (7)

ŚAKUNTALĀ: Friends, who else can I tell? May I burden you?
BOTH FRIENDS: We insist! Sharing sorrow with loving friends
makes it bearable.
KING:

Friends who share her joy and sorrow
discover the love concealed in her heart—
though she looked back longingly at me,
now I am afraid to hear her response.   (8)

ŚAKUNTALĀ: Friend, since my eyes first saw the guardian of
the hermits' retreat, I've felt such strong desire for him!
KING: I have heard what I want to hear.

My tormentor, the god of love,
has soothed my fever himself,
like the heat of late summer
allayed by early rain clouds.   (9)

ŚAKUNTALĀ: If you two think it's right, then help me to win
the king's pity. Otherwise, you'll soon pour sesame oil and
water on my corpse . . .
KING: Her words destroy my doubt.
PRIYAṂVADĀ (*in a stage whisper*): She's so dangerously in love
that there's no time to lose. Since her heart is set on the
ornament of the Puru dynasty, we should rejoice that she
desires him.
ANASŪYĀ: What you say is true.
PRIYAṂVADĀ (*aloud*): Friend, by good fortune your desire is
in harmony with nature. A great river can only descend to the
ocean. A jasmine creeper can only twine around a mango
tree.
KING: Why is this surprising when the twin stars of spring
serve the crescent moon?

ANASŪYĀ: What means do we have to fulfill our friend's desire secretly and quickly?

PRIYAMVADĀ: "Secretly" demands some effort. "Quickly" is easy.

ANASŪYĀ: How so?

PRIYAMVADĀ: The king was charmed by her loving look; he seems thin these days from sleepless nights.

KING: It's true . . .

> This golden armlet
> slips to my wrist
> without touching the scars
> my bowstring has made;
> its gemstones are faded
> by tears of secret pain
> that every night wets my arm
> where I bury my face. (10)

PRIYAMVADĀ (*thinking*): Compose a love letter and I'll hide it in a flower. I'll deliver it to his hand on the pretext of bringing an offering to the deity.

ANASŪYĀ: This subtle plan pleases me. What does Śakuntalā say?

ŚAKUNTALĀ: I'll try my friend's plan.

PRIYAMVADĀ: Then compose a poem to declare your love!

ŚAKUNTALĀ: I'm thinking, but my heart trembles with fear that he'll reject me.

KING (*delighted*):

> The man you fear will reject you
> waits longing to love you, timid girl—
> a suitor may lose or be lucky,
> but the goddess always wins. (11)

BOTH FRIENDS: Why do you belittle your own virtues? Who would cover his body with a piece of cloth to keep off cool autumn moonlight?

ŚAKUNTALĀ (*smiling*): I'm trying to follow your advice.
(*She sits thinking.*)

KING: As I gaze at her, my eyes forget to blink.

> She arches an eyebrow,
> struggling to compose the verse—
> the down rises on her cheek,
> showing the passion she feels. (12)

ŚAKUNTALĀ: I've thought of a verse, but I have nothing to write it on.

PRIYAṀVADĀ: Engrave the letters with your nail on this lotus leaf! It's as delicate as a parrot's breast.

ŚAKUNTALĀ (*miming what Priyaṁvadā described*): Listen and tell me if this makes sense!

BOTH FRIENDS: We're both paying attention.

ŚAKUNTALĀ (*singing*):

> I don't know
> your heart,
> but day and night
> for wanting you,
> love violently
> tortures
> my limbs,
> cruel man. (13)

KING (*suddenly revealing himself*):

> Love torments you, slender girl,
> but he completely consumes me—
> daylight spares the lotus pond
> while it destroys the moon. (14)

BOTH FRIENDS (*looking, rising with delight*): Welcome to the swift success of love's desire!

(*Śakuntalā tries to rise.*)

KING: Don't exert yourself!

> Limbs lying among crushed petals
> like fragile lotus stalks
> are too weakened by pain
> to perform ceremonious acts. (15)

ANASŪYĀ: Then let the king sit on this stone bench!

(*The king sits; Śakuntalā rises in embarrassment.*)

PRIYAṀVADĀ: The passion of two young lovers is clear. My affection for our friend makes me speak out again now.

KING: Noble lady, don't hesitate! It is painful to keep silent when one must speak.

PRIYAṀVADĀ: We're told that it is the king's duty to ease the pain of his suffering subjects.

KING: My duty, exactly!

PRIYAṀVADĀ: Since she first saw you, our dear friend has been reduced to this sad condition. You must protect her and save her life.

KING: Noble lady, our affection is shared and I am honored by all you say.

ŚAKUNTALĀ (*looking at Priyaṁvadā*): Why are you keeping the king here? He must be anxious to return to his palace.

KING:

> If you think that my lost heart
> could love anyone but you,
> a fatal blow strikes a man
> already wounded by love's arrows! (16)

ANASŪYĀ: We've heard that kings have many loves. Will our dear friend become a sorrow to her family after you've spent time with her?

KING: Noble lady, enough of this!

> Despite my many wives,
> on two the royal line rests—
> sea-bound earth
> and your friend. (17)

BOTH FRIENDS: You reassure us.

PRIYAṀVADĀ (*casting a glance*): Anasūyā, this fawn is looking for its mother. Let's take it to her!

(*They both begin to leave.*)

ŚAKUNTALĀ: Come back! Don't leave me unprotected!

BOTH FRIENDS: The protector of the earth is at your side.

ŚAKUNTALĀ: Why have they gone?
KING: Don't be alarmed! I am your servant.

> Shall I set moist winds in motion
> with lotus-leaf fans to cool your pain,
> or rest your soft red lotus feet
> on my lap to stroke them, my love? (18)

ŚAKUNTALĀ: I cannot sin against those I respect!
(*Standing as if she wants to leave.*)
KING: Beautiful Śakuntalā, the day is still hot.

> Why should your frail limbs
> leave this couch of flowers
> shielded by lotus leaves
> to wander in the heat? (19)

(*Saying this, he forces her to turn around.*)
ŚAKUNTALĀ: Puru king, control yourself! Though I'm burning with love, how can I give myself to you?
KING: Don't fear your elders! The father of your family knows the law. When he finds out, he will not blame you.

> The daughters of royal sages often marry
> in secret and then their fathers bless them. (20)

ŚAKUNTALĀ: Release me! I must ask my friends' advice!
KING: Yes, I shall release you.
ŚAKUNTALĀ: When?
KING:

> Only let my thirsting mouth
> gently drink from your lips,
> the way a bee sips nectar
> from a fragile virgin blossom. (21)

(*Saying this, he tries to raise her face. Śakuntalā evades him with a dance.*)
VOICE OFFSTAGE: Red goose, bid farewell to your gander! Night has arrived!

ŚAKUNTALĀ (*flustered*): Puru king, Mother Gautamī is surely coming to ask about my health. Hide behind this tree!

KING: Yes.

(*He conceals himself and waits. Then Gautamī enters with a vessel in her hand, accompanied by Śakuntalā's two friends.*)

BOTH FRIENDS: This way, Mother Gautamī!

GAUTAMĪ (*approaching Śakuntalā*): Child, does the fever in your limbs burn less?

ŚAKUNTALĀ: Madam, I do feel better.

GAUTAMĪ: Kuśa grass and water will soothe your body.

(*She sprinkles Śakuntalā's head.*)

Child, the day is ended. Come, let's go back to our hut!

(*She starts to go.*)

ŚAKUNTALĀ (*to herself*): My heart, even when your desire was within reach, you were bound by fear. Now you'll suffer the torment of separation and regret.

(*Stopping after a few steps, she speaks aloud.*)

Bower of creepers, refuge from my torment, I say goodbye until our joy can be renewed . . .

(*Sorrowfully, Śakuntalā exits with the other women.*)

KING (*coming out of hiding*): Fulfillment of desire is fraught with obstacles.

> Why didn't I kiss her face
> as it bent near my shoulder,
> her fingers shielding lips
> that stammered lovely warning?   (22)

Should I go now? Or shall I stay here in this bower of creepers that my love enjoyed and then left?

> I see the flowers her body pressed
> on this bench of stone,
> the letter her nails inscribed
> on the faded lotus leaf,
> the lotus-fiber bracelet
> that slipped from her wrist—
> my eyes are prisoners
> in this empty house of reeds.   (23)

VOICE IN THE AIR: King!

> When the evening rituals begin,
> shadows of flesh-eating demons swarm
> like amber clouds of twilight,
> raising terror at the altar of fire. (24)

KING: I am coming.
(*He exits.*)

END OF ACT THREE

ACT FOUR

(The two friends enter, miming the gathering of flowers.)

ANASŪYĀ: Priyaṃvadā, I'm delighted that Śakuntalā chose a suitable husband for herself, but I still feel anxious.

PRIYAṂVADĀ: Why?

ANASŪYĀ: When the king finished the sacrifice, the sages thanked him and he left. Now that he has returned to his palace women in the city, will he remember us here?

PRIYAṂVADĀ: Have faith! He's so handsome, he can't be evil. But I don't know what Father Kanva will think when he hears about what happened.

ANASŪYĀ: I predict that he'll give his approval.

PRIYAṂVADĀ: Why?

ANASŪYĀ: He's always planned to give his daughter to a worthy husband. If fate accomplished it so quickly, Father Kanva won't object.

PRIYAṂVADĀ *(looking at the basket of flowers)*: We've gathered enough flowers for the offering ceremony.

ANASŪYĀ: Shouldn't we worship the goddess who guards Śakuntalā?

PRIYAṂVADĀ: I have just begun.

(She begins the rite.)

VOICE OFFSTAGE: I am here!

ANASŪYĀ *(listening)*: Friend, a guest is announcing himself.

PRIYAṂVADĀ: Śakuntalā is in her hut nearby, but her heart is far away.

ANASŪYĀ: You're right! Enough of these flowers!

(They begin to leave.)

VOICE OFFSTAGE: So . . . you slight a guest . . .

> Since you blindly ignore
> a great sage like me,
> the lover you worship
> with mindless devotion
> will not remember you,
> even when awakened—
> like a drunkard who forgets
> a story he just composed! (1)

PRIYAṀVADĀ: Oh! What a terrible turn of events! Śakuntalā's distraction has offended someone she should have greeted.
(*Looking ahead.*)
Not just an ordinary person, but the angry sage Durvāsas himself cursed her and went away in a frenzy of quivering, mad gestures. What else but fire has such power to burn?
ANASŪYĀ: Go! Bow at his feet and make him return while I prepare the water for washing his feet!
PRIYAṀVADĀ: As you say.
(*She exits.*)
ANASŪYĀ (*after a few steps, she mimes stumbling*): Oh! The basket of flowers fell from my hand when I stumbled in my haste to go.
(*She mimes the gathering of flowers.*)
PRIYAṀVADĀ (*entering*): He's so terribly cruel! No one could pacify him! But I was able to soften him a little.
ANASŪYĀ: Even that is a great feat with him! Tell me more!
PRIYAṀVADĀ: When he refused to return, I begged him to forgive a daughter's first offense, since she didn't understand the power of his austerity.
ANASŪYĀ: Then? Then?
PRIYAṀVADĀ: He refused to change his word, but he promised that when the king sees the ring of recollection, the curse will end. Then he vanished.
ANASŪYĀ: Now we can breathe again. When he left, the king himself gave her the ring engraved with his name. Śakuntalā will have her own means of ending the curse.

PRIYAṀVADĀ: Come friend! We should finish the holy rite we're performing for her.

(*The two walk around, looking.*)

Anasūyā, look! With her face resting on her hand, our dear friend looks like a picture. She is thinking about her husband's leaving, with no thought for herself, much less for a guest.

ANASŪYĀ: Priyaṁvadā, we two must keep all this a secret between us. Our friend is fragile by nature; she needs our protection.

PRIYAṀVADĀ: Who would sprinkle a jasmine with scalding water?

(*They both exit; the interlude ends. Then a disciple of Kaṇva enters, just awakened from sleep.*)

DISCIPLE: Father Kaṇva has just returned from his pilgrimage and wants to know the exact time. I'll go into a clearing to see what remains of the night.

(*Walking around and looking.*)

It is dawn.

> The moon sets over the western mountain
> as the sun rises in dawn's red trail—
> rising and setting, these two bright powers
> portend the rise and fall of men.   (2)
>
> When the moon disappears, night lotuses
> are but dull souvenirs of its beauty—
> when her lover disappears, the sorrow
> is too painful for a frail girl to bear.   (3)

ANASŪYĀ (*throwing aside the curtain and entering*): Even a person withdrawn from worldly life knows that the king has treated Śakuntalā badly.

DISCIPLE: I'll inform Father Kaṇva that it's time for the fire oblation.

(*He exits.*)

ANASŪYĀ: Even when I'm awake, I'm useless. My hands and feet don't do their work. Love must be pleased to have made our innocent friend put her trust in a liar . . . but perhaps it was the curse of Durvāsas that changed him . . . otherwise, how could the king have made such promises and not sent even a message by now? Maybe we should send the ring to remind him. Which of these ascetics who practice austerities can we ask? Father Kaṇva has just returned from his pilgrimage. Since we feel that our friend was also at fault, we haven't told him that Śakuntalā is married to Duṣyanta and is pregnant. The problem is serious. What should we do?

PRIYAṀVADĀ (*entering, with delight*): Friend, hurry! We're to celebrate the festival of Śakuntalā's departure for her husband's house.

ANASŪYĀ: What's happened, friend?

PRIYAṀVADĀ: Listen! I went to ask Śakuntalā how she had slept. Father Kaṇva embraced her and though her face was bowed in shame, he blessed her: "Though his eyes were filled with smoke, the priest's oblation luckily fell on the fire. My child, I shall not mourn for you . . . like knowledge given to a good student I shall send you to your husband today with an escort of sages."

ANASŪYĀ: Who told Father Kaṇva what happened?

PRIYAṀVADĀ: A bodiless voice was chanting when he entered the fire sanctuary.

(*Quoting in Sanskrit.*)

> Priest, know that your daughter
> carries Dusyanta's potent seed
> for the good of the earth—
> like fire in mimosa wood.   (4)

ANASŪYĀ: I'm joyful, friend. But I know that Śakuntalā must leave us today and sorrow shadows my happiness.

PRIYAṀVADĀ: Friend, we must chase away sorrow and make this hermit girl happy!

ANASŪYĀ: Friend, I've made a garland of mimosa flowers. It's in the coconut-shell box hanging on a branch of the mango tree. Get it for me! Meanwhile I'll prepare the special ointments of deer musk, sacred earth, and blades of dūrvā grass.

PRIYAṀVADĀ: Here it is!

(*Anasūyā exits; Priyaṁvadā gracefully mimes taking down the box.*)

VOICE OFFSTAGE: Gautamī! Śārṅgarava and some others have been appointed to escort Śakuntalā.

PRIYAṀVADĀ (*listening*): Hurry! Hurry! The sages are being called to go to Hastināpura.

ANASŪYĀ (*reentering with pots of ointments in her hands*): Come, friend! Let's go!

PRIYAṀVADĀ (*looking around*): Śakuntalā stands at sunrise with freshly washed hair while the female ascetics bless her with handfuls of wild rice and auspicious words of farewell. Let's go to her together.

(*The two approach as Śakuntalā enters with Gautamī and other female ascetics, and strikes a posture as described. One after another, the female ascetics address her.*)

FIRST FEMALE ASCETIC: Child, win the title "Chief Queen" as a sign of your husband's high esteem!

SECOND FEMALE ASCETIC: Child, be a mother to heroes!

THIRD FEMALE ASCETIC: Child, be honored by your husband!

BOTH FRIENDS: This happy moment is no time for tears, friend.

(*Wiping away her tears, they calm her with dance gestures.*)

PRIYAṀVADĀ: Your beauty deserves jewels, not these humble things we've gathered in the hermitage.

(*Two boy ascetics enter with offerings in their hands.*)

BOTH BOYS: Here is an ornament for you!

(*Everyone looks amazed.*)

GAUTAMĪ: Nārada, my child, where did this come from?

FIRST BOY: From Father Kaṇva's power.

GAUTAMĪ: Was it his mind's magic?

SECOND BOY: Not at all! Listen! You ordered us to bring flowers from the forest trees for Śakuntalā.

> One tree produced this white silk cloth,
> another poured resinous lac to redden her feet—
> the tree nymphs produced jewels in hands
> that stretched from branches like young shoots.   (5)

PRIYAMVADĀ (*watching Śakuntalā*): This is a sign that royal fortune will come to you in your husband's house.
(*Śakuntalā mimes modesty.*)
FIRST BOY: Gautama, come quickly! Father Kanva is back from bathing. We'll tell him how the trees honor her.
SECOND BOY: As you say.
(*The two exit.*)
BOTH FRIENDS: We've never worn them ourselves, but we'll put these jewels on your limbs the way they look in pictures.
ŚAKUNTALĀ: I trust your skill.
(*Both friends mime ornamenting her. Then Kanva enters, fresh from his bath.*)
KANVA:

> My heart is touched with sadness
> since Śakuntalā must go today,
> my throat is choked with sobs,
> my eyes are dulled by worry—
> if a disciplined ascetic
> suffers so deeply from love,
> how do fathers bear the pain
> of each daughter's parting?   (6)

(*He walks around.*)
BOTH FRIENDS: Śakuntalā, your jewels are in place; now put on the pair of silken cloths.
(*Standing, Śakuntalā wraps them.*)
GAUTAMĪ: Child, your father has come. His eyes filled with tears of joy embrace you. Greet him reverently!
ŚAKUNTALĀ (*modestly*): Father, I welcome you.
KANVA: Child,

> May your husband honor you
> the way Yayāti honored Śarmiṣṭhā.
> As she bore her son Puru,
> may you bear an imperial prince.   (7)

GAUTAMĪ: Sir, this is a blessing, not just a prayer.
KANVA: Child, walk around the sacrifical fires!

(All walk around; Kanva intoning a prayer in Vedic meter.)

> Perfectly placed around the main altar,
> fed with fuel, strewn with holy grass,
> destroying sin by incense from oblations,
> may these sacred fires purify you! (8)

You must leave now!
(Looking around.)
Where are Śārṅgarava and the others?
DISCIPLE *(entering)*: Here we are, sir!
KANVA: You show your sister the way!
ŚĀRṄGARAVA: Come this way!
(They walk around.)
KANVA: Listen, you trees that grow in our grove!

> Until you were well watered
> she could not bear to drink;
> she loved you too much
> to pluck your flowers for her hair;
> the first time your buds bloomed,
> she blossomed with joy—
> may you all bless Śakuntalā
> as she leaves for her husband's house. (9)

(Miming that he hears a cuckoo's cry.)

> The trees of her forest family
> have blessed Śakuntalā—
> the cuckoo's melodious song
> announces their response. (10)

VOICE IN THE AIR:

> May lakes colored by lotuses mark her path!
> May trees shade her from the sun's burning rays!
> May the dust be as soft as lotus pollen!
> May fragrant breezes cool her way! (11)

(All listen astonished.)

GAUTAMĪ: Child, the divinities of our grove love you like your family and bless you. We bow to you all!

ŚAKUNTALĀ (*bowing and walking around; speaking in a stage whisper*): Priyaṁvadā, though I long to see my husband, my feet move with sorrow as I start to leave the hermitage.

PRIYAṀVADĀ: You are not the only one who grieves. The whole hermitage feels this way as your departure from our grove draws near.

> Grazing deer
> drop grass,
> peacocks
> stop dancing,
> vines loose
> pale leaves
> falling
> like tears. (12)

ŚAKUNTALĀ (*remembering*): Father, before I leave, I must see my sister, the vine Forestlight.

KAṆVA: I know that you feel a sister's love for her. She is right here.

ŚAKUNTALĀ: Forestlight, though you love your mango tree, turn to embrace me with your tendril arms! After today, I'll be so far away . . .

KAṆVA:

> Your merits won you the husband
> I always hoped you would have
> and your jasmine has her mango tree—
> my worries for you both are over. (13)

Start your journey here!

ŚAKUNTALĀ (*facing her two friends*): I entrust her care to you.

BOTH FRIENDS: But who will care for us?

(*They wipe away their tears.*)

KAṆVA: Anasūyā, enough crying! You should be giving Śakuntalā courage!

(*All walk around.*)

ŚAKUNTALĀ: Father, when the pregnant doe who grazes near my hut gives birth, please send someone to give me the good news.

KAṆVA: I shall not forget.

ŚAKUNTALĀ (*miming the interrupting of her gait*): Who is clinging to my skirt?

(*She turns around.*)

KAṆVA: Child,

> The buck whose mouth you healed with oil
> when it was pierced by a blade of kuśa grass
> and whom you fed with grains of rice—
> your adopted son will not leave the path. (14)

ŚAKUNTALĀ: Child, don't follow when I'm abandoning those I love! I raised you when you were orphaned soon after your birth, but now I'm deserting you too. Father will look after you. Go back!

(*Weeping, she starts to go.*)

KAṆVA: Be strong!

> Hold back the tears that blind
> your long-lashed eyes—
> you will stumble if you cannot see
> the uneven ground on the path. (15)

ŚĀRṄGARAVA: Sir, the scriptures prescribe that loved ones be escorted only to the water's edge. We are at the shore of the lake. Give us your message and return!

ŚAKUNTALĀ: We shall rest in the shade of this fig tree.

(*All walk around and stop; Kaṇva speaks to himself.*)

What would be the right message to send to King Duṣyanta?

(*He ponders.*)

ŚAKUNTALĀ (*in a stage whisper*): Look! The wild goose cries in anguish when her mate is hidden by lotus leaves. What I'm suffering is much worse.

ANASŪYĀ: Friend, don't speak this way!

This goose spends
every long night
in sorrow
without her mate,
but hope lets her
survive
the deep pain
of loneliness.   (16)

KANVA: Śārṅgarava, speak my words to the king after you
present Śakuntalā!
ŚĀRṄGARAVA: As you command, sir!
KAṆVA:

Considering our discipline,
the nobility of your birth
and that she fell in love with you
before her kinsmen could act,
acknowledge her with equal rank
among your wives—
what more is destined for her,
the bride's family will not ask.   (17)

ŚĀRṄGARAVA: I grasp your message.
KAṆVA: Child, now I must instruct you. We forest hermits
know something about worldly matters.
ŚĀRṄGARAVA: Nothing is beyond the scope of wise men.
KAṆVA: When you enter your husband's family:

Obey your elders, be a friend to the other wives!
If your husband seems harsh, don't be impatient!
Be fair to your servants, humble in your happiness!
Women who act this way become noble wives;
sullen girls only bring their families disgrace.   (18)

But what does Gautamī think?
GAUTAMĪ: This is good advice for wives, child. Take it all to
heart!
KAṆVA: Child, embrace me and your friends!

ŚAKUNTALĀ: Father, why must Priyaṁvadā and my other friends turn back here?

KAṆVA: They will also be given in marriage. It is not proper for them to go there now. Gautamī will go with you.

ŚAKUNTALĀ (*embracing her father*): How can I go on living in a strange place, torn from my father's side, like a vine torn from the side of a sandalwood tree growing on a mountain slope?

KAṆVA: Child, why are you so frightened?

> When you are your husband's honored wife,
> absorbed in royal duties and in your son,
> born like the sun to the eastern dawn,
> the sorrow of separation will fade. (19)

(*Śakuntalā falls at her father's feet.*)
Let my hopes for you be fulfilled!

ŚAKUNTALĀ (*approaching her two friends*): You two must embrace me together!

BOTH FRIENDS (*embracing her*): Friend, if the king seems slow to recognize you, show him the ring engraved with his name!

ŚAKUNTALĀ: Your suspicions make me tremble!

BOTH FRIENDS: Don't be afraid! It's our love that fears evil.

ŚĀRṄGARAVA: The sun is high in the afternoon sky. Hurry, please!

ŚAKUNTALĀ (*facing the sanctuary*): Father, will I ever see the grove again?

KAṆVA:

> When you have lived for many years
> as a queen equal to the earth
> and raised Duṣyanta's son
> to be a matchless warrior,
> your husband will entrust him
> with the burdens of the kingdom
> and will return with you
> to the calm of this hermitage. (20)

GAUTAMĪ: Child, the time for our departure has passed. Let

your father turn back! It would be better, sir, if you turn back yourself. She'll keep talking this way forever.

KAṆVA: Child, my ascetic practice has been interrupted.

ŚAKUNTALĀ: My father's body is already tortured by ascetic practices. He must not grieve too much for me!

KAṆVA (*sighing*):

> When I see the grains of rice
> sprout from offerings you made
> at the door of your hut,
> how shall I calm my sorrow! (21)

(*Śakuntalā exits with her escort.*)

BOTH FRIENDS (*watching Śakuntalā*): Śakuntalā is hidden by forest trees now.

KAṆVA: Anasūyā, your companion is following her duty. Restrain yourself and return with me!

BOTH FRIENDS: Father, the ascetics' grove seems empty without Śakuntalā. How can we enter?

KAṆVA: The strength of your love makes it seem so.

(*Walking around in meditation.*)

Good! Now that Śakuntalā is on her way to her husband's family, I feel calm.

> A daughter belongs to another man—
> by sending her to her husband today,
> I feel the satisfaction
> one has on repaying a loan. (22)

(*All exit.*)

END OF ACT FOUR

ACT FIVE

(*The king and the buffoon enter; both sit down.*)

BUFFOON: Pay attention to the music room, friend, and you'll hear the notes of a song strung into a delicious melody . . . the lady Haṁsapadikā is practicing her singing.
KING: Be quiet so I can hear her!
VOICE IN THE AIR (*singing*):

> Craving sweet
> new nectar,
> you kissed
> a mango bud once—
> how could you
> forget her, bee,
> to bury your joy
> in a lotus? (1)

KING: The melody of the song is passionate.
BUFFOON: But did you get the meaning of the words?
KING: I once made love to her. Now she reproaches me for loving Queen Vasumatī. Friend Mādhavya, tell Haṁsapadikā that her words rebuke me soundly.
BUFFOON: As you command!
(*He rises.*)
But if that woman grabs my hair tuft, it will be like a heavenly nymph grabbing some ascetic . . . there go my hopes of liberation!
KING: Go! Use your courtly charm to console her.
BUFFOON: What a fate!
(*He exits.*)

KING (*to himself*): Why did hearing the song's words fill me with such strong desire? I'm not parted from anyone I love . . .

> Seeing rare beauty,
> hearing lovely sounds,
> even a happy man
> becomes strangely uneasy . . .
> perhaps he remembers,
> without knowing why,
> loves of another life
> buried deep in his being. (2)

(*He stands bewildered. Then the king's chamberlain enters.*)
CHAMBERLAIN: At my age, look at me!

> Since I took this ceremonial bamboo staff
> as my badge of office in the king's chambers
> many years have passed; now I use it
> as a crutch to support my faltering steps. (3)

A king cannot neglect his duty. He has just risen from his seat of justice and though I am loath to keep him longer, Sage Kaṇva's pupils have just arrived. Authority to rule the world leaves no time for rest.

> The sun's steeds were yoked before time began,
> the fragrant wind blows night and day,
> the cosmic serpent always bears earth's weight,
> and a king who levies taxes has his duty. (4)

Therefore, I must perform my office.
(*Walking around and looking.*)

> Weary from ruling them like children,
> he seeks solitude far from his subjects,
> like an elephant bull who seeks cool shade
> after gathering his herd at midday. (5)

(*Approaching.*)
Victory to you, king! Some ascetics who dwell in the forest at

the foothills of the Himālayas have come. They have women with them and bring a message from Sage Kaṇva. Listen, king, and judge!

KING (*respectfully*): Are they Sage Kaṇva's messengers?

CHAMBERLAIN: They are.

KING: Inform the teacher Somarāta that he should welcome the ascetics with the prescribed rites and then bring them to me himself. I'll wait in a place suitable for greeting them.

CHAMBERLAIN: As the king commands.

(*He exits.*)

KING (*rising*): Vetravatī, lead the way to the fire sanctuary.

DOORKEEPER: Come this way, king!

KING (*walking around, showing fatigue*): Every other creature is happy when the object of his desire is won, but for kings success contains a core of suffering.

> High office only leads to greater greed;
> just perfecting its rewards is wearisome—
> a kingdom is more trouble than it's worth,
> like a royal umbrella one holds alone. (6)

TWO BARDS OFFSTAGE: Victory to you, king!

FIRST BARD:

> You sacrifice your pleasures every day
> to labor for your subjects—
> as a tree endures burning heat
> to give shade from the summer sun. (7)

SECOND BARD:

> You punish villains with your rod of justice,
> you reconcile disputes, you grant protection—
> most relatives are loyal only in hope of gain,
> but you treat all your subjects like kinsmen. (8)

KING: My weary mind is revived.

(*He walks around.*)

DOORKEEPER: The terrace of the fire sanctuary is freshly washed and the cow is waiting to give milk for the oblation.

Let the king ascend!
KING: Vetravatī, why has Father Kanva sent these sages to me?

Does something hinder their ascetic life?
Or threaten creatures in the sacred forest?
Or do my sins stunt the flowering vines?
My mind is filled with conflicting doubts.   (9)

DOORKEEPER: I would guess that these sages rejoice in your virtuous conduct and come to honor you.
(*The ascetics enter; Śakuntalā is in front with Gautamī; the chamberlain and the king's priest are in front of her.*)
CHAMBERLAIN: Come this way, sirs!
ŚĀRṄGARAVA: Śāradvata, my friend:

I know that this renowned king is righteous
and none of the social classes follows evil ways,
but my mind is so accustomed to seclusion
that the palace feels like a house in flames.   (10)

ŚĀRADVATA: I've felt the same way ever since we entered the city.

As if I were freshly bathed, seeing a filthy man,
pure while he's defiled, awake while he's asleep,
as if I were a free man watching a prisoner,
I watch this city mired in pleasures.   (11)

ŚAKUNTALĀ (*indicating she feels an omen*): Why is my right eye twitching?
GAUTAMĪ: Child, your husband's family gods turn bad fortune into blessings!
(*They walk around.*)
PRIEST (*indicating the king*): Ascetics, the guardian of sacred order has left the seat of justice and awaits you now. Behold him!
ŚĀRṄGARAVA: Great priest, he seems praiseworthy, but we expect no less.

Boughs bend, heavy with ripened fruit,
clouds descend with fresh rain,
noble men are gracious with wealth—
this is the nature of bountiful things. (12)

DOORKEEPER: King, their faces look calm. I'm sure that the
sages have confidence in what they're doing.
KING (*seeing Śakuntalā*):

Who is she? Carefully veiled
to barely reveal her body's beauty,
surrounded by the ascetics
like a bud among withered leaves. (13)

DOORKEEPER: King, I feel curious and puzzled too. Surely
her form deserves closer inspection.
KING: Let her be! One should not stare at another man's wife!
ŚAKUNTALĀ (*placing her hand on her chest, she speaks to herself*):
My heart, why are you quivering? Be quiet while I learn my
noble husband's feelings.
PRIEST (*going forward*): These ascetics have been honored with
due ceremony. They have a message from their teacher. The
king should hear them!
KING: I am paying attention.
SAGES (*raising their hands in a gesture of greeting*): May you be
victorious, king!
KING: I salute you all!
SAGES: May your desires be fulfilled!
KING: Do the sages perform austerities unhampered?
SAGES:

Who would dare obstruct the rites
of holy men whom you protect—
how can darkness descend
when the sun's rays shine? (14)

KING: My title "king" is more meaningful now. Is the world
blessed by Father Kanva's health?

SAGES: Saints control their own health. He asks about your welfare and sends this message . . .

KING: What does he command?

ŚĀRṄGARAVA: At the time you secretly met and married my daughter, affection made me pardon you both.

> We remember you to be a prince of honor;
> Śakuntalā is virtue incarnate—
> the creator cannot be condemned
> for mating the perfect bride and groom.   (15)

And now that she is pregnant, receive her and perform your sacred duty together.

GAUTAMĪ: Sir, I have something to say, though I wasn't appointed to speak:

> She ignored her elders
> and you failed to ask her kinsmen—
> since you acted on your own,
> what can I say to you now?   (16)

ŚAKUNTALĀ: What does my noble husband say?

KING: What has been proposed?

ŚAKUNTALĀ (*to herself*): The proposal is as clear as fire.

ŚĀRṄGARAVA: What's this? Your Majesty certainly knows the ways of the world!

> People suspect a married woman who stays
> with her kinsmen, even if she is chaste—
> a young wife should live with her husband,
> no matter how he despises her.   (17)

KING: Did I ever marry you?

ŚAKUNTALĀ (*visibly dejected, speaking to herself*): Now your fears are real, my heart!

ŚĀRṄGARAVA:

> Does one turn away from duty in contempt
> because his own actions repulse him?   (18a)

KING: Why ask this insulting question?

ŚĀRŃGARAVA:

> Such transformations take shape
> when men are drunk with power. (18b)

KING: This censure is clearly directed at me.
GAUTAMĪ: Child, this is no time to be modest. I'll remove your veil. Then your husband will recognize you.
(*She does so.*)
KING (*staring at Śakuntalā*):

> Must I judge whether I ever married
> the flawless beauty they offer me now?
> I cannot love her or leave her, like a bee
> near a jasmine filled with frost at dawn. (19)

(*He shows hesitation.*)
DOORKEEPER: Our king has a strong sense of justice. Who else would hesitate when beauty like this is handed to him?
ŚĀRŃGARAVA: King, why do you remain silent?
KING: Ascetics, even though I'm searching my mind, I don't remember marrying this lady. How can I accept a woman who is visibly pregnant when I doubt that I am the cause?
ŚAKUNTALĀ (*in a stage whisper*): My lord casts doubt on our marriage. Why were my hopes so high?
ŚĀRŃGARAVA: It can't be!

> Are you going to insult the sage
> who pardons the girl you seduced
> and bids you keep his stolen wealth,
> treating a thief like you with honor? (20)

ŚĀRADVATA: Śārṅgarava, stop now! Śakuntalā, we have delivered our message and the king has responded. He must be shown some proof.
ŚAKUNTALĀ (*in a stage whisper*): When passion can turn to this, what's the use of reminding him? But, it's up to me to prove my honor now.
(*Aloud.*)
My noble husband . . .

(*She breaks off when this is half-spoken.*)
Since our marriage is in doubt, this is no way to address him.
Puru king, you do wrong to reject a simple-hearted person
with such words after you deceived her in the hermitage.
KING (*covering his ears*): Stop this shameful talk!

> Are you trying to stain my name
> and drag me to ruin—
> like a river eroding her own banks,
> soiling water and uprooting trees? (21)

ŚAKUNTALĀ: Very well! If it's really true that fear of taking
another man's wife turns you away, then this ring will revive
your memory and remove your doubt.
KING: An excellent idea!
ŚAKUNTALĀ (*touching the place where the ring had been*): I'm
lost! The ring is gone from my finger.
(*She looks despairingly at Gautamī.*)
GAUTAMĪ: The ring must have fallen off while you were
bathing in the holy waters at the shrine of the goddess near
Indra's grove.
KING (*smiling*): And so they say the female sex is cunning.
ŚAKUNTALĀ: Fate has shown its power. Yet, I will tell you
something else.
KING: I am still obliged to listen.
ŚAKUNTALĀ: One day, in a jasmine bower, you held a lotus-
leaf cup full of water in your hand.
KING: We hear you.
ŚAKUNTALĀ: At that moment the buck I treated as my son
approached. You coaxed it with the water, saying that it
should drink first. But he didn't trust you and wouldn't drink
from your hand. When I took the water, his trust returned.
Then you jested, "Every creature trusts what its senses know.
You both belong to the forest."
KING: Thus do women further their own ends by attracting
eager men with the honey of false words.

GAUTAMĪ: Great king, you are wrong to speak this way. This child raised in an ascetics' grove doesn't know deceit.

KING: Old woman,

> When naive female beasts show cunning,
> what can we expect of women who reason?
> Don't cuckoos let other birds nurture
> their eggs and teach the chicks to fly?   (22)

ŚAKUNTALĀ (*angrily*): Evil man! you see everything distorted by your own ignoble heart. Who would want to imitate you now, hiding behind your show of justice, like a well overgrown with weeds?

KING (*to himself*): Her anger does not seem feigned; it makes me doubt myself.

> When the absence of love's memory
> made me deny a secret affair with her,
> this fire-eyed beauty bent her angry brows
> and seemed to break the bow of love.   (23)

(*Aloud.*)

Lady, Duṣyanta's conduct is renowned, so what you say is groundless.

ŚAKUNTALĀ: All right! I may be a self-willed wanton woman! But it was faith in the Puru dynasty that brought me into the power of a man with honey in his words and poison in his heart.

(*She covers her face at the end of the speech and weeps.*)

ŚĀRṄGARAVA: A willful act unchecked always causes pain.

> One should be cautious
> in forming a secret union—
> unless a lover's heart is clear,
> affection turns to poison.   (24)

KING: But sir, why do you demean me with such warnings? Do you trust the lady?

ŚĀRṄGARAVA (*scornfully*): You have learned everything back-
wards.

> If you suspect the word of one
> whose nature knows no guile,
> then you can only trust
> people who practice deception.   (25)

KING: I presume you speak the truth. Let us assume so. But
what could I gain by deceiving this woman?
ŚĀRṄGARAVA: Ruin.
KING: Ruin? A Puru king has no reason to want his own ruin!
ŚĀRADVATA: Śārṅgarava, this talk is pointless. We have deliv-
ered our master's message and should return.

> Since you married her, abandon her or take her—
> absolute is the power a husband has over his wife.   (26)

GAUTAMĪ: You go ahead.
(*They start to go.*)
ŚAKUNTALĀ: What? Am I deceived by this cruel man and
then abandoned by you?
(*She tries to follow them.*)
GAUTAMĪ (*stopping*): Śārṅgarava my son, Śakuntalā is follow-
ing us, crying pitifully. What will my child do now that her
husband has refused her?
ŚĀRṄGARAVA (*turning back angrily*): Bold woman, do you still
insist on having your way?
(*Śakuntalā trembles in fear.*)

> If you are what the king says you are,
> you don't belong in Father Kaṇva's family—
> if you know that your marriage vow is pure,
> you can bear slavery in your husband's house.   (27)

Stay! We must go on!
KING: Ascetic, why do you disappoint the lady too?

> The moon only makes lotuses open,
> the sun's light awakens lilies—
> a king's discipline forbids him
> to touch another man's wife.   (28)

ŚĀRṄGARAVA: If you forget a past affair because of some present attachment, why do you fear injustice now?

KING (*to the priest*): Sir, I ask you to weigh the alternatives:

> Since it's unclear whether I'm deluded
> or she is speaking falsely—
> should I risk abandoning a wife
> or being tainted by another man's? (29)

PRIEST (*deliberating*): I recommend this . . .

KING: Instruct me! I'll do as you say.

PRIEST: Then let the lady stay in our house until her child is born. If you ask why: the wise men predict that your first son will be born with the marks of a king who turns the wheel of empire. If the child of the sage's daughter bears the marks, congratulate her and welcome her into your palace chambers. Otherwise, send her back to her father.

KING: Whatever the elders desire.

PRIEST: Child, follow me!

ŚAKUNTALĀ: Mother earth, open to receive me!

(*Weeping, Śakuntalā exits with the priest and the hermits. The king, his memory lost through the curse, thinks about her.*)

VOICE OFFSTAGE: Amazing! Amazing!

KING (*listening*): What could this be?

PRIEST (*reentering, amazed*): King, something marvelous has occurred!

KING: What?

PRIEST: When Kaṇva's pupils had departed,

> The girl threw up her arms and wept,
> lamenting her misfortune . . . then . . . (30a)

KING: Then what?

PRIEST:

> Near the nymph's shrine a ray of light
> in the shape of a woman carried her away. (30b)

(*All mime amazement.*)

KING: We've already settled the matter. Why discuss it further?

PRIEST (*observing the king*): May you be victorious!
(*He exits.*)
KING: Vetravatī, I am bewildered. Lead the way to my chamber!
DOORKEEPER: Come this way, my lord!
(*She walks forward.*)
KING:

> I cannot remember marrying
> the sage's abandoned daughter,
> but the pain my heart feels
> makes me suspect that I did. (31)

(*All exit.*)

END OF ACT FIVE

ACT SIX

(The king's wife's brother, who is city magistrate, enters with two policemen leading a man whose hands are tied behind his back.)

BOTH POLICEMEN *(beating the man)*: Speak, thief! Where'd you steal this handsome ring with the king's name engraved in the jewel?

MAN *(showing fear)*: Peace, sirs! I wouldn't do a thing like that.

FIRST POLICEMAN: Don't tell us the king thought you were some famous priest and gave it to you as a gift!

MAN: Listen, I'm a humble fisherman who lives near Indra's grove.

SECOND POLICEMAN: Thief, did we ask you about your caste?

MAGISTRATE: Sūcaka, let him tell it all in order! Don't interrupt him!

BOTH POLICEMEN: Whatever you command, chief!

MAN: I feed my family by catching fish with nets and hooks.

MAGISTRATE *(mocking)*: What a pure profession!

MAN:

> The work I do
> may be vile
> but I won't deny
> my birthright—
> a priest
> doing his holy rites
> pities the animals
> he kills.

(1)

MAGISTRATE: Go on!

MAN: One day as I was cutting up a red carp, I saw the shining stone of this ring in its belly. When I tried to sell it, you grabbed me. Kill me or let me go! That's how I got it!

MAGISTRATE: Jānuka, I'm sure this ugly butcher's a fisherman by his stinking smell. We must investigate how he got the ring. We'll go straight to the palace.

BOTH POLICEMEN: Okay. Go in front, you pickpocket!

(*All walk around.*)

MAGISTRATE: Sūcaka, guard this villain at the palace gate! I'll report to the king how we found the ring, get his orders, and come back.

BOTH POLICEMEN: Chief, good luck with the king!

(*The magistrate exits.*)

FIRST POLICEMAN: Jānuka, the chief's been gone a long time.

SECOND POLICEMAN: Well, there are fixed times for seeing kings.

FIRST POLICEMAN: Jānuka, my hands are itching to tie on his execution garland.

(*He points to the man.*)

MAN: You shouldn't think about killing a man for no reason.

SECOND POLICEMAN (*looking*): I see our chief coming with a letter in his hand. It's probably an order from the king. You'll be thrown to the vultures or you'll see the face of death's dog again . . .

MAGISTRATE (*entering*): Sūcaka, release this fisherman! I'll tell you how he got the ring.

FIRST POLICEMAN: Whatever you say, chief!

SECOND POLICEMAN: The villain entered the house of death and came out again.

(*He unties the prisoner.*)

MAN (*bowing to the magistrate*): Master, how will I make my living now?

MAGISTRATE: The king sends you a sum equal to the ring.

(*He gives the money to the man.*)

MAN (*bowing as he grabs it*): The king honors me.

FIRST POLICEMAN: This fellow's certainly honored. He was lowered from the execution stake and raised up on a royal elephant's back.

SECOND POLICEMAN: Chief, the reward tells me this ring was special to the king.

MAGISTRATE: I don't think the king valued the stone, but when he caught sight of the ring, he suddenly seemed to remember someone he loved, and he became deeply disturbed.

FIRST POLICEMAN: You served him well, chief!

SECOND POLICEMAN: I think you better served this king of fish.

(*Looking at the fisherman with jealousy.*)

MAN: My lords, half of this is yours for your good will.

FIRST POLICEMAN: It's only fair!

MAGISTRATE: Fisherman, now that you are my greatest and dearest friend, we should pledge our love over kadamba-blossom wine. Let's go to the wine shop!

(*They all exit together; the interlude ends. Then a nymph named Sānumatī enters by the skyway.*)

SĀNUMATĪ: Now that I've performed my assigned duties at the nymph's shrine, I'll slip away to spy on King Duṣyanta while the worshipers are bathing. My friendship with Menakā makes me feel a bond with Śakuntalā. Besides, Menakā asked me to help her daughter.

(*Looking around.*)

Why don't I see preparations for the spring festival in the king's palace? I can learn everything by using my mental powers, but I must respect my friend's request. So be it! I'll make myself invisible and spy on these two girls who are guarding the pleasure garden.

(*Sānumatī mimes descending and stands waiting. Then a maid servant named Parabhṛtikā, "Little Cuckoo," enters, looking at a mango bud. A second maid, named Madhukarikā, "Little Bee," is following her.*)

FIRST MAID:

> Your pale green stem
> tinged with pink
> is a true sign
> that spring has come—
> I see you,
> mango-blossom bud,
> and I pray
> for a season of joy. (2)

SECOND MAID: What are you muttering to yourself?

FIRST MAID: A cuckoo goes mad when she sees a mango bud.

SECOND MAID (*joyfully rushing over*): Has the sweet month of spring come?

FIRST MAID: Now's the time to sing your songs of love.

SECOND MAID: Hold me while I pluck a mango bud and worship the god of love.

FIRST MAID: Only if you'll give me half the fruit of your worship.

SECOND MAID: That goes without saying . . . our bodies may be separate, but our lives are one . . .

(*Leaning on her friend, she stands and plucks a mango bud.*)

The mango flower is still closed, but this broken stem is fragrant.

(*She makes the dove gesture with her hands.*)

> Mango-blossom bud,
> I offer you to Love
> as he lifts
> his bow of passion.
> Be the first
> of his flower arrows
> aimed at lonely girls
> with lovers far away! (3)

(*She throws the mango bud.*)

CHAMBERLAIN (*angrily throwing aside the curtain and entering*): Not now, stupid girl! When the king has banned the festival of spring, how dare you pluck a mango bud!

BOTH MAIDS (*frightened*): Please forgive us, sir. We don't know what you mean.

CHAMBERLAIN: Did you not hear that even the spring trees and the nesting birds obey the king's order?

> The mango flowers bloom without spreading pollen,
> the red amaranth buds, but will not bloom,
> cries of cuckoo cocks freeze though frost is past,
> and out of fear, Love holds his arrow half-drawn.   (4)

BOTH MAIDS: There is no doubt about the king's great power!

FIRST MAID: Sir, several days ago we were sent to wait on the queen by Mitrāvasu, the king's brother-in-law. We were assigned to guard the pleasure garden. Since we're newcomers, we've heard no news.

CHAMBERLAIN: Let it be! But don't do it again!

BOTH MAIDS: Sir, we're curious. May we ask why the spring festival was banned?

SĀNUMATĪ: Mortals are fond of festivals. The reason must be serious.

CHAMBERLAIN: It is public knowledge. Why should I not tell them? Has the scandal of Śakuntalā's rejection not reached your ears?

BOTH MAIDS: We only heard from the king's brother-in-law that the ring was found.

CHAMBERLAIN (*to himself*): There is little more to tell.
(*Aloud.*)
When he saw the ring, the king remembered that he had married Śakuntalā in secret and had rejected her in his delusion. Since then the king has been tortured by remorse.

> Despising what he once enjoyed,
> he shuns his ministers every day
> and spends long sleepless nights
> tossing at the edge of his bed—
> when courtesy demands that
> he converse with palace women,
> he stumbles over their names,
> and then retreats in shame.   (5)

SĀNUMATĪ: This news delights me.

CHAMBERLAIN: The festival is banned because of the king's melancholy.

BOTH MAIDS: It's only right.

VOICE OFFSTAGE: This way, sir!

CHAMBERLAIN (*listening*): The king is coming. Go about your business!

BOTH MAIDS: As you say.

(*Both maids exit. Then the king enters, costumed to show his grief, accompanied by the buffoon and the doorkeeper.*)

CHAMBERLAIN (*observing the king*): Extraordinary beauty is appealing under all conditions. Even in his lovesick state, the king is wonderful to see.

> Rejecting his regal jewels,
> he wears one golden bangle
> above his left wrist;
> his lips are pale with sighs,
> his eyes wan from brooding at night—
> like a gemstone ground in polishing,
> the fiery beauty of his body
> makes his wasted form seem strong. (6)

SĀNUMATĪ (*seeing the king*): I see why Śakuntalā pines for him though he rejected and disgraced her.

KING (*walking around slowly, deep in thought*):

> This cursed heart slept
> when my love came to wake it,
> and now it stays awake
> to suffer the pain of remorse. (7)

SĀNUMATĪ: The girl shares his fate.

BUFFOON (*in a stage whisper*): He's having another attack of his Śakuntalā disease. I doubt if there's any cure for that.

CHAMBERLAIN (*approaching*): Victory to the king! I have inspected the grounds of the pleasure garden. Let the king visit his favorite spots and divert himself.

KING: Vetravatī, deliver a message to my noble minister

Piśuna: "After being awake all night, we cannot sit on the seat of justice today. Set in writing what your judgment tells you the citizens require and send it to us!"

DOORKEEPER: Whatever you command!

(*She exits.*)

KING: Vātāyana, attend to the rest of your business!

CHAMBERLAIN: As the king commands!

(*He exits.*)

BUFFOON: You've cleared out the flies. Now you can rest in some pretty spot. The garden is pleasant now in this break between morning cold and noonday heat.

KING: Dear friend, the saying "Misfortunes rush through any crack" is absolutely right:

> Barely freed by the dark force
> that made me forget Kaṇva's daughter,
> my mind is threatened by an arrow
> of mango buds fixed on Love's bow. (8)

BUFFOON: Wait, I'll destroy the love god's arrow with my wooden stick.

(*Raising his staff, he tries to strike a mango bud.*)

KING (*smiling*): Let it be! I see the majesty of brahman bravery. Friend, where may I sit to divert my eyes with vines that remind me of my love?

BUFFOON: Didn't you tell your maid Caturikā, "I'll pass the time in the jasmine bower. Bring me the drawing board on which I painted a picture of Śakuntalā with my own hand!"

KING: Such a place may soothe my heart. Show me the way!

BUFFOON: Come this way!

(*Both walk around; the nymph Sānumatī follows.*)

The marble seat and flower offerings in this jasmine bower are certainly trying to make us feel welcome. Come in and sit down!

(*Both enter the bower and sit.*)

SĀNUMATĪ: I'll hide behind these creepers to see the picture he's drawn of my friend. Then I'll report how great her husband's passion is.

(She does as she says and stands waiting.)

KING: Friend, now I remember everything. I told you about my first meeting with Śakuntalā. You weren't with me when I rejected her, but why didn't you say anything about her before? Did you suffer a loss of memory too?

BUFFOON: I didn't forget. You did tell me all about it once, but then you said, "It's all a joke without any truth." My wit is like a lump of clay, so I took you at your word . . . or it could be that fate is powerful . . .

SĀNUMATĪ: It is!

KING: Friend, help me!

BUFFOON: What's this? It doesn't become you! Noblemen never take grief to heart. Even in storms, mountains don't tremble.

KING: Dear friend, I'm defenseless when I remember the pain of my love's bewilderment when I rejected her.

> When I cast her away, she followed her kinsmen,
> but Kanva's disciple harshly shouted, "Stay!"
> The tearful look my cruelty provoked
> burns me like an arrow tipped with poison. (9)

SĀNUMATĪ: The way he rehearses his actions makes me delight in his pain.

BUFFOON: Sir, I guess that the lady was carried off by some celestial creature or other.

KING: Who else would dare to touch a woman who worshiped her husband? I was told that Menakā is her mother. My heart suspects that her mother's companions carried her off.

SĀNUMATĪ: His delusion puzzled me, but not his reawakening.

BUFFOON: If that's the case, you'll meet her again in good time.

KING: How?

BUFFOON: No mother or father can bear to see a daughter parted from her husband.

KING:

> Was it dream or illusion or mental confusion,
> or the last meager fruit of my former good deeds?
> It is gone now, and my heart's desires are
> like riverbanks crumbling of their own weight. (10)

BUFFOON: Stop this! Isn't the ring evidence that an unexpected meeting is destined to take place?

KING (*looking at the ring*): I only pity it for falling from such a place.

> Ring, your punishment is proof
> that your fate is as flawed as mine—
> you were placed in her lovely fingers,
> glowing with crimson nails, and you fell. (11)

SĀNUMATĪ: The real pity would have been if it had fallen into some other hand.

BUFFOON: What prompted you to put the signet ring on her hand?

SĀNUMATĪ: I'm curious too.

KING: I did it when I left for the city. My love broke into tears and asked, "How long will it be before my noble husband sends news to me?"

BUFFOON: Then? What then?

KING: Then I placed the ring on her finger with this promise:

> One by one, day after day,
> count each syllable of my name!
> At the end, a messenger will come
> to bring you to my palace. (12)

But in my cruel delusion, I never kept my word.

SĀNUMATĪ: Fate broke their charming agreement!

BUFFOON: How did it get into the belly of the carp the fisherman was cutting up?

KING: While she was worshiping at the shrine of Indra's wife, it fell from her hand into the Gaṅgā.

BUFFOON: It's obvious now!

SĀNUMATĪ: And the king, doubtful of his marriage to Śakun-talā, a female ascetic, was afraid to commit an act of injustice. But why should such passionate love need a ring to be remembered?

KING: I must reproach the ring for what it's done.

BUFFOON (*to himself*): He's gone the way of all madmen . . .

KING:

Why did you leave her delicate finger
and sink into the deep river? (13a)

Of course . . .

A mindless ring can't recognize virtue,
but why did I reject my love? (13b)

BUFFOON (*to himself again*): Why am I consumed by a craving for food?

KING: Oh ring! Have pity on a man whose heart is tormented because he abandoned his love without cause! Let him see her again!

(*Throwing the curtain aside, the maid Caturikā enters, with the drawing board in her hand.*)

CATURIKĀ: Here's the picture you painted of the lady.

(*She shows the drawing board.*)

BUFFOON: Dear friend, how well you've painted your feelings in this sweet scene! My eyes almost stumble over the hollows and hills.

SĀNUMATĪ: What skill the king has! I feel as if my friend were before me.

KING:

The picture's imperfections are not hers,
but this drawing does hint at her beauty. (14)

SĀNUMATĪ: Such words reveal that suffering has increased his modesty as much as his love.

BUFFOON: Sir, I see three ladies now and they're all lovely to look at. Which is your Śakuntalā?

SĀNUMATĪ: Only a dim-witted fool like this wouldn't know such beauty!

KING: You guess which one!

BUFFOON: I guess Śakuntalā is the one you've drawn with flowers falling from her loosened locks of hair, with drops of sweat on her face, with her arms hanging limp and tired as she stands at the side of a mango tree whose tender shoots are gleaming with the fresh water she poured. The other two are her friends.

KING: You are clever! Look at these signs of my passion!

> Smudges from my sweating fingers
> stain the edges of the picture
> and a tear fallen from my cheek
> has raised a wrinkle in the paint. (15)

Caturikā, the scenery is only half-drawn. Go and bring my paints!

CATURIKĀ: Noble Mādhavya, hold the drawing board until I come back!

KING: I'll hold it myself.

(*He takes it, the maid exits.*)

> I rejected my love when she came to me,
> and now I worship her in a painted image—
> having passed by a river full of water,
> I'm longing now for an empty mirage. (16)

BUFFOON (*to himself*): He's too far gone for a river now! He's looking for a mirage!

(*Aloud.*)

Sir, what else do you plan to draw here?

SĀNUMATĪ: He'll want to draw every place my friend loved.

KING:

> I'll draw the river Mālinī
> flowing through Himālaya's foothills
> where pairs of wild geese nest in the sand
> and deer recline on both riverbanks,

where a doe is rubbing her left eye
on the horn of a black buck antelope
under a tree whose branches
have bark dresses hanging to dry.   (17)

BUFFOON (*to himself*): Next he'll fill the drawing board with mobs of ascetics wearing long grassy beards.

KING: Dear friend, I've forgotten to draw an ornament that Śakuntalā wore.

BUFFOON: What is it?

SĀNUMATĪ: It will suit her forest life and her tender beauty.

KING:

I haven't drawn the mimosa flower on her ear,
its filaments resting on her cheek,
or the necklace of tender lotus stalks,
lying on her breasts like autumn moonbeams.   (18)

BUFFOON: But why does the lady cover her face with her red lotus-bud fingertips and stand trembling in fear?
(*Looking closely.*)
That son-of-a-bee who steals nectar from flowers is attacking her face.

KING: Drive the impudent rogue away!

BUFFOON: You have the power to punish criminals. You drive him off!

KING: All right! Bee, favored guest of the flowering vines, why do you frustrate yourself by flying here?

A female bee waits on a flower,
thirsting for your love—
she refuses to drink
the sweet nectar without you.   (19)

SĀNUMATĪ: How gallantly he's driving him away!

BUFFOON: When you try to drive it away, this creature becomes vicious.

KING: Why don't you stop when I command you?

Bee, if you touch the lips of my love
that lure you like a young tree's virgin buds,
lips I gently kissed in festivals of love,
I'll hold you captive in a lotus flower cage.   (20)

BUFFOON: Why isn't he afraid of your harsh punishment?
(*Laughing, he speaks to himself.*)
He's gone crazy and I'll be the same if I go on talking like this.
(*Aloud.*)
But sir, it's just a picture!
KING: A picture? How can that be?
SĀNUMATĪ: When I couldn't tell whether it was painted, how
could he realize he was looking at a picture?
KING: Dear friend, are you envious of me?

My heart's affection made me feel
the joy of seeing her—
but you reminded me again
that my love is only a picture.   (21)

(*He wipes away a tear.*)
SĀNUMATĪ: The effects of her absence make him quarrel-
some.
KING: Dear friend, why do I suffer this endless pain?

Sleepless nights prevent our meeting in dreams;
her image in a picture is ruined by my tears.   (22)

SĀNUMATĪ: You have clearly atoned for the suffering your
rejection caused Śakuntalā.
CATURIKĀ (*entering*): Victory my lord! I found the paint box
and started back right away . . . but I met Queen Vasumatī
with her maid Taralikā on the path and she grabbed the box
from my hand, saying, "I'll bring it to the noble lord myself!"
BUFFOON: You were lucky to get away!
CATURIKĀ: The queen's shawl got caught on a tree. While
Taralikā was freeing it, I made my escape.
KING: Dear friend, the queen's pride can quickly turn to anger. Save this picture!

BUFFOON: You should say, "Save yourself!"

(*Taking the picture, he stands up.*)

If you escape the woman's deadly poison, then send word to me in the Palace of the Clouds.

(*He exits hastily.*)

SĀNUMATĪ: Even though another woman has taken his heart and he feels indifferent to the queen, he treats her with respect.

DOORKEEPER (*entering with a letter in her hand*): Victory, king!

KING: Vetravatī, did you meet the queen on the way?

DOORKEEPER: I did, but when she saw the letter in my hand, she turned back.

KING: She knows that this is official and would not interrupt my work.

DOORKEEPER: King, the minister requests that you examine the contents of this letter. He said that the enormous job of reckoning the revenue in this one citizen's case had taken all his time.

KING: Show me the letter!

(*The girl hands it to him and he reads barely aloud.*)

What is this? "A wealthy merchant sea captain named Dhanamitra has been lost in a shipwreck and the laws say that since the brave man was childless, his accumulated wealth all goes to the king." It's terrible to be childless! A man of such wealth probably had several wives. We must find out if any one of his wives is pregnant!

DOORKEEPER: King, it's said that one of his wives, the daughter of a merchant of Ayodhyā, has performed the rite to ensure the birth of a son.

KING: The child in her womb surely deserves his paternal wealth. Go! Report this to my minister!

DOORKEEPER: As the king commands!

(*She starts to go.*)

KING: Come here a moment!

DOORKEEPER: I am here.

KING: Is it his offspring or not?

> When his subjects lose a kinsman,
> Duṣyanta will preserve the estates—
> unless there is some crime.
> Let this be proclaimed.   (23)

DOORKEEPER: It shall be proclaimed loudly.
(*She exits; reenters.*)
The king's order will be as welcome as rain in the right season.

KING (*sighing long and deeply*): Families without offspring whose lines of succession are cut off lose their wealth to strangers when the last male heir dies. When I die, this will happen to the wealth of the Puru dynasty.

DOORKEEPER: Heaven forbid such a fate!

KING: I curse myself for despising the treasure I was offered.

SĀNUMATĪ: He surely has my friend in mind when he blames himself.

KING:

> I abandoned my lawful wife, the holy ground
> where I myself planted my family's glory,
> like earth sown with seed at the right time,
> ready to bear rich fruit in season.   (24)

SĀNUMATĪ: But your family's line will not be broken.

CATURIKĀ (*in a stage whisper*): The king is upset by the story of the merchant. Go and bring noble Mādhavya from the Palace of the Clouds to console him!

DOORKEEPER: A good idea!
(*She exits.*)

KING: Duṣyanta's ancestors are imperiled.

> Our fathers drink the yearly libation
> mixed with my childless tears,
> knowing that there is no other son
> to offer the sacred funeral waters.   (25)

(*He falls into a faint.*)

CATURIKĀ (*looking at the bewildered king*): Calm yourself, my lord!

SĀNUMATĪ: Though a light shines, his separation from Śakuntalā keeps him in a state of dark depression. I could make him happy now, but I've heard Indra's consort consoling Śakuntalā with the news that the gods are hungry for their share of the ancestral oblations and will soon conspire to have her husband welcome his lawful wife. I'll have to wait for the auspicious time, but meanwhile I'll cheer my friend by reporting his condition.

(*She exits, flying into the air.*)

VOICE OFFSTAGE: Help! Brahman-murder!

KING (*regaining consciousness, listening*): Is it Mādhavya's cry of pain? Who's there?

DOORKEEPER: King, your friend is in danger. Help him!

KING: Who dares to threaten him?

DOORKEEPER: Some invisible spirit seized him and dragged him to the roof of the Palace of the Clouds.

KING (*getting up*): Not this! Even my house is haunted by spirits.

> When I don't even recognize
> the blunders I commit every day,
> how can I keep track
> of where my subjects stray? (26)

VOICE OFFSTAGE: Dear friend! Help! Help!

KING (*breaking into a run*): Friend, don't be afraid! I'm coming!

VOICE OFFSTAGE (*repeating the call for help*): Why shouldn't I be afraid? Someone is trying to split my neck in three, like a stalk of sugar cane.

KING (*casting a glance*): Quickly, my bow!

BOW-BEARER (*entering with a bow in hand*): Here are your bow and quiver.

(*The king takes his bow and arrows.*)

VOICE OFFSTAGE:

> I'll kill you as a tiger kills struggling prey!
> I'll drink fresh blood from your tender neck!
> Take refuge now in the bow Duṣyanta lifts
> to calm the fears of the oppressed! (27)

KING (*angrily*): How dare you abuse my name? Stop, carrion-eater! Or you will not live!
(*He strings his bow.*)
Vetravatī, lead the way to the stairs!
DOORKEEPER: This way, king.
(*All move forward in haste.*)
KING (*searching around*): There is no one here!
VOICE OFFSTAGE: Help! Help! I see you. Don't you see me? I'm like a mouse caught by a cat! My life is hopeless!
KING: Don't count on your powers of invisibility! My magical arrows will find you. I aim this arrow:

> It will strike its doomed target
> and spare the brahman it must save—
> a wild goose can extract the milk
> and leave the water untouched. (28)

(*He aims the arrow. Then Indra's charioteer Mātali enters, having released the buffoon.*)
MĀTALI: King!

> Indra sets demons as your targets;
> draw your bow against them!
> Send friends gracious glances
> rather than deadly arrows! (29)

KING (*withdrawing his arrow*): Mātali, welcome to great Indra's charioteer!
BUFFOON (*entering*): He tried to slaughter me like a sacrifical beast and this king is greeting him with honors!
MĀTALI (*smiling*): Your Majesty, hear why Indra has sent me to you!
KING: I am all attention.
MĀTALI: There is an army of demons descended from one-hundred-headed Kālanemi, known to be invincible . . .
KING: I have already heard it from Nārada, the gods' messenger.

MĀTALI:

> He is invulnerable to your friend Indra,
> so you are appointed to lead the charge—
> the moon dispels the darkness of night
> since the sun cannot drive it out.　　　　　　　(30)

Take your weapon, mount Indra's chariot, and prepare for victory!

KING: Indra favors me with this honor. But why did you attack Mādhavya?

MĀTALI: I'll tell you! From the signs of anguish Your Majesty showed, I knew that you were despondent. I attacked him to arouse your anger.

> A fire blazes when fuel is added;
> a cobra provoked raises its hood—
> men can regain lost courage
> if their emotions are roused.　　　　　　　　(31)

KING (*in a stage whisper*): Dear friend, I cannot disobey a command from the lord of heaven. Inform my minister Piśuna of this and tell him this for me:

> Concentrate your mind on guarding my subjects!
> My bow is strung to accomplish other work.　　(32)

BUFFOON: Whatever you command!
(*He exits.*)
MĀTALI: Mount the chariot, Your Majesty!
(*The king mimes mounting the chariot; all exit.*)

END OF ACT SIX

ACT SEVEN

(The king enters with Mātali by the skyway, mounted on a chariot.)

KING: Mātali, though I carried out his command, I feel unworthy of the honors Indra gave me.

MĀTALI *(smiling)*: Your Majesty, neither of you seems satisfied.

> You belittle the aid you gave Indra
> in face of the honors he conferred,
> and he, amazed by your heroic acts,
> deems his hospitality too slight. (1)

KING: No, not so! When I was taking leave, he honored me beyond my heart's desire and shared his throne with me in the presence of the gods:

> Indra gave me a garland of coral flowers
> tinged with sandalpowder from his chest,
> while he smiled at his son Jayanta,
> who stood there barely hiding his envy. (2)

MĀTALI: Don't you deserve whatever you want from Indra?

> Indra's heaven of pleasures has twice
> been saved by rooting out thorny demons—
> your smooth-jointed arrows have now done
> what Visnu once did with his lion claws. (3)

KING: Here too Indra's might deserves the praise.

> When servants succeed in great tasks,
> they act in hope of their master's praise—
> would dawn scatter the darkness
> if he were not the sun's own charioteer? (4)

MĀTALI: This attitude suits you well!
(*He moves a little distance.*)
Look over there, Your Majesty! See how your own glorious fame has reached the vault of heaven!

> Celestial artists are drawing your exploits
> on leaves of the wish-granting creeper
> with colors of the nymphs' cosmetic paints,
> and bards are moved to sing of you in ballads. (5)

KING: Mātali, in my desire to do battle with the demons, I did not notice the path we took to heaven as we climbed through the sky yesterday. Which course of the winds are we traveling?
MĀTALI:

> They call this path of the wind Parivaha—
> freed from darkness by Visnu's second stride,
> it bears the Gaṅgā's three celestial streams
> and turns stars in orbit, dividing their rays. (6)

KING: Mātali, this is why my soul, my senses, and my heart feel calm.
(*He looks at the chariot wheels.*)
We've descended to the level of the clouds.
MĀTALI: How do you know?
KING:

> Crested cuckoos fly between the spokes,
> lightning flashes glint off the horses' coats,
> and a fine mist wets your chariot's wheels—
> all signs that we go over rain-filled clouds. (7)

MĀTALI: In a moment you'll be back in your own domain, Your Majesty.
KING (*looking down*): Our speeding chariot makes the mortal world appear fantastic. Look!

> Mountain peaks emerge as the earth descends,
> branches spread up from a sea of leaves,
> fine lines become great rivers to behold—
> the world seems to hurtle toward me. (8)

MĀTALI: You observe well! (*He looks with great reverence.*)
The beauty of earth is sublime.
KING: Mātali, what mountain do I see stretching into the
eastern and western seas, rippled with streams of liquid gold,
like a gateway of twilight clouds?
MĀTALI: Your Majesty, it is called the "Golden Peak," the
mountain of the demigods, a place where austerities are practiced to perfection.

> Mārīca, the descendant of Brahmā,
> a father of both demons and gods,
> lives the life of an ascetic here
> in the company of Aditi, his wife.   (9)

KING: One must not ignore good fortune! I shall perform the
rite of circumambulating the sage.
MĀTALI: An excellent idea!
(*The two mime descending.*)
KING (*smiling*):

> The chariot wheels make no sound,
> they raise no clouds of dust,
> they touch the ground unhindered—
> nothing marks the chariot's descent.   (10)

MĀTALI: It is because of the extraordinary power that you and
Indra both possess.
KING: Mātali, where is Mārīca's hermitage?
MĀTALI (*pointing with his hand*):

> Where the sage stands staring at the sun,
> as immobile as the trunk of a tree,
> his body half-buried in an ant hill,
> with a snake skin on his chest,
> his throat pricked by a necklace
> of withered thorny vines,
> wearing a coil of long matted hair
> filled with nests of śakunta birds.   (11)

KING: I do homage to the sage for his severe austerity.

MĀTALI (*pulling hard on the chariot reins*): Great king, let us enter Mārīca's hermitage, where Aditi nurtures the celestial coral trees.

KING: This tranquil place surpasses heaven. I feel as if I'm bathing in a lake of nectar.

MĀTALI (*stopping the chariot*): Dismount, Your Majesty!

KING (*dismounting*): Mātali, what about you?

MĀTALI: I have stopped the chariot. I'll dismount too.

(*He does so.*)

This way, Your Majesty!

(*He walks around.*)

You can see the grounds of the ascetics' grove ahead.

KING: I am amazed!

> In this forest of wish-fulfilling trees
> ascetics live on only the air they breathe
> and perform their ritual ablutions
> in water colored by golden lotus pollen.
> They sit in trance on jeweled marble slabs
> and stay chaste among celestial nymphs,
> practicing austerities in the place
> that others seek to win by penances. (12)

MĀTALI: Great men always aspire to rare heights!

(*He walks around, calling aloud.*)

O venerable Śākalya, what is the sage Mārīca doing now? What do you say? In response to Aditi's question about the duties of a devoted wife, he is talking in a gathering of great sages' wives.

KING (*listening*): We must wait our turn.

MĀTALI (*looking at the king*): Your Majesty, rest at the foot of this aśoka tree. Meanwhile, I'll look for a chance to announce you to Indra's father.

KING: As you advise . . .

(*He stops.*)

MĀTALI: Your Majesty, I'll attend to this.

(*He exits.*)

KING (*indicating he feels an omen*):

> I have no hope for my desire.
> Why does my arm throb in vain?
> Once good fortune is lost,
> it becomes constant pain. (13)

VOICE OFFSTAGE: Don't be so wild! Why is his nature so stubborn?

KING (*listening*): Unruly conduct is out of place here. Whom are they reprimanding?

(*Looking toward the sound, surprised.*)

Who is this child, guarded by two female ascetics? A boy who acts more like a man.

> He has dragged this lion cub
> from its mother's half-full teat
> to play with it, and with his hand
> he violently tugs its mane. (14)

(*The boy enters as described, with two female ascetics.*)

BOY: Open your mouth, lion! I want to count your teeth!

FIRST ASCETIC: Nasty boy, why do you torture creatures we love like our children? You're getting too headstrong! The sages gave you the right name when they called you "Sarvadamana, Tamer-of-everything."

KING: Why is my heart drawn to this child, as if he were my own flesh? I don't have a son. That is why I feel tender toward him . . .

SECOND ASCETIC: The lioness will maul you if you don't let go of her cub!

BOY (*smiling*): Oh, I'm scared to death!

(*Pouting.*)

KING:

> This child appears to be
> the seed of hidden glory,
> like a spark of fire
> awaiting fuel to burn. (15)

FIRST ASCETIC: Child, let go of the lion cub and I'll give you another toy!
BOY: Where is it? Give it to me!
(*He reaches out his hand.*)
KING: Why does he bear the mark of a king who turns the wheel of empire?

> A hand with fine webs connecting the fingers
> opens as he reaches for the object greedily,
> like a single lotus with faint inner petals
> spread open in the red glow of early dawn.　　　　　(16)

SECOND ASCETIC: Suvratā, you can't stop him with words! The sage Mārkandeya's son left a brightly painted clay bird in my hut. Get it for him!
FIRST ASCETIC: I will!
(*She exits.*)
BOY: But until it comes I'll play with this cub.
KING: I am attracted to this pampered boy . . .

> Lucky are fathers whose laps give refuge
> to the muddy limbs of adoring little sons
> when childish smiles show budding teeth
> and jumbled sounds make charming words.　　　　　(17)

SECOND ASCETIC: Well, he ignores me.
(*She looks back.*)
Is one of the sage's sons here?
(*Looking at the king.*)
Sir, please come here! Make him loosen his grip and let go of the lion cub! He's tormenting it in his cruel child's play.
KING (*approaching the boy, smiling*): Stop! You're a great sage's son!

> When self-control is your duty by birth,
> why do you violate the sanctuary laws
> and ruin the animals' peaceful life,
> like a young black snake in a sandal tree?　　　　　(18)

SECOND ASCETIC: Sir, he's not a sage's son.

KING: His actions and his looks confirm it. I based my false assumption on his presence in this place.
(*He does what she asked; responding to the boy's touch, he speaks to himself.*)

> Even my limbs feel delighted
> from the touch of a stranger's son—
> the father at whose side he grew
> must feel pure joy in his heart. (19)

SECOND ASCETIC (*examining them both*): It's amazing! Amazing!
KING: What is it, madam?
SECOND ASCETIC: This boy looks surprisingly like you. He doesn't even know you, and he's acting naturally.
KING (*fondling the child*): If he's not the son of an ascetic, what lineage does he belong to?
SECOND ASCETIC: The family of Puru.
KING (*to himself*): What? His ancestry is the same as mine . . . so this lady thinks he resembles me. The family vow of Puru's descendants is to spend their last days in the forest.

> As world protectors they first choose
> palaces filled with sensuous pleasures,
> but later, their homes are under trees
> and one wife shares the ascetic vows. (20)

(*Aloud.*)
But mortals cannot enter this realm on their own.
SECOND ASCETIC: You're right, sir. His mother is a nymph's child. She gave birth to him here in the hermitage of Mārīca.
KING (*in a stage whisper*): Here is a second ground for hope!
(*Aloud.*)
What famed royal sage claims her as his wife?
SECOND ASCETIC: Who would even think of speaking the name of a man who rejected his lawful wife?
KING (*to himself*): Perhaps this story points to me. What if I ask the name of the boy's mother? No, it is wrong to ask about another man's wife.

FIRST ASCETIC (*returning with a clay bird in her hand*): Look, Sarvadamana, a śakunta! Look! Isn't it lovely?

BOY: Where's my mother?

BOTH ASCETICS: He's tricked by the similarity of names. He wants his mother.

SECOND ASCETIC: Child, she told you to look at the lovely clay śakunta bird.

KING (*to himself*): What? Is his mother's name Śakuntalā? But names can be the same. Even a name is a mirage . . . a false hope to herald despair.

BOY: I like this bird!

(*He picks up the toy.*)

FIRST ASCETIC (*looking frantically*): Oh, I don't see the amulet-box on his wrist!

KING: Don't be alarmed! It broke off while he was tussling with the lion cub.

(*He goes to pick it up.*)

BOTH ASCETICS: Don't touch it! Oh, he's already picked it up!

(*With their hands on their chests, they stare at each other in amazement.*)

KING: Why did you warn me against it?

FIRST ASCETIC: It contains the magical herb called Aparājitā, honored sir. Mārīca gave it to him at his birth ceremony. He said that if it fell to the ground no one but his parents or himself could pick it up.

KING: And if someone else does pick it up?

FIRST ASCETIC: Then it turns into a snake and strikes.

KING: Have you two seen it so transformed?

BOTH ASCETICS: Many times.

KING (*to himself, joyfully*): Why not rejoice in the fulfillment of my heart's desire?

(*He embraces the child.*)

SECOND ASCETIC: Suvratā, come, let's tell Śakuntalā that her penances are over.

(*Both ascetics exit*).

BOY: Let me go! I want my mother!

KING: Son, you will greet your mother with me.

BOY: My father is Duṣyanta, not you!

KING: This contradiction confirms the truth.

(*Śakuntalā enters, wearing the single braid of a woman in mourning.*)

ŚAKUNTALĀ: Even though Sarvadamana's amulet kept its natural form instead of changing into a snake, I can't hope that my destiny will be fulfilled. But maybe what my friend Sānumatī reports is right.

KING (*looking at Śakuntalā*): It is Śakuntalā!

> Wearing dusty gray garments,
> her face gaunt from penances,
> her bare braid hanging down—
> she bears with perfect virtue
> the trial of long separation
> my cruelty forced on her.　　　　　　　　　　(21)

ŚAKUNTALĀ (*seeing the king pale with suffering*): He doesn't resemble my noble husband. Whose touch defiles my son when the amulet is protecting him?

BOY (*going to his mother*): Mother, who is this stranger who calls me "son"?

KING: My dear, I see that you recognize me now. Even my cruelty to you is transformed by your grace.

ŚAKUNTALĀ (*to herself*): Heart, be consoled! My cruel fate has finally taken pity on me. It is my noble husband!

KING:

> Memory chanced to break my dark delusion
> and you stand before me in beauty,
> like the moon's wife Rohiṇī
> as she rejoins her lord after an eclipse.　　　　(22)

ŚAKUNTALĀ: Victory to my noble husband! Vic . . .

(*She stops when the word is half-spoken, her throat choked with tears.*)

KING: Beautiful Śakuntalā,

> Even choked by your tears,
> the word "victory" is my triumph
> on your bare pouting lips,
> pale-red flowers of your face.   (23)

BOY: Mother, who is he?
ŚAKUNTALĀ: Child, ask the powers of fate!
KING (*falling at Śakuntalā's feet*):

> May the pain of my rejection
> vanish from your heart;
> delusion clouded my weak mind
> and darkness obscured good fortune—
> a blind man tears off a garland,
> fearing the bite of a snake.   (24)

ŚAKUNTALĀ: Noble husband, rise! Some crime I had committed in a former life surely came to fruit and made my kind husband indifferent to me.
(*The king rises.*)
But how did my noble husband come to remember this woman who was doomed to pain?
KING: I shall tell you after I have removed the last barb of sorrow.

> In my delusion I once ignored
> a teardrop burning your lip—
> let me dry the tear on your lash
> to end the pain of remorse!   (25)

(*He does so.*)
ŚAKUNTALĀ (*seeing the signet ring*): My noble husband, this is the ring!
KING: I regained my memory when the ring was recovered.
ŚAKUNTALĀ: When it was lost, I tried in vain to convince my noble husband who I was.

KING: Let the vine take back this flower as a sign of her union with spring.

ŚAKUNTALĀ: I don't trust it. Let my noble husband wear it! (*Mātali enters.*)

MĀTALI: Good fortune! This meeting with your lawful wife and the sight of your son's face are reasons to rejoice.

KING: The sweet fruit of my desire! Mātali, didn't Indra know about all this?

MĀTALI: What is unknown to the gods? Come, Your Majesty! The sage Mārīca grants you an audience.

KING: Śakuntalā, hold our son's hand! We shall go to see Mārīca together.

ŚAKUNTALĀ: I feel shy about appearing before my elders in my husband's company.

KING: But it is customary at a joyous time like this. Come! Come!

(*They all walk around. Then Mārīca enters with Aditi; they sit.*)

MĀRĪCA (*looking at the king*):

Aditi, this is king Duṣyanta,
who leads Indra's armies in battle;
his bow lets your son's thunderbolt
lie ready with its tip unblunted.   (26)

ADITI: He bears himself with dignity.

MĀTALI: Your Majesty, the parents of the gods look at you with affection reserved for a son. Approach them!

KING: Mātali, the sages so describe this pair:

Source of the sun's twelve potent forms,
parents of Indra, who rules the triple world,
birthplace of Visnu's primordial form,
sired by Brahmā's sons, Marīci and Dakṣa.   (27)

MĀTALI: Correct!

KING (*bowing*): Indra's servant, Duṣyanta, bows to you both.

MĀRĪCA: My son, live long and protect the earth!

ADITI: My son, be an invincible warrior!

ŚAKUNTALĀ: I worship at your feet with my son.
MĀRĪCA:

> Child, with a husband like Indra
> and a son like his son Jayanta,
> you need no other blessing.
> Be like Indra's wife Paulomī! (28)

ADITI: Child, may your husband honor you and may your child live long to give both families joy! Be seated!
(*All sit near Mārīca.*)
MĀRĪCA (*pointing to each one*):

> By the turn of fortune,
> virtuous Śakuntalā, her noble son,
> and the king are reunited—
> faith and wealth with order. (29)

KING: Sir, first came the success of my hopes, then the sight of you. Your kindness is unparalleled.

> First flowers appear, then fruits,
> first clouds rise, then rain falls,
> but here the chain of events is reversed—
> first came success, then your blessing. (30)

MĀTALI: This is the way the creator gods give blessings.
KING: Sir, I married your charge by secret marriage rites. When her relatives brought her to me after some time, my memory failed and I sinned against the sage Kaṇva, your kinsman. When I saw the ring, I remembered that I had married his daughter. This is all so strange!

> Like one who doubts the existence
> of an elephant who walks in front of him
> but feels convinced by seeing footprints,
> my mind has taken strange turns. (31)

MĀRĪCA: My son, you need not take the blame. Even your delusion has another cause. Listen!
KING: I am attentive.

MĀRĪCA: When Menakā took her bewildered daughter from the steps of the nymphs' shrine and brought her to my wife, I knew through meditation that you had rejected this girl as your lawful wife because of Durvāsas' curse, and that the curse would end when you saw the ring.

KING (*sighing*): So I am freed of blame.

ŚAKUNTALĀ (*to herself*): And I am happy to learn that I wasn't rejected by my husband without cause. But I don't remember being cursed. Maybe the empty heart of love's separation made me deaf to the curse . . . my friends did warn me to show the ring to my husband . . .

MĀRĪCA: My child, I have told you the truth. Don't be angry with your husband!

> You were rejected when the curse
> that clouded memory made him cruel,
> but now darkness is lifted
> and your power is restored—
> a shadow has no shape
> in a badly tarnished mirror,
> but when the surface is clean
> it can easily be seen. (32)

KING: Sir, here is the glory of my family!

(*He takes the child by the hand.*)

MĀRĪCA: Know that he is destined to turn the wheel of your empire!

> His chariot will smoothly cross
> the ocean's rough waves
> and as a mighty warrior
> he will conquer the seven continents.
> Here he is called Sarvadamana,
> Tamer-of-everything;
> later when his burden is the world,
> men will call him Bharata, Sustainer. (33)

KING: Since you performed his birth ceremonies, we can hope for all this.

ADITI: Sir, let Kanva be told that his daughter's hopes have been fulfilled. Menakā, who loves her daughter, is here in attendance.

ŚAKUNTALĀ (*to herself*): The lady expresses my own desire.

MĀRĪCA: He knows everything already through the power of his austerity.

KING: This is why the sage was not angry at me.

MĀRĪCA: Still, I want to hear his response to this joyful reunion. Who is there?

DISCIPLE (*entering*): Sir, it is I.

MĀRĪCA: Gālava, fly through the sky and report the joyous reunion to Kanva in my own words: "The curse is ended. Śakuntalā and her son are embraced by Dusyanta now that his memory is restored."

DISCIPLE: As you command, sir!

(*He exits.*)

MĀRĪCA: My son, mount your friend Indra's chariot with your wife and son and return to your royal capital!

KING: As you command, sir!

MĀRĪCA: My son, what other joy can I give you?

KING: There is no greater joy, but if you will:

> May the king serve nature's good!
> May priests honor the goddess of speech!
> And may Śiva's dazzling power
> destroy my cycle of rebirths!   (34)

(*All exit.*)

END OF ACT SEVEN AND OF THE PLAY
ŚAKUNTALĀ AND THE RING OF RECOLLECTION

Tr. Barbara Stoler Miller

Islamic

Literature

Arabian Literature

Abdallah ibn al-Muqaffa (d. ca. 760)
From *Fables of Bidpai* (*Kalila wa Dimna*)

Introduction
by Esin Atil

The history of the *Kalila wa Dimna*, also called the *Fables of Bidpai*, is as fascinating as the stories included in the book. The original work, written in Sanskrit, was a compilation of parables taken from the Indian classics. The title is derived from a corruption of the names of the two jackals, Karataka and Damanaka, who are the protagonists of the first story. The book, thought to have been written down around the year 300 by an unknown Vishnuite Brahman living in Kashmir, was later attributed to an Indian sage named Bidpai. It was intended to instruct princes and contains several chapters, which teach a particular moral principle or rule of conduct.

Each chapter begins with the king asking the philosopher the consequences of a certain mode of behavior; the philosopher explains the effects of such an action and illustrates his advice with stories enacted by animals who are caught in a similar predicament. A chapter encompasses a number of parenthetical episodes, tales, sayings, and discourses that emphasize the moral of the story. The animals used in the tales display the full range of human emotion and thought; they speak and behave as if they are living in human societies and are punished or rewarded for their actions.

Although the significance of the work lies in the moral lessons taught by these tales, the didactic theme is often overshadowed by the personalities of the animals who solve their problems with cunning, wit, and ingenuity. The reader tends to remember only the fables, and the fact that these are stories told by the philosopher to the king to illustrate an ethical question becomes a secondary element. Yet this feature is of great structural importance since it provides coherence to the book and links the otherwise independent chapters with each other.

The *Kalila wa Dimna* was introduced to the Near East in the middle of the sixth century. The book was brought from India to Iran by a physician named Burzoe, who had been requested by a Sasanian king to translate the text into Pahlavi (Middle Persian). Burzoe's version was rendered into Arabic by Abdallah ibn al-Muqaffa two hundred years later. Ibn al-Muqaffa's *Kalila wa Dimna* was exceedingly popular and it became the source for subsequent translations. Many later Arabic, Persian, and Turkish renditions were profusely illustrated in the Islamic courts throughout the Near East.

The copy in the Bodleian Library in Oxford, completed in 1354, is

among the earliest illustrated Arabic versions of the work. Its anonymous painter invites us to enter a world of fantasy where human
emotions, attitudes, and ideas are expressed by anthropomorphic creatures who have established highly structured societies. The individuals
inhabiting the sky, sea, and land are as believable and real as the men and
women included in the stories. In fact, the human figures, who are
represented in a stylized manner, frequently converse with the animals
and are a part of this fantastic world, thus prohibiting us from differentiating
between man and beast.

The behavior of the animals reflects human weaknesses and strengths,
ambitions and achievements. We can relate to the justice and injustice of
their world and to the cruelty and kindness shown by friends and
enemies since we face similar circumstances in our own lives. We are
touched by their endearing personalities; we appreciate their intelligence, resourcefulness, and compassion.

This psychological rapport between protagonist and reader is immensely enhanced by the illustrations, which with their simple compo-
sitions, abstracted settings, and charming character portrayals visually
transport us into the world of animals.

The *Kalila wa Dimna* is more than a book of parables or a mirror for
princes. It symbolizes man's search for truth and justice, challenging his
perception of reality on the one hand and the extent of his imagination
on the other. The underlying theme of the work is that all creatures, big
or small, are a part of creation and each society is a microcosm of a much
larger entity that controls the destiny of its members. This perhaps was
the essence of the worldwide popularity of the *Kalila wa Dimna*, appealing to all peoples at all times.

The Lion and the Ox

Dabshalim, the king of India, asked his minister and advisor,
who was a philosopher, to tell him stories that contained instructions
on governing his kingdom. His first request to the philosopher was
to explain how a false and cunning person can come between two
friends and cause dissension, turning their love and trust to hatred
and enmity.

The philosopher began by telling the story of the merchant and
his three sons.

There was a well-to-do merchant with three extravagant and

irresponsible sons. When the sons squandered their father's money, the merchant admonished them and gave the following advice: everyone desired three things in life—ample sustenance, respect, and provisions for life hereafter—which could be obtained through four means—to amass wealth by lawful procedures, put this wealth to good use, care for one's own interests, and be generous to the less fortunate.

The sons followed their father's counsel, and the oldest set out on a trading venture with a wagon drawn by two oxen called Shanzabeh and Banzabeh. When they reached a marshy terrain, Shanzabeh, exhausted from pulling the heavy wagon, got stuck in the mud. The young merchant, who was in a hurry, decided to leave the ox with an attendant assigned to free the animal. The attendant waited for a while and then left the ox. When he caught up with his master, he lied and said that the ox had died.

Meanwhile Shanzabeh was able to free himself from the marsh. He found a good pasture near a stream and soon recovered his strength and became fat and healthy. Although he had plenty of food and water, Shanzabeh was lonely. He would bellow pathetically whenever he felt sad and alone.

Not too far from Shanzabeh's meadow was the court of the lion, which included two jackals, Kalila and Dimna, who were employed at the royal gate. The jackals were crafty and bright as well as wise and learned. Dimna was particularly ambitious and not at all content with his present position. He was constantly on the look out to improve his status and be closer to the king.

Every time the lion heard the ox bellow, he cringed in fright, not knowing who was making this dreadful sound. Ashamed of his fear, the lion hid in his den whenever he heard the noise. Dimna noticed that the lion kept close to his den and rarely ventured far from court. He requested an audience with the king and presented himself. He started telling stories, which put the lion at ease, and quickly won the king's confidence. But as soon as the bellow of the ox was heard, the lion became terrified and confessed that he was afraid of whoever was making this noise. Dimna understood the lion's dilemma and began to tell him the story of the fox and the drum.

A hungry fox was walking through the forest when he heard a deafening sound. It was coming from a large drum suspended from a tree; whenever the wind blew, branches hit the drum, thereby producing a loud noise. The fox followed the direction of the sound and when he saw the drum, he attacked it, thinking that it contained food. When he found nothing inside, he realized that it was the insignificant things that were bigger in size and louder in sound.

Dimna finished the story of the fox and the drum by saying that perhaps the terrible sound disturbing the lion was also from an insignificant creature. He volunteered to go and seek its source.

The lion anxiously awaited Dimna's return. When the jackal came back, he reported that the noise was coming from an ox who was big but lacked the power of the lion; he also said that the lion had no reason to fear this creature. The lion, greatly relieved, asked to see this ox. Dimna went once again to the meadow and told Shanzabeh that the lion, the king of the beasts, summoned him to appear at his court. The ox, alarmed at this request, said that he would go with Dimna, provided the jackal promise that no harm would befall him. Upon being reassured by the jackal, he set out to meet the lion.

After Dimna introduced Shanzabeh to the lion, the king asked the ox how he came to this part of the world. Shanzabeh related the story of his falling into the marsh and being abandoned by his master. The lion invited him to stay at his court and soon a great friendship developed between the two. They roamed the forest, held counsel, and thoroughly enjoyed each other's company.

Dimna became jealous of their friendship and felt that his influence with the lion was quickly being replaced by that of the ox. He decided to resort to cunning and treachery to put an end to this affair. He revealed his intentions to his brother, Kalila, who advised him not to complain since it was his fault that the lion met the ox; besides, Kalila said, these two animals were much stronger than a jackal. Dimna, not convinced that defeat should be his fate, told Kalila several stories proving that strength is no match for cunning.

One of these stories was about the lion and the hare. The lion, a fearsome creature, lived in a forest inhabited by many kinds of animals who were terrified of him. They agreed among themselves that if they sent the lion one animal each day, he would leave the others in peace and not prey upon them. The lion agreed to this arrangement and every day the animals drew lots to determine which one would be fed to the lion the following day.

One day the lot fell on a certain hare, who was exceptionally clever and had no intention of being the lion's next meal. She devised a plan to trick the lion and asked to be sent to him very slowly so that she would be late for the meal. The hungry lion, annoyed that his food was late, was in an ugly mood. When the hare approached him he wanted to know who she was. She said that she was a messenger; the fat hare sent to him by the animals had been seized by another lion. Furious that his territory was invaded by another lion, the lion asked to see his rival.

The hare took him to a deep well filled with water and told him to look down. The lion did as he was instructed and saw his own reflection together with that of the hare. He thought that he was seeing the rival lion with the fat hare intended for him. He leaped at his reflection to snatch his food, fell into the well, and drowned.

At the conclusion of the story Kalila told Dimna that if he could destroy the ox without harming the lion, then he should do so. But Kalila was worried that the lion would become terribly distressed by the loss of his friend.

Dimna, oblivious to his brother's advice, went on with his plans. He stayed away from the lion for several days. When he finally appeared at the court, the lion asked him why he had been absent. Dimna replied that he had heard dreadful news and could not bring himself to face the lion. After pretending to evade the issue, Dimna announced that Shanzabeh was plotting against the lion. At first the lion refused to believe him, but Dimna was able to convince him that the ox was indeed planning to eliminate the king. The jackal suggested that the lion attack the ox before Shanzabeh had a chance to kill him. The lion said that if the story was true, he would order Shanzabeh to leave his court and expel him from his kingdom. But his suspicion was aroused when Dimna warned him to be cautious if the ox approached with his head held down and horns thrust out.

Dimna then sought out the ox and told him the same story. He tried to convince Shanzabeh that the lion was planning to kill him. When Shanzabeh refused to believe this rumor, Dimna said that he was just as naive as the honest and trusting camel, and proceeded to tell the story of the lion, the crow, the wolf, and the jackal.

The lion dwelt near a public road and had three companions: the crow, the wolf, and the jackal. The lion hunted regularly and his companions fed well on his leftovers. One day some merchants passing by left behind them a camel, who wandered into the marsh where the lion lived. The lion decided to spare the camel and give him protection since the animal was harmless and ate only grass. The camel joined the other companions and was very happy to be in their company.

During one of his outings, the lion ran into a powerful elephant who attacked him. They fought furiously and the lion was so badly wounded that he crawled back to his home and lay sick for days. He became weaker and weaker, unable to hunt and eat. The crow, the wolf, and the jackal, accustomed to being fed by the lion, could not find food and decided that the easiest catch was the camel. When they told the lion they intended to eat the camel, the lion was indignant; he had promised to protect the camel and would not go back on his word. The three companions then devised a plan to trick the camel. They told him that since the lion was wounded and could not hunt, he was in desperate need of food. They were willing to offer themselves to the lion who had protected and befriended them. First the crow asked to be eaten, but the others objected, saying that he was small and scrawny and could not satisfy the lion's hunger. The the wolf offered himself, but he, too, was rejected since his meat was indigestible and gave cramps and pain. When it was the jackal's turn, they told him that his flesh was stinking and foul and thus inedible. Then the simple-minded camel said that his flesh was the sweetest and asked that the lion eat him, thinking that the others would make excuses for him as well. But this was exactly what the three companions had planned; they fell upon the unsuspecting camel and tore him to pieces. The lion, seeing that the camel and offered himself willingly and it was not too late to save him, joined the others.

When Shanzabeh heard this story, he wondered whether he would come to a similar end. Dimna continued to persuade the ox that the lion was determined to kill him. The jackal said that if Shanzabeh did not take the advice of friends, his fate would be like that of the tortoise who did not profit from wise counsel.

The tortoise lived in a marsh together with two geese. They were good friends and enjoyed one another's company. But, when the marsh began to dry up, the geese decided to seek another lake to build their nest. The tortoise asked them to devise a plan so that he, too, could go with them and not be left behind to die. The geese told him that if he took hold of the middle of a stick with his mouth and they held its ends in their beaks, they could transport him. But, they warned, he would have to observe absolute silence during the flight.

The tortoise promised to keep quiet and took the stick in his mouth. The geese began to fly, carrying the tortoise with them. They passed over a group of villagers who were amazed by this strange sight; they began to laugh and make fun of the tortoise. The tortoise forgot his promise and opened his mouth to answer them. He let go of the stick and fell to his death.

Shanzabeh, now totally convinced that Dimna was telling the truth, decided to go to the lion peacefully and affectionately and try to persuade him to change his mind. This, naturally, would have upset Dimna's plans. He told the ox to watch the lion's mood: if the lion's ears were extended like arrows and his paws were stamping the ground, then he was ready for the kill.

Shanzabeh, terrified of the lion, approached him cautiously. The lion saw him and became nervous; he extended his ears like arrows and began to stamp the ground with his paws. The ox saw this change in his friend and became even more frightened; he held his head down and thrust out his horns. Things were exactly as Dimna had predicted and each was now sure that the other was out to destroy him. The lion and the ox engaged in a ferocious battle that lasted a long time.

Kalila and Dimna came to see the outcome of this fierce encounter. During the course of the battle Dimna told his brother several stories. Kalila scolded him for breaking up the friendship between the lion and the ox and warned him that if his treachery were ever discovered, Dimna would be severely punished.

Finally the battle was over and the lion had fatally wounded the ox. Soon after Shanzabeh died, the lion repented and missed his friend. Dimna tried to justify the kill by saying that when a poisonous snake has bitten a man's finger or toe, he cuts off his hand or foot so that it does not infect the entire body.

Later the lion learned that it was Dimna' envy and deceit that had caused the death of Shanzabeh. Thus, a lying confidant and a false friend had caused a friendship to be severed and had turned the love between two friends into hatred.

The Monkey and the Tortoise

After he had heard the parable of the deceitful enemies and how one should guard against them, the king said to the philosopher that he would like to hear about a man who acquires wealth but does not know how to manage it.

The philosopher replied that acquiring was easier than keeping. The man who amasses wealth without knowing how to manage it is like the monkey and the tortoise. The tortoise had the monkey in his grasp but could not handle him; the monkey slipped away and the tortoise was left with disappointment.

One of the islands in the ocean was inhabited by monkeys. Their ailing and aged king was ousted by an ambitious young monkey. The old king crept away and arrived at a region where there was a pond with plenty of fruit trees growing on its shores. The monkey moved into one of the fig trees and feasted on the fruit. As he ate, he would drop some of the figs into the pond, delighted by the sound they made when they splashed in the water.

One day he saw a tortoise in the pond eating the figs. The tortoise, thinking that the monkey was throwing the figs for him, wanted to become friends with the former king. They started talking and eventually became devoted to one another. Like the monkey, the tortoise was separated from his family, having left his wife and children on another island.

The wife of the tortoise began to complain of her husband's attachment to the monkey and told a friend he was neglecting her because of this relationship. The friend advised her that if the monkey were eliminated, her husband would return. They devised a sinister plan to dispose of the monkey. The wife wrote to the tortoise saying that she was gravely ill. When he came to see her she pretended that she was too sick to talk. Her friend told the tortoise that the only cure for her ailment was the heart of an ape; otherwise, she would die.

The tortoise distressed by his wife's illness and disturbed that the only medicine was his friend's heart, decided that he had to destroy the monkey to save his mate. He planned to take the monkey to an isolated island, leave him there without food or drink until he died, and then remove his heart and give it to his wife.

When he came back to the pond, the monkey inquired about his wife. The tortoise implored his friend to come home with him so that his children might serve him and his wife might recover by his company. He said that his home was in a dense forest with cool waters and delicious fruit. The monkey, lusting after the fruit, agreed to go with the tortoise.

The monkey climbed onto the back of the tortoise, who began to swim toward his home. Lost in thought, he would paddle for a while and then stop. The monkey sensed something was wrong and asked him what was amiss. The tortoise, who had begun regretting his evil plans, confessed that the only cure for his wife's ailment was the heart of an ape. When the monkey heard this, he realized that his life was in danger and tried to find a way out of his dilemma.

The monkey said that he sympathized with the tortoise and knew how precious his wife was to his friend. Their women were also afflicted with a similar disease but recovered when they received an ape's heart. The monkeys were not injured when they gave up their hearts; they were in pain for a while but soon recovered. He said that he would happily give his heart to the wife, except that he left it on the fig tree next to their pond. He suggested that they go back so that he could retrieve it.

The foolish tortoise was so relieved that he did not have to hurt his friend that he gladly brought the monkey back to the pond. The monkey leaped ashore and climbed his tree. When the tortoise urged him to come down, the monkey laughed and accused the tortoise of being a false friend. The tortoise confessed his sins and begged forgiveness.

The monkey forgave the tortoise and said that if the tortoise wished to remain on the island, he would feed his friend as before; but if the tortoise desired to go home, he would wish him peace; and if in the future the tortoise wanted to come back to the pond, he would have the monkey's blessings. Thus parted two old friends and the tortoise went home in humiliation and shame.

Al-Hariri of Basrah (1054-1122)
From *The Assemblies*
Samarkand

Introduction
by James Kritzeck

The twin strains of Arabic folk literature and more sophisticated *adab* never came closer to fusion than they did in the *maqamah* form. What the *maqāmah* did, one authority explains, "was to invest with the literary graces of *saj‘* [rhymed prose] and the glamour of impromptu composition the old-time tale in alternate prose and verse...and, by a stroke of genius, to adopt as the mouthpiece of [its] art that familiar figure in popular story, the witty vagabond."

The greatest writer in the *maqāmah* form, and one of the most respected figures in Arabic literature, was Al-Hariri of Basrah, who was born in 1054 and died in 1122. He produced a set of maqāmahs in which his *rāwi*, Al-Harith, meets Abu Zayd Seruj, a clever trickster, who appears in many situations and guises to display his talent. Unabashed imitations of the work of Al-Hamadhani a century before, they clearly surpass their predecessors in all respects. It is, in fact, difficult to imagine that the Arabic language has ever been handled with more consummate skill under such restrictions. There are sections composed exclusively of words with double meanings, series of sentences ending in rhyming syllables or with regular combinations of consonants throughout, and poems utilizing only certain letters of the alphabet.

The following selection may serve at least to illustrate the fact that the rigidity of form did not prevent amusing stories from being told. For all their cleverness, indeed, they did not escape outcries of moral indignation over their cavalier plots and favoritism toward the trickster. It is easily granted that they were not intended to be edifying, but they are certainly far from frivolous.

Al Hârith, son Hammâm, related: In one of my journeys I chose sugar-candy for a merchandise, making with the same for Samarcand, and in those days I was upright of build, brimful of sprightliness, taking sight from the bow of enjoyment at the target of pleasures, and seeking in the sap of my youth help against the glamours of the water-semblance [mirage]. Now I reached her on a Friday morn, after I had endured hardship, and I bestirred myself without tarrying, until a nightstead was got, and when I had carried there my sugar-candy, and was entitled to say "at home with me," I wended forthwith towards a bath, when I put from me the weariness of travel, and took to the washing of the congregation-day comformably to tradition. Then I hastened with the bearing of the humble to the cathedral mosque, so as to join those who were near the prayer-leader, and offer [as it were] the fattened camel, and happily I was foremost in the race, and elected the central place for hearing the sermon. Meanwhile people ceased not to enter in troops into the faith of Allah, and to arrive singly and in pairs, until, when the mosque was crowded with its assembly, and a person had waxed equal with his shadow, the preacher sallied forth, swaggering in the wake of his acolyths, and straightway mounted the steps of the pulpit of the [divine] call, until he stood at its summit, when he gave blessing with a wave of his right hand, sitting down thereafter until the ritual of the cry to prayer was completed. Then he rose and spoke: "Praise be to Allah, the exalted of names, the praised for His bounties, the abundant in gifts, the called upon for the rescinding of calamity;—king of the nations, restorer of rotten bones, honourer of the folks of forbearance and generosity, destroyer of Âd and Irem;—whose cognizance comes up with every secret, whose compassion encompasses every obdurate in sin, whose munificence comprises all the world, whose power breaks down every revolter.—I praise him with the praise of one who proclaims [God's] unity and professes Islâm, I pray to Him with the prayer of the hopeful, the trusting, for He is the God, there is no God but He, the unique, the one, the just, the eternal, there is none begotten to Him, and no begetter, no companion with Him and no helpmate.—He sent forth Mohammed to spread about Islâm, to consolidate religion, to confirm the guidance of the apostles, to straighten the black-hued and the red.—He united womb-connections, he taught the fundamentals of truth, he set a stamp on the lawful and the forbidden, he regulated [laid down the rules for] the doffing and the donning of the pilgrim-cloak.—May Allah exalt his place, and perfect the blessing and benediction upon him, may He have compassion on his race, the worthy, and on his progeny, the uterine, as long as the pile-cloud pours, as long as the dove coos, as long as the cattle graze, as long as the sword assaults.—Work ye, may Allah have mercy upon you, the work of the pious, exert yourselves towards your return[on the resurrection day] with the exertion of the sound, curb your lusts with the curbing of enemies, make ready for your departure with the readiness of the blissful.—Put ye on the robes of abstinence, and put away the ailings of greed, make straight the crookedness of your dealings, and resist the whisperings of hope.—Portray ye to your imaginings the vicissitudes of circumstances, and the alighting of terrors, and the attacks of sickness, and the cutting off from pelf and kin:—Bethink ye yourselves of death, and the agony of its throwing-place, of the tomb and the awfulness of that which is sighted there, of the grave-niche and the loneliness of the one deposed in it, of the angel and the frightfulness of his questioning and of his advent.— Look ye at fortune and the baseness of its onslaught, and the evil of its deceit and cunning:—How many road-marks has it effaced, how many viands embittered! how many a host has it scattered, how many an honoured king has it overthrown.—Its striving is to strike deaf the ears, to make flow the tear-founts, to baffle desires, to destroy the songster and the listener to the song. Its decree is the same for kings and subjects, for the lord and the henchman, for the envied and the envier, for serpents and for lions.—It enriches not, but to turn away, and reverse hopes; it bestows not, but to outrage and cut into the limbs; it gladdens not, but to sadden, and revile, and injure; it grants no health, but to engender disease and frighten friends.—Fear ye Allah! fear ye Allah! May Allah keep you! How long this persistency in levity, this perseverance in thoughtlessness, this stubbornness in sin, this loading yourselves with crime, this rejection of the word of the wise, this rebellion against the God of heaven?—Is not senility your harvest, and the clod your couch? Is not death your capturer, and [the bridge] Sirât your path? Is not the hour [of resurrection] your tryst, and the plain [or hell] your goal? Are not the terrors of doomsday laid in ambush for you? Is not the

abode of transgressors Al-Ḥutamah, the firmly [safely] locked?—
Their warder Mâlik, their comeliness raven blackness, their food
poison, their breathing-air the scorching blast!—No wealth prospers
them, no offspring; no numbers protect them, and no equipments.—
But lo, Allah has mercy upon the man who rules his passion, and
who treads the paths of His Guidance; who makes firm his obedi-
ence towards his Lord, and strives for the restfulness of his place of
refuge; who works while life lasts obedient, and fortune at truce
with him, and health perfect and welfare at hand;—Lest he be
overtaken by the frustration of his wish, by the faltering of speech,
by the alighting of afflictions, by the fulfillment of fate, by the
blunting of senses, by the remedy of the sepulchres. Alack on them
for a misery whose woefulness is assured, whose term is infinite! He
who is remedied thereby is wretched, his distractedness has none to
allay it, his regret none to pity it; there is not one to ward off that
which befalls him. May then Allah inspire you with the
praiseworthiest of inspirations! May He robe you with the robe of
glory! May He cause you to alight in the abode of peace! Of Him I
ask mercy upon you and on the people of the religion of Islâm, for
He is the most forgiving of the generous, the saviour, and peace by
with you."—Said Al Hârith, son of Hammâm: Now, when I saw
that the sermon was a choice thing without a flaw, and a bride
without a spot, the wonderment at its admirable strain urged me on
to look at the preacher's face, and I began to scan it narrowly, and to
let my glance range over him carefully, when it became clear to me
by the truth of tokens, that it was our Shaykh, the author of the
Assemblies.—There was, however, no help from keeping silent for
the time being; so I withheld until he had left off praying, and "the
dispersing on the earth" had come. Then I turned towards him, and
hastened to meet him, and when he spied me he quickened his pace,
and was profuse in doing me honour, bidding me to accompany
him to his abode and making me a confidant of the particulars of his
intimate affairs.—Now, when the wing of darkness had spread, and
the time for sleep had come, he brought forth wineflasks secured
with plug, whereupon I said to him: "Dost thou quaff it before sleep,
and thou the prayer-leader of the people?" But he replied: "Hush! I

by day am preacher, but by night make merry."—Said I: "By Allah, I know not whether to wonder more at thy unconcernedness as to thy kinsfolk and thy birthplace, or at thy preacher-office with thy foul habits, and the rotation of thy wine-cup."—Thereupon he turned his face in disgust from me, and presently he said:—Listen to me:

"Weep not for a friend that is distant, nor for an abode, but turn thyself about with fortune as it turns about.

Reckon thou all mankind thy dwelling-place, and fancy all the earth thy home.

Forbear with the ways of him with whom thou dealest, and humor him, for it is the wise that humors.

Miss thou no chance of enjoyment, for thou knowest not if thou live a day, or if an age.

Know thou that death is going round, and the moon-halos circle above all created beings,

Swearing that they will not cease chasing them, as long as morn and even turn and re-turn.

How then mayest thou hope to escape from a net from which neither Kisrá escaped, nor Dârâ."

Said he [the narrator]: And when the cups went between us from hand to hand, and the vital spirits waxed gleeful, he dragged from me the oath that allows no exception, that I would screen his repute [secret]. So I complied with his wish, and kept faith with him, and ranked him before the great in the rank of Al Fuzail, and let down the skirt over the turpitudes of the night; and this continued to be his wont and my wont, until the time for my return came, when I took leave from him, while he persisted in hypocrisy and in secretly quaffing old wine.

(Tr. F. Steingass)

Persian Literature

Firdawsi (ca. 940-1020)
From *The Book of Kings (Shah-nameh)*
Rustam and Sohrab

Introduction
by James Kritzeck

Firdawsi is one of Iran's great heroes. His long epic poem, *Shāh-nāmeh*, is read by every school child in Iran and may still be heard recited in the coffeehouses and gymnasiums of the country. A. J. Arberry has printed an interesting letter which Mirza Muhammad Ali Furughi, a scholar and prime minister, wrote on the millenary of Firdawsi's birth, trying to explain his feelings about the poet and the poem.

He wrote in part: "Firdausi's *Shāh-nāmeh,,* considered both quantitatively and qualitatively, is the greatest work in Persian literature and poetry; indeed, one can say that it's one of the world's literary masterpieces..[Firdawsi] rescued from oblivion and preserved for all time our national history... [and] our Persian language."[1]

Firdawsi was born in Tus. His family were rich landowners, and he lived most of his life on his estates. The poem was begun by Daqiqi, and when he died, Firdawsi took up his work, incorporated and acknowledged one thousand of his finished lines, and spent some twenty-five years completing it. The finished work contains over sixty thousand couplets; one standard edition of the Persian text fills ten volumes. Firdawsi deliberately tried to use Persian words and avoid the Arabic vocabulary which had already flooded his native tongue.

The subject of the *Shāh-nāmeh,*is the history of Iran, its heroes and glory, from legendary times to those of the Sassanian kings.[2] It is decidedly not an Islamic work, although the general theme of the warfare between the descendants of Irj (the Persians) and Tur (the Turks) had a very contemporary meaning. The major source for the poem, in which legend and history are almost inextricably mixed, seems to have been an old Pahlavi history of the early kings. Like most of the older epics, it is a fiercely patriotic work. The famous story of Firdawsi's experiences with Sultan Mahmud of Ghaznah in connection with the work [is to be found in] the *Chāhar Maqālah* of Samarqandi. The poem was completed about 1010.

[1]*Classical Persian Literature* (London, 1958), pp. 45-50.
[2]In volume 9 of *The Shāhnáma of Firdausí,* tr. A. G. and Edmond Warner (London, 1906), there is a very useful "General Table of Contents," by means of which one can study the exceedingly complex arrangement of the poem and locate the following selection with respect to the whole.

The following episode from the *Shah-nameh* is already somewhat familiar to English readers because of its treatment by Matthew Arnold. It comes as close to genuine tragedy as anything in Islamic literature.

The bright sun shone, the raven night flew low,
Great Rustam donned his tiger-skin cuirass
And mounted on his fiery dragon-steed.
Two leagues divided host from host, and all
Stood ready-armed. The hero with a casque
Of iron on his head came on the field.
Suhráb on his side revelling with comrades
Had thus addressed Húmán: "That lion-man,
Who striveth with me, is as tall as I am
And hath a dauntless heart. He favoreth me
In shoulder, breast, and arm, and thou wouldst say
That some skilled workman laid us out by line.
His very feet and stirrups move my love
And make me blush, for I perceive in him
The marks whereof my mother spake. Moreover
My heart presageth that he must be Rustam,
For few resemble him. I may not challenge
My sire or lightly meet him in the combat."
    Húmán said: "Rustam oft hath countered me:
This charger is like his, except in action."
    At sunrise, when they woke, Suhráb arrayed
Himself in mail and mirthful though resolved
Set forward shouting, ox-head mace in hand.
He greeted Rustam smiling, thou hadst said
That they had passed the night in company:
"How went the night? How is't with thee to-day?
Why so intent on strife? Fling down thine arrows
And scimitar, and drop the hand of wrong.
Let us dismount and, sitting, clear our faces
With wine, and, leaguing in God's sight, repent

Our former strife. Until some other cometh
To battle, feast with me because I love thee,
And weep for shamefastness. In sooth thou comest
From heroes and wilt tell me of they stock,
For as my foe thou shouldst not hide thy name.
Art thou the famous Rustam of Zábul,
The son of valiant Zál the son of Sám?"
    Then Rustam: "Young aspirant! heretofore
We talked not thus but spake last night of wrestling.
I am not to be gulled, attempt it not.
Though thou art young I am no child myself,
But girt to wrestle, and the end shall be
According to the will of Providence.
I have known ups and downs, and am not one
To practice guile upon."
                Suhráb replied:
"Old man! if thou rejectest my proposals...!
I wished that thou shouldst die upon thy bed,
And that thy kin should tomb thy soulless corpse,
But I will end thee if it be God's will."
    They lighted, tied their chargers to a rock,
And cautiously advanced in mail and casque
With troubled hearts. They wrestled like two lions
Until their bodies ran with sweat and blood.
From sunrise till the shadows grew they strove
Until Suhráb, that maddened Elephant,
Reached out, up-leaping with a lion's spring,
Caught Rustam's girdle, tugged amain as though
Thou wouldst have said, to rend the earth, and shouting
With rage and vengeance hurled him to the ground,
Raised him aloft and, having dashed him down,
Sat on his breast with visage, hand, and mouth
Besmirched with dust, as when a lion felleth
An onager, then drew a bright steel dagger
To cut off Rustam's head, who seeing this
Exclaimed: "Explain I must! O warrior

That takest Lions captive and art skilled
With lasso, mace, and scimitar! the customs
And laws of arms with us are not as yours.
In wrestling none may take a foeman's head
The first time that his back is on the ground,
But having thrown him twice and won the name
Of Lion then he may behead the foe:
Such is our custom."
                Thus he sought to 'scape
The Dragon's clutches and get off with life.
The brave youth hearkened to the old man's words.
In part through confidence, in part through fate,
In part no doubt through magnanimity,
Suhráb let Rustam go, turned toward the plain,
Pursued an antelope that crossed his path,
And utterly forgot his recent foe.
When he was far away Húmán came up
As swift as dust and asked about the fight.
He told Húmán what had been said and done,
Who cried: "Alas! young man! art thou indeed
So weary of thy life? Woe for thy breast,
Mien, stature, stirrups, and heroic feet!
The mighty Lion whom thou hadst ensnared
Thou hast let go and all is still to do.
Mark how he will entreat thee on the day
Of battle owing to thy senseless act.
A king once spake a proverb to the point:
'Despise not any foe however weak.'"
    He took the very life out of Suhráb,
Who standing sorrowing and amazed replied:
"Let us dismiss such fancies from our hearts,
For he will come to fight with me tomorrow,
And thou shalt see a yoke upon his neck."
    He went to camp in dudgeon at his deed.
When Rustam had escaped his foeman's clutch
He was again as 'twere a mount of steel.

He went toward a rivulet as one
Who having fainted is himself again.
He drank and bathed, then prayed to God for strength
And victory, not knowing what the sun
And moon decreed, or how the turning sky
Would rob him of the Crown upon his head.
    The tale is told that Rustam had at first
Such strength bestowed by Him who giveth all
That if he walked upon a rock his feet
Would sink therein. Such puissance as that
Proved an abiding trouble, and he prayed
To God in bitterness of soul to minish
His strength that he might walk like other men.
According to his prayer his mountain-strength
Had shrunk, but face to face with such a task,
And pierced by apprehension of Suhráb,
He cried to God and said: "Almighty Lord!
Protect Thy slave in his extremity.
O holy Fosterer! I ask again
My former strength."
                 God granted him his prayer,
The strength which once had waned now waxed in him.
He went back to the field perturbed and pale
While, like a maddened elephant, Suhráb,
With lasso on his arm and bow in hand,
Came in his pride and roaring like a lion,
His plunging charger flinging up the soil.
When Rustam saw the bearing of his foe
He was astound and gazing earnestly
Weighed in his mind the chances of the fight.
Suhráb, puffed up with youthful arrogance,
On seeing Rustam in his strength and grace,
Cried: "Thou that didst escape the Lion's claws!
Why com'st thou boldly to confront me? Speak!
Hast thou no interests of thine own to seek?"

They tied their steeds while fate malignantly
Revolved o'erhead, and when dark fate is wroth
Flint rocks become like wax. The two began
To wrestle, holding by their leathern belts.
As for Suhráb thou wouldst have said: "High heaven
Hath hampered him," while Rustam reaching clutched
That warrior-leopard by the head and neck,
Bent down the body of the gallant youth,
Whose time was come and all whose strength was gone,
And like a lion dashed him to the ground;
Then, knowing that Suhráb would not stay under,
Drew lightly from his waist his trenchant sword
And gashed the bosom of his gallant son.
   Whenever thou dost thirst for blood and stain
Therewith thy glittering dagger, destiny
   Will be athirst for thy blood, and ordain
Each hair of thine to be a sword for thee.
     Suhráb cried: "Ah!" and writhed. Naught recked
       he then
Of good or ill. "I am alone to blame,"
He said to Rustam. "Fate gave thee my key.
This hump-backed sky reared me to slay me soon.
Men of my years will mock me since my neck
Hath thus come down to dust. My mother told me
How I should recognise my father. I
Sought him in love and die of my desire.
Alas! my toils are vain, I have not seen him.
Now wert thou fish, or wrapped like night in gloom,
Or quit of earth wast soaring like a star,
My father would avenge me when he seeth
My pillow bricks. Some chief will say to Rustam:
'Suhráb was slain and flung aside in scorn
While seeking thee.'"
               Then Rustam grew distraught,
The world turned black, his body failed; o'ercome
He sank upon the ground and swooned away;

Till coming to himself he cried in anguish:
"Where is the proof that thou art Rustam's son?
May his name perish from among the great,
For I am Rustam! Be my name forgotten,
And may the son of Sám sit mourning me!"
    He raved, his blood seethed, and with groans he
            plucked
His hair up by the roots, while at the sight
Suhráb sank swooning till at length he cried:
"If thou indeed art Rustam thou hast slain me
In wanton malice, for I made advances,
But naught that I could do would stir thy love.
Undo my breastplate, view my body bare,
Behold thy jewel, see how sires treat sons!
The drums beat at my gate, my mother came
With blood-stained cheeks and stricken to the soul
Because I went. She bound this on mine arm
And said: 'Preserve this keepsake of thy father's
And mark its virtue.' It is mighty now,
Now when the strife is over and the son
Is nothing to his sire."
                  When Rustam loosed
The mail and saw the gem he rent his clothes,
And cried: "Oh! my brave son, approved by all
And slain by me!"
              With dust upon his head
And streaming face he rent his locks until
His blood ran down.
            "Nay, this is worse and worse,"
Suhráb said, "Wherefore weep? What will it profit
To slay thyself? What was to be hath been."
    When day declined and Rustam came not back
There went forth twenty trusty warriors
To learn the issue. Both the steeds were standing
Bemoiled with dust, but Rustam was not there.
The nobles, thinking that he had been slain,

Went to Káús in consternation saying:
"The throne of majesty is void of Rustam!"
    A cry went up throughoutt the host and all
Was in confusion. Then Káús bade sound
The drums and trumpets, Tús came, and the Sháh
Said to the troops: "Dispatch a messenger
That he may find out what Suhráb hath done,
And if there must be mourning through Irán.
None will confront him with brave Rustam dead.
We must attack in force and speedily."
    While clamour raged Suhráb said thus to Rustam:
"The Turkmans' case is altered since my day
Is done. Use all thine influence that the Sháh
May not attack them. They approached Irán
Through trust in me, and I encouraged them.
How could I tell, O famous paladin!
That I should perish by my father's hand?
Let them depart unscathed, and treat them kindly.
I had a warrior in yonder hold
Caught by my lasso. Him I often asked
To point thee out: mine eyes looked ever for thee.
He told me all but this. His place is void.
His words o'er-cast my day, and I despaired.
See who he is and let him not be harmed.
I marked in thee the tokens that my mother
Described but trusted not mine eyes. The stars
Decreed that I should perish by thy hand.
I came like lightning and like wind I go.
In heaven I may look on thee with joy."
    Then Rustam choked, his heart was full of fire,
His eyes of tears. He mounted quick as dust
And came with lamentations to the host
In grievous consternation at his deed.
The Iránians catching sight of him fell prostrate
And gave God praise that Rustam had returned,
But when they saw the dust upon his head,

His clothes and bosom rent, they questioned him:
"What meaneth this? For whom art thou thus troubled?"
　He told the fearful deed, and all began
To mourn aloud with him. His anguish grew.
He told the nobles: "I have lost to-day
All strength and courage. Fight not with Túrán:
I have done harm enough."

(Tr. Arthur and Edmond Warner)

Farid ad-Din Attar (died ca. 1229)
From *Mantiq al-Tayr*
(The Conference of the Birds)
The Bird Parliament

Introduction
by James Kritzcek

Even the dates of Attar's life cannot be fixed with any certainty, and in his works the editorial problem appears like the very devil. Recently it has been shown that eight of the twenty-five works believed to have been his were forgeries. Hellmut Ritter, the European scholar who has done the most work on Attar, wrote: "The works attributed to him fall into three groups which differ so considerably in content and style that it is difficult to ascribe all three to the same person."

Overlooking this perplexing situation, let us say that Attar was by early trade a druggist, as his name would indicate, who lived in Khurasan during the second half of the twelfth century and well into the thirteenth, a Sufi master who wrote much and well concerning the mystical search for God. That is more than we know about many Persian poets.

The Bird Parliament is Attar's most famous work. It is an allegory, of course, of man's contemplative journey—if he chooses to take it—toward union with God. The main story is clear and well-constructed, and it is interspersed throughout with a variety of subsidiary tales. It is this combination of the planned and the random, in fact, which lends the book its distinctive character within Sufi literature.

All of the birds of the world, known and unknown, were assembled together. They said: "No country in the world is without a king. How comes it, then, that the kingdom of the birds is without a ruler? This state of things cannot last. We must make effort together and search for one; for no country can have a good administration and a good organization without a king."

So they began to consider how to set out on their quest. The Hoopoe, excited and full of hope, came forward and placed herself in the middle of the assembled birds. On her breast was the ornament which symbolized that she had entered the way of spiritual knowledge; the crest on her head was as the crown of truth, and she had knowledge of both good and evil.

"Dear Birds," she began, "I am one who is engaged in divine warfare, and I am a messenger of the world invisible. I have knowledge of God and of the secrets of creation. When one carries on his beak, as I do, the name of God, Bismillah, it follows that one must have knowledge of many hidden things. Yet my days pass restlessly and I am concerned with no person, for I am wholly occupied by love for the King. I can find water by instinct, and I know many other secrets. I talk with Solomon and am the foremost of his followers. It is astonishing that he neither asked nor sought for those who were absent from his kingdom, yet when I was away from him for a day he sent his messengers everywhere, and, since he could not be without me for a moment, my worth is established forever. I carried his letters, and I was his confidential companion. The bird who is sought after by the prophet Solomon merits a crown for his head. The bird who is well spoken of by God, how can he trail his feathers in the dust? For years I have travelled by sea and land, over mountains and valleys. I covered an immense space in the time of the deluge; I accompanied Solomon on his journeys, and I have measured the bounds of the world.

"I know well my King, but alone I cannot set out to find him. Abandon your timidity, your self-conceit and your unbelief, for he

who makes light of his own life is delivered from himself; he is
delivered from good and evil in the way of his beloved. Be generous
with your life. Set your feet upon the earth and step out joyfully for
the court of the King. We have a true King, he lives behind the
mountains called Kāf. His name is Simurgh and he is the King of
birds. He is close to us, but we are far from him. The place where he
dwells is inaccessible, and no tongue is able to utter his name. Before
him hang a hundred thousand veils of light and darkness, and in the
two worlds no one has power to dispute his kingdom. He is the
sovereign lord and is bathed in the perfection of his majesty. He
does not manifest himself completely even in the place of his
dwelling, and to this no knowledge or intelligence can attain. The
way is unknown, and no one has the steadfastness to seek it, though
thousands of creatures spend their lives in longing. Even the purest
soul cannot describe him, neither can the reason comprehend: these
two eyes are blind. The wise cannot discover his perfection nor can
the man of understanding perceive his beauty. All creatures have
wished to attain to this perfection and beauty by imagination. But
how can you tread that path with thought? How measure the moon
from the fish? So thousands of heads go here and there, like the ball
in polo, and only lamentations and sighs of longing are heard. Many
lands and seas are on the way. Do not imagine that the journey is
short; and one must have the heart of a lion to follow this unusual
road, for it is very long and the sea is deep. One plods along in a state
of amazement, sometimes smiling, sometimes weeping. As for me,
I shall be happy to discover even a trace of him. That would indeed
be something, but to live without him would be a reproach. A man
must not keep his soul from the beloved, but must be in a fitting
state to lead his soul to the court of the King. Wash your hand of this
life if you would be called a man of action. For your beloved,
renounce this dear life of yours, as worthy men. If you submit with
grace, the beloved will give his life for you.

"An astonishing thing! The first manifestation of the Simurgh
took place in China in the middle of the night. One of his feathers fell
on China and his reputation filled the world. Everyone made a
picture of this feather, and from it formed his own system of ideas,

and so fell into a turmoil. This feather is still in the picture-gallery of that country; hence the saying, 'Seek knowledge, even in China!'

"But for his manifestation there would not have been so much noise in the world concerning this mysterious Being. This sign of his existence is token of his glory. All souls carry an impression of the image of his feather. Since the description of it has neither head nor tail, beginning nor end, it is not necessary to say more about it. Now, any of you who are for this road, prepare yourselves, and put your feet on the Way."

When the Hoopoe had finished, the birds began excitedly to discuss the glory of this King, and seized with longing to have him for their own sovereign, they were all impatient to be off. They resolved to go together; each became a friend to the other and an enemy to himself. But when they began to realize how long and painful their journey was to be, they hesitated, and in spite of their apparent good will began to excuse themselves, each according to his type.

One bird said to the Hoopoe: "O you who know the road of which you have told us and on which you wish us to accompany you, to me the way is dark, and in the gloom it appears to be very difficult, and many parasangs in length."

The Hoopoe replied: "We have seven valleys to cross, and only after we have crossed them shall we discover the Simurgh. No one has ever come back into the world who has made this journey, and it is impossible to say how many parasangs there are in front of us. Be patient, O fearful one, since all those who went by this road were in your state.

"The first valley is the Valley of the Quest, the second the Valley of Poverty and Nothingness, beyond which one can go no farther."

When the birds had listened to this discourse of the Hoopoe their heads dropped down, and sorrow pierced their hearts. Now they understood how difficult it would be for a handful of dust like themselves to bend such a bow. So great was their agitation that numbers of them died then and there. But others, in spite of their distress, decided to set out on the long road. For years they travelled over mountains and valleys, and a great part of their life flowed past on this journey. But how is it possible to relate all that happened to them? It would be necessary to go with them and see their difficulties for oneself, and to follow the wanderings of this long road. Only then could one realize what the birds suffered.

In the end, only a small number of all this great company arrived at that sublime place to which the Hoopoe had led them. Of the thousands of birds, almost all had disappeared. Many had been lost in the ocean; others had perished on the summits of the high mountains, tortured by thirst; others had had their wings burnt and their hearts dried up by the fire of the sun; others were devoured by tigers and panthers; others died of fatigue in the deserts and in the wilderness, their lips parched and their bodies overcome by the heat. Some went mad and killed each other for a grain of barley; others, enfeebled by suffering and weariness, dropped on the road, unable to go farther; others, bewildered by the things they saw, stopped where they were, stupefied; and many who had started out from curiosity or pleasure, perished without an idea of what they had set out to find.

So then out of all those thousands of birds, only thirty reached the end of the journey. And even these were bewildered, weary and dejected, with neither feathers nor wings. But now they were at the door of this Majesty that cannot be described, whose essence is incomprehensible—that Being who is beyond human reason and knowledge. Then flashed the lightning of fulfillment, and a hundred worlds were consumed in a moment. They saw thousands of suns, each more resplendent than the other, thousands of moons and stars all equally beautiful, and seeing all this they were amazed and agitated like a dancing atom of dust, and they cried out: "O Thou who art more radiant than the sun! Thou who has reduced the sun to an atom, how can we appear before Thee? Ah, why have we so uselessly endured all this suffering on the Way? Having renounced ourselves and all things, we now cannot obtain that for which we have striven. Here it little matters whether we exist or not."

Then the birds, who were so disheartened that they resembled a cock half-killed, sank into despair. A long time passed. When, at a propitious moment, the door suddenly opened, there stepped out a noble Chamberlain, one of the courtiers of the Supreme Majesty. He looked them over and saw that out of thousands, only these thirty birds were left.

He said: "Now then, O Birds, where have you come from, and what are you doing here? What is your name? O you who are destitute of everything, where is your home? What do they call you in the world? What can be done with a feeble handful of dust like you?"

"We have come," they said, "to acknowledge the Simurgh as our King. Through love and desire for him we have lost our reason and our peace of mind. Very long ago, when we started on this journey, we were thousands, and now only thirty of us have arrived at this sublime court. We cannot believe that the King will scorn us after all the sufferings we have gone through. Ah, no! He cannot but look on us with the eye of benevolence!"

The Chamberlain replied: "O you whose mind and hearts are troubled, whether you exist or do not exist in the universe, the King has his being always and eternally. Thousands of worlds of creatures are no more than an ant at his gate. You bring nothing but moans and lamentations. Return then to whence you came, O vile handful of earth!"

At this the birds were petrified with astonishment. Nevertheless, when they came to themselves a little, they said: "Will this great King reject us so ignominiously? And if he really has this attitude to us, may he not change it to one of honour? Remember Majnūn, who said: 'If all the people who dwell on earth wished to sing my praises, I would not accept them; I would rather have the insults of Laila. One of her insults is more to me than a hundred compliments from another woman!'"

"The lightning of his glory manifests itself," said the Chamberlain, "and it lifts up the reason of all souls. What benefit is there if the soul be consumed by a hundred sorrows? What benefit is there at this moment in either greatness or littleness?"

The birds, on fire with love, said: "How can the moth save itself from the flame when it wishes to be one with the flame? The friend we seek will content us by allowing us to be united to him. If now we are refused, what is there left for us to do? We are like the moth who wished for union with the flame of the candle. They begged him not to sacrifice himself so foolishly and for such an impossible aim, but he thanked them for their advice and told them that since his heart was given to the flame forever, nothing else mattered."

Then the Chamberlain, having tested them, opened the door; and as he drew aside a hundred curtains, one after the other, a new world beyond the veil was revealed. Now was the light of lights manifested, and all of them sat down on the masnad, the seat of the Majesty and Glory. They were given a writing which they were told to read through; and reading this, and pondering, they were able to understand their state. When they were completely at peace and detached from all things, they became aware that the Simurgh was there with them, and a new life began for them in the Simurgh. All that they had done previously was washed away. The sun of Majesty sent forth his rays, and in the reflection of each other's faces these thirty birds (*si-murgh*) of the outer world contemplated the face of the Simurgh of the inner world. This so astonished them that they did not know if they were still themselves or if they had become the Simurgh. At last, in a state of contemplation, they realized that they were the Simurgh and that the Simurgh was the thirty birds. When they gazed at the Simurgh they saw that it was truly the Simurgh who was there, and when they turned their eyes toward themselves they saw that they themselves were the Simurgh. And perceiving both at once, themselves and Him, they realized that they and the Simurgh were one and the same being. No one in the world has ever heard of anything to equal it.

Then they gave themselves up to meditation, and after a little they asked the Simurgh, without the use of tongues, to reveal to them the secret of the mystery of the unity and plurality of beings. The Simurgh, also without speaking, made this reply: "The sun of my majesty is a mirror. He who sees himself therein sees his soul and his body, and sees them completely. Since you have come as thirty birds, *si-murgh*,[1] you will see thirty birds in this mirror. If forty or fifty were to come, it would be the same. Although you are now completely changed, you see yourselves as you were before.

"Can the sight of an ant reach to the far-off Pleiades? And can this insect lift an anvil? Have you ever seen a gnat seize an elephant in its teeth? All that you have known, all that you have seen, all that you have said or heard—all this is no longer that. When you crossed the valleys of the Spiritual Way and when you performed good tasks, you did all this by my action; and you were able to see the valleys of my essence and my perfections. You, who are only thirty birds, did well to be astonished, impatient and wondering. But I am more than thirty birds. I am the very essence of the true Simurgh. Annihilate then yourselves gloriously and joyfully in me, and in me you shall find yourselves."

Thereupon the birds at last lost themselves forever in the Simurgh—the shadow was lost in the sun, and that is all.

All that you have heard or seen or known is not even the beginning of what you must know, and since the ruined habitation of this world is not your place you must renounce it. Seek the trunk of the tree, and do not worry about whether the branches do or do not exist.

When a hundred thousand generations had passed, the mortal birds surrendered themselves spontaneously to total annihilation. No man, neither young nor old, can speak fittingly of death or immortality. Even as these things are far from us, so the description of them is beyond all explanation or definition. If my readers wish for an allegorical explanation of the immortality that follows annihilation, it will be necessary for me to write another book. So long as you are identified with the things of the world you will not set out on the Path, but when the world no longer binds you, you enter as in a dream, and knowing the end, you see the benefit. A germ is

[1] *Simurgh*, as "God," and s̄imurgh, "thirty birds," although not a very subtle play on words, determined the plot of the work. [S.C. Nott]

nourished among a hundred cares and loves so that it may become an intelligent and acting being. It is instructed and given the necessary knowledge. Then death comes and everything is effaced, its dignity is thrown down. This that was a being has become the dust of the street. It has several times been annihilated; but in the meanwhile it has been able to learn a hundred secrets of which previously it had not been aware, and in the end it receives immortality, and is given honour in place of dishonour. Do you know what you possess? Enter into yourselves and reflect on this. So long as you do not realize your nothingness and so long as you do not renounce your self-pride, your vanity and your self-love, you will never reach the heights of immortality. On the Way you are cast down in dishonour and raised in honour.

And now my story is finished; I have nothing more to say.

(Tr. S.C. Nott)

Nur ad-Din Abd ar-Rahman Jami (1414-1492)
From Yūsuf u Zulaikhā
(Joseph and Zulaikha)
The Women of Memphis

Introduction
by James Kritzeck

Jami, born in 1414 in a village near Samarkand, is commonly considered the last great classical Persian writer. While he lived, he was highly praised, and his work had great authority and many imitators after he died. He was a member of the Naqshbandi order, and one of his more famous works is a book of Sufi biographies. He was versatile, prolific, and proud. He wrote: "I have found no master with whom I have read superior to myself. On the contrary, I have invariably found that in argument I could defeat them all. I acknowledge, therefore, the obliga-

tions of a pupil to his master to none of them; for if I am a pupil of anyone
it is of my own father, who taught me the language."

He was, first and foremost, a poet, writing many poems of many
kinds. He collected three separate *dīvāns* of his poems, not including his
seven *masnavīs*. The theme of Joseph and Potiphar's wife (known as
Zulaykha in Islamic tradition) was an extremely popular one with the
Persian poets. Embellishing the Koranic account, they turned it into a
tragic love story, exonerating Zulaykha on the ground that Joseph's
beauty was irresistible. Jami's poem on the subject is one of his best
works and one of the best treatments of it in all of Islamic literature. The
episode described in the following selection was derived from the two
verses in the Koran 12.30-31.

Love is ill suited with peace and rest:
Scorn and reproaches become him best.
Rebuke gives strength to his tongue, and blame
Wakes the dull spark to a brighter flame.
Blame is the censor of Love's bazaar:
It suffers no rust the pure splendour to mar.
Blame is the whip whose impending blow
Speeds the willing lover and wakes the slow;
And the weary steed who can hardly crawl
Is swift of foot when reproaches fall.
When the rose of the secret had opened and blown,
The voice of reproach was a bulbul in tone.[1]

The women of Memphis, who heard the tale first,
The whispered slander received and nursed.
Then, attacking Zulaikha for right and wrong,
Their uttered reproaches were loud and long:
"Heedless of honour and name she gave
The love of her heart to the Hebrew slave,

---

[1]An allusion to the bulbul's love of the rose, whose beauty,
according to Persian legend, he sings.

Who lies so deep in her soul enshrined
That to sense and religion her eyes are blind.
She loves her servant. 'Tis strange to think
That erring folly so low can sink;
But stranger still that the slave she woos
Should scorn her suit and her love refuse.
His cold eye to hers he never will raise;
He never will walk in the path where she strays.
He stops if before him her form he sees;
If she lingers a moment he turns and flees.
When her lifted veil leaves her cheek exposed,
With the stud of his eyelash his eye is closed.
If she weeps in her sorrow he laughs at her pain,
And closes each door that she opens in vain.
It may be that her form is not fair in his eyes,
And his cold heart refuses the proffered prize.
If once her beloved one sat with us
He would sit with us ever, not treat us thus.
Our sweet society ne'er would he leave,
But joy unending would give and receive.
But not all have this gift in their hands: to enthral
The heart they would win is not given to all.
There is many a woman, fair, good, and kind,
To whom never the heart of a man inclined;
And many a Laila with soft black eye.
The tears of whose heart-blood are never dry."
    Zulaikha heard, and resentment woke
To punish the dames for the words they spoke.
She summoned them all from the city to share
A sumptuous feast which she bade prepare.
A delicate banquet meet for kings
Was spread with the choicest of dainty things.
Cups filled with sherbet of every hue
Shone as rifts in a cloud when the sun gleams through.
There were goblets of purest crystal filled
With wine and sweet odours with art distilled.

The golden cloth blazed like the sunlight; a whole
Cluster of stars was each silver bowl.
From goblet and charger rare odours came;
There was strength for the spirit and food for the frame.
All daintiest fare that your lip would taste,
From fish to fowl, on the cloth was placed.
It seemed that the fairest their teeth had lent
For almonds, their lips for the sugar sent.
A mimic palace rose fair to view
Of a thousand sweets of each varied hue,
Where instead of a carpet the floor was made
With bricks of candy and marmalade.
Fruit in profusion, of sorts most rare,
Piled in baskets, bloomed fresh and fair.
Those who looked on their soft transparency felt
That the delicate pulp wold dissolve and melt.
Bands of boys and young maidens, fine
As mincing peacocks, were ranged in line;
And the fair dames of Memphis, like Peris eyed,
In a ring on their couches sat side by side.
They tasted of all that they fancied, and each
Was courteous in manner and gentle in speech.

The feast was ended; the cloth was raised,
And Zulaikha sweetly each lady praised.
Then she set, as she planned in her wily breast,
A knife and an orange beside each guest:
An orange, to purge the dark thoughts within
Each jaundiced heart with its golden skin.
One hand, as she bade them, the orange clasped,
The knife in the other was firmly grasped.
Thus she addressed them: "Dames fair and sweet,
Most lovely of all when the fairest meet,
Why should my pleasure your hearts annoy?
Why blame me for loving my Hebrew boy?
If your eyes with the light of his eyes were filled,

Each tongue that blames me were hushed and stilled.
I will bid him forth, if you all agree,
And bring him near for your eyes to see."
"This, even this," cried each eager dame,
"Is the dearest wish that our hearts can frame.
Bid him come; let us look on the lovely face
That shall stir our hearts with its youthful grace.
Already charmed, though our eyes never fell
On the youth we long for, we love him well.
These oranges still in our hands we hold,
To sweeten the spleen with their skins of gold.
But they please us not, for he is not here:
Let not one be cut till the boy appear."

  She sent the nurse to address him thus:
"Come, free-waving cypress, come forth to us.
Let us worship the ground which they dear feet press,
And bow down at the sight of thy loveliness.
Let'our love-stricken hearts be thy chosen retreat,
And our eyes a soft carpet beneath thy feet."

  But he came not forth, like a lingering rose
Which the spell of the charmer has failed to unclose.
Then Zulaikha flew to the house where he dwelt,
And in fond entreaty before him knelt:
"My darling, the light of these longing eyes,
Hope of my heart," thus she spoke with sighs,
"I fed on the hope which thy words had given;
But that hope from my breast by despair is driven.
For thee have I forfeited all: my name
Through thee has been made a reproach and shame.
I have found no favour: thou wouldst not fling
One pitying look on so mean a thing.
Yet let not the women of Memphis see
That I am so hated and scorned by thee.
Come, sprinkle the salt of thy lip to cure

The wounds of my heart and the pain I endure.
Let the salt be sacred: repay the debt
Of the faithful love thou shouldst never forget."

The heart of Yusuf grew soft at the spell
Of her gentle words, for she charmed so well.
Swift as the wind from her knees she rose,
And decked him gay with the garb she chose.
Over his shoulders she drew with care,
The scented locks of his curling hair,
Like serpents of jet-black lustre seen
With their twisted coils where the grass is green.
A girdle gleaming with gold, round the waist
That itself was fine as a hair, she braced.
I marvel so dainty a waist could bear
The weight of the jewels that glittered there.
She girt his brow with bright gems; each stone
Of wondrous beauty enhanced his own.
On his shoes were rubies and many a gem,
And pearls on the latchets that fastened them.
A scarf, on whose every thread was strung
A loving heart, on his arm was hung.
A golden ewer she gave him to hold,
And a maid brow-bound with a fillet of gold
In her hand a basin of silver bore,
And shadow-like moved as he walked before.
If a damsel had looked, she at once had resigned
All joy of her life, all the peace of her mind.
Too weak were my tongue if it tried to express
The charm of his wonderful loveliness.

Like a bed of roses in perfect bloom
The secret treasure appeared in the room.
The women of Memphis beheld him, and took
From that garden of glory the rose of a look.
One glance at his beauty o'erpowered each soul

And drew from their fingers the reins of control.
Each lady would cut through the orange she held,
As she gazed on that beauty unparalleled.
But she wounded her finger, so moved in her heart,
That she knew not her hand and orange apart.
One made a pen of her finger, to write
On her soul his name who had ravished her sight—
A reed which, struck with the point of the knife,
Poured out a red flood from each joint in the strife.
One scored a calendar's lines in red
On the silver sheet of her palm outspread,
And each column, marked with the blood-drops, showed
Like a brook when the stream o'er the bank has flowed.

When they saw that youth in his beauty's pride:
"No mortal is he," in amaze they cried.
"No clay and water composed his frame,
But, a holy angel, from heaven he came."
"'Tis my peerless boy," cried Zulaikha, "long
For him have I suffered reproach and wrong.
I told him my love for him, called him the whole
Aim and desire of my heart and soul.
He looked on me coldly; I bent not his will
To give me his love and my hope fulfill.
He still rebelled: I was forced to send
To prison the boy whom I could not bend.
In trouble and toil, under lock and chain,
He passed long days in affliction and pain.
But his spirit was tamed by the woe he felt,
And the heart that was hardened began to melt.
Keep your wild bird in a cage and see
How soon he forgets that he once was free."

Of those who wounded their hands, a part
Lost reason and patience, and mind and heart.
To weak the sharp sword of his love to stay,
They gave up their souls ere they moved away.
The reason of others grew dark and dim,
And madness possessed them for love of him.
Bare-headed, bare-footed, they fled amain,
And the light that had vanished ne'er kindled again.
To some their senses at length returned,
But their hearts were wounded, their bosoms burned.
They were drunk with the cup which was full to the brim.
And the birds of their hearts were ensnared by him.
Nay, Yusuf's love was a mighty bowl
With varied power to move the soul.
One drank the wine till her senses reeled;
To another, life had no joy to yield;
One offered her soul his least wish to fulfil;
One dreamed of him ever, but mute and still.
But only the woman to whom no share
Of the wine was vouchsafed could be pitied there.

                              (Tr. Ralph T. H. Griffith)

Japanese
Literature

A Guide to the Pronunciation of Japanese

There are five vowels in Japanese. Each vowel can be long or short. Long vowels are indicated by macrons when in romanized form; for example, ō or ū. Rough equivalents with English pronunciation are as follows:

a as in *father*

i as in *machine*

u as in *rhubarb*

e as in *get*

o as in *horse*

The consonants are pronounced as in English.

Introduction

by Thomas Rimer

I

The history of Japanese poetry is long and rich; poetic possibilities first explored in the earliest examples recorded continue to unfold today. The earliest fragments of Japanese poetry are preserved in ancient historical works such as the *Kojiki* (Record of Ancient Matters), compiled early in the eighth century, and those poems doubtless represent an oral literature that extends back many centuries. They are short, quite free in form, and simple in utterance, seemingly spontaneous outbursts inspired by the beauties of nature, the passions of love, or the power of the ruler and his court.

The *Man'yōshū* (Collection of Myriad Leaves), a vast anthology containing over four thousand poems composed, according to traditional attributions, over a period of several centuries, was compiled late in the eighth century. The *Man'yōshū* marks the real beginning of the tradition of Japanese poetry and contains poems so powerful in artistic and emotional appeal that they have seldom if ever been surpassed in later periods. Although the anthology was compiled by court officials, the authors of the poems range from emperors and priests to anonymous soldiers and peasants. From the evidence provided by the poems themselves, the art of poetry at this period was neither a hereditary calling nor the function of a particular social class. Nor was the composition of poetry reserved to particular gifted individuals. Rather, poetry was a part of daily life, a means of expression for anyone who felt the need to manifest emotion through ordered language. The underlying tone of the *Man'yōshū* was true to the national character; its virtues were those of openness, directness of expression, and intensity of feeling. (In later periods, when poetic tastes came to be dominated by members of the court aristocracy, these qualities were overlaid with an emphasis on artifice and indirection. In such an atmosphere, displays of wit and verbal cleverness were much admired, but genuine sensibility and sincerity of feeling, or *makoto*, remained the ultimate virtues.) Subjects first treated in the *Man'yōshū* have continued to find powerful expression down to the present century. The beauty and awesomeness of nature, love and separation, laments for the dead and the impermanence of life, affairs of the common people, and the loneliness of soldiers far away from home and family all echo through poetry composed in generation after generation.

The *Man'yōshū* employs two major poetic forms: the tanka (short poem), which consists of 31 syllables arranged in units of 5, 7, 5, 7, and 7 syllables, and the chōka (long poem), which uses the same basic units of 5 and 7 syllables but is unlimited in length, although it seldom exceeds a hundred units or lines. Nothing comparable to an epic form of poetry developed in Japan.

The precise identity of the compiler or compilers of the *Man'yōshū* is uncertain. In succeeding centuries, the court took an increasingly active role in encouraging poetry and defining canons of taste, and for some reason not yet fully understood, tanka verse of 31 syllables became the standard form of court poetry. Poetry contests were held, and a series of anthologies were compiled on imperial command to preserve the best works of the time. For a man or woman of the aristocracy, poetry became an undertaking of intense seriousness, a means of attracting notice or advancing a career, and to have a work included in an imperial anthology might well represent the crowning achievement of a lifetime. The conception of poetry as a group activity, rather than as a solitary pursuit—a principle so important in the composition of renga or linked verse—had its beginnings in the court tradition.

In addition to the imperial anthologies, works of individual poets were compiled, and schools of poetry appeared to teach those who aspired to write poetry, often espousing rival esthetic ideals and handing down carefully guarded secrets of the art. Poetry of the kind recognized in court circles thus became less a form of spontaneous expression than the product of long practice and careful study of the works of the past, an art that only the upper classes had the leisure to pursue. In addition, the court, as the repository for the highest cultural ideals and accomplishments, was also responsible for the development of literary works in prose and poetry written directly in Chinese. As early as the *Man'yōshū* influences from Chinese poetry and culture can be found in Japanese poetry. At that time, China was enjoying one of its greatest periods of artistic, political, and cultural maturity during the T'ang Dynasty (618-907), and Japan learned an enormous amount in the spheres of linguistic and poetic modes of expression from its continental neighbor. Court officials and other highly educated persons expressed their thoughts and feelings in Chinese in somewhat the same fashion that medieval clerics in Europe used Latin. The tradition of kanshi or poems written in classical Chinese has continued on and off until the present century.

The development of these sophisticated traditions did not mean, however, that poetry ceased to play a part in the lives of the common people. Examples begin with selections of poems by border guards and other anonymous figures in the *Man'yōshū* followed by Shinto dance songs, then by excerpts from the *Ryōjin hishō* (Secret Selection of Songs) and other collections from the Heian period [ca. 794-ca. 1185]... The kind of popular sentiment expressed in this poetry remains just as genuine, and is just as effective in its own way, as much that was written in the high literary forms.

The tanka became the dominant form of poetry in the Heian and medieval periods, and because of this the supposition has sometimes been made—incorrectly—that Japanese poetry is invariably brief. At the time of the *Man'yōshū* , Japanese poetry included long poems, and the tradition produced a resurgence of extended forms in the twentieth century. The preference for tanka and later for the 5-7-5 syllable hokku popular in the Tokugawa period [ca. 1600-ca. 1868] has often been explained, or explained away, through linguistic configurations and limitations. Nevertheless, there has always existed a tension in the tradition between the self contained brevity of a single poetic unit and the larger scope of a more general poetic conception. Even in the *Man'yōshū*, headnotes were sometimes provided in order to give the setting of a poem as a proper background to the lyrical impulse (see, for example, the various poems by Ōtomo no Yakamochi). In imperial and other anthologies, more systematic designs were imposed by the editors, who selected and arranged poems by different authors in seasonal or other sequences in order to suggest, by means of juxtaposition, association, and progression, a composite image larger than, and sometimes slightly at variance with, any one of its particular aspects. Fujiwara no Teika's compilation of one hundred three tanka [shows] this technique.

Toward the end of the Heian period, poets composing in the tanka form began to follow a tendency to divide the 31-syllable form and organize images into two smaller parts of 5-7-5 and 7-7 syllables. By the fourteenth century, such a division had made dominant the poetic form of renga, in which usually two or more poets wrote alternating 5-7-5 and 7-7 syllable parts. Although any two consecutive parts—but not more—of a renga were to relate directly, such linking did permit the development of longer poetic structures. The rules for the composition of these verse became exceedingly complex and required extensive training and practice on the part of the participants. The amount of concentration and cooperation required for successful renga composition might be compared with the challenge of playing chamber music: in both cases, each participant must listen carefully to his companions as well as to himself in order to keep the momentum going. The pleasure of "performing" poetry in a group, already an important element in the tanka contests of the imperial court, flowered in the cooperative esthetic of the renga.

In content, there were two kinds of renga: the formal, serious kind that stressed elegance in the court poetry tradition, and the light, humorous kind that stressed earthiness and realism. The latter, known as haikai no renga or simply haikai, often overwhelmed the serious renga in sheer popularity in the fourteenth and fifteenth centuries and became predominant thereafter. In the Edo period Matsuo Bashō elevated haikai no renga to high art, giving it a spirit that, while still lyrical, was playful and contemporary in feeling, vocabulary, and theme.

In renga, the opening part, or hokku, made up 5-7-5 syllables, was intended to set the general tone of the links that followed. By tradition, and because renga composition was essentially a group activity, a sequence was usually required to begin in a propitious, congratulatory, lofty, or otherwise affirmative tone. Often, the principal guest would use the hokku to compliment the host, who in turn would write the following part, the wakiku, deprecating himself or returning the compliment. Mainly because of this practice, hokku remained positive in outlook long after they came to be written independently as they did early in the development of renga. In the modern period, independent hokku were given the designation of haiku and are so referred to today.

II

In order to give some idea of the musical and esthetic effect of Japanese poetry, a simple description of the language in which it is written may be useful. although Japanese has gone through many changes since the time of the *Man'yōshū*, particularly in the writing system, certain general principles apply to much of the poetic tradition. Japanese is an agglutinative language that strings together short semantic elements to create long and often very complex word formations. Japanese verbs in particular are often highly inflected through the addition of suffixes expressing variations of mood and probability concerning the action. A single verb form may thus occupy an entire 5- or 7-syllable unit of a poem. In addition, the language employs a variety of emotive particles used to vary the tone and to add to the exclamatory force of an utterance. The result is a flowing syntax that, although often imprecise in meaning, is capable of expressing subtle shades of emotion.

The sound system of Japanese is quite simple, although it was evidently slightly more complex in the early periods. Nearly all the syllables in the language, when represented in a Western alphabet, consist of a consonant followed by a vowel. There is no stress accent, each syllable being pronounced with more or less equal emphasis. Meters based on stress, familiar to readers of English poetry, become virtually impossible. Since nearly every syllable ends in a vowel, of which there are only five, rhyming becomes so simple that it is pointless, so end rhyme has never become an important technique in Japanese poetry. And while pitch accent may serve a a factor in poetic diction, there seems little general agreement among scholars as to what its effect might be on the prosody or other aspects of Japanese poetry.

As noted above, the basic form employed in traditional poetry is distinguished by its use of units of 5 and 7 syllables, and nearly all its poetic forms are of a fixed length. Tanka is restricted to 31 syllables, and what is now called haiku in 17 syllables is constructed of a pattern of 5, 7, and 5 syllables. Other literary devices include parallelism, conventional epithets prefixed to certain nouns, and particularly in later poetry, double entendres, word associations, and allusive variations on phrases from earlier poetry.

Burton Watson has supplied the following example by way of illustrating some of these characteristics:

Here is a well-known work by a semi-legendary poet of the Heian period named Semimaru. It is in tanka form and describes a famous barrier or checkpoint near Kyoto on the road connecting the capital with eastern Japan. Friends or relatives of persons journeying east frequently accompanied the travelers as far as the barrer before taking leave of them.

The barrier was located at a place named Ausaka (Osaka in modern pronunciation), which means "meeting slope."

> *Kore ya kono*
> *yuku mo kaeru mo*
> *wakaretsutsu*
> *shiru mo shiranu mo*
> *Ausaka no seki*

> This is the spot—
> where those going, those returning
> take their leave,
> those who know each other, those who don't
> the barrier at Meeting Slope

The poem plays on the meaning of the place name Ausaka (meeting slope, contrary to its name, is really a place of parting), and through its rapid succession of verbs suggests the bustling activity of the barrier and the bitterness of the leave-takings conducted there. But the real beauty of the poem lies in the repetition of the *mo* particle and the wonderful interweaving of "k" and "s" sounds. It is euphonies and musical resonances of this type, and the intrinsic flowing quality of the language, rather than elaborate prosodic devices, that in most cases account for the particular appeal of Japanese poetry in the original.

III

Within the Japanese tradition, there exists a remarkable variety of thematic and artistic concerns, yet there remains some suggestion of an implicit unity as well. What gives this sense of cohesion? An examination — and reexamination — of the various poems included here will reveal a resonance of forms, images, and ideas which may help define the special sense of the world that hovers unseen behind the different texts.

The first and most obvious source of unity has to do with the close relationship poets in all periods show for the manifestations and processes of nature. Some aspect or phenomenon of the natural world, as witnessed by the poet, often serves as a kernel for individual insight. Even when such personal observation seems to lie well within the canons of precedent and taste so important in court poetry, it is the presence of this close and genuinely felt observation that invariable gives a good poem both its emotional center and its sharpness of focus. True, the subject matter of much nature poetry seems, superficially, to be restricted, but the natural images themselves possess a history of their own. Bamboo is as important in the *Kojiki* of the eighth century as it is in the poetry of Hagiwara Sakutarō (1886-1942), and the image of dew is as moving for Saigyō (1118-1190) ("Drops of dew") as it is for Kobayashi Issa (1763-1827) ("The world of dew").

Tradition and the individual talent of the poet are meant to come together to produce a poem that, while within the boundaries of literary taste and possibility, also gives sufficient scope to the poet to observe and comment both on what he has personally felt and on how he responds to what he has read and learned of earlier literary reactions to the same sort of natural stimulus. A new poem on, say, cherry blossoms can thus serve not only as a record of the poet's own observations on nature, but also as his personal commentary on the way in which others before him have responded to a similar scene. A contemporary English language reader will doubtless grasp the beauty of the individual observation quickly, but may quite understandably find difficulty in placing that observation in the larger scheme of literary precedent. This anthology helps document the growth of the tradition and provides some record of how the central natural images in Japanese poetry grew and changed...

The literary purposes behind a close observation of nature changed and expanded as the tradition grew more sophisticated. The assumptions about nature and its purposes revealed in the *Man'yōshū* are rather artless and certainly less self-conscious than they were to become in the work of later poets. Still, even in that earliest collection, the first stirrings of an esthetic that makes use of nature as a metaphor for the transcendental can easily be seen. In a beautiful tanka by an eighth century priest, Mansei, the mechanism for creating a linguistic and spiritual bridge from observation to abstraction is constructed with consummate art:

> To what shall I compare this world? A boat that rows off with
> morning, leaving no trace behind.

As such methods grew in sophistication in the later Heian and Kamakura [ca. 1185-ca. 1392] periods, they came to be defined as an artistic quality or virtue called *yūgen*, the representation of the ineffable or the unseen, a summoning up of what lies beneath the surface of perceived nature. Yūgen, as described by the poet and critic Kamo no Chōmei (1153-1216), became a central principle in a metaphysical concept of the poetic art:

> [T]hose who have attained the state say it is in essence an overtone that does not appear in words, a feeling that is not visible in form....For example, the evening sky in autumn has no color, no voice, and yet, though there seems to be no reason why this should happen, you find tears welling up in your eyes. But those without heart think nothing of such a sight, appreciating only the blossoms and crimson leaves that are so obvious to the eye....Again, when you look at the autumn hills through rifts in the mist, what you can see is vague, but what lies beyond enchants you, making you wonder endlessly how interesting the whole spread of crimson leaves must be; such a view is superior to seeing it all too clearly.
>
> (Tr. Sato)

In such an esthetic scheme a poem was intended to remain grounded on one level in a directly felt observation of nature, behind or beyond which some intimation of the existence of a different or higher reality was suggested. Poems fully given over to abstraction, such as the following by Minamoto Sanetomo (1192-1219), the Third Kamakura shogun and a student of Jujiwara no Teika (1162-1241), did not challenge the dominant esthetic:

> This world —
>   call it an image
>   caught in a mirror —
>   real it is not,
>   nor unreal either.

Rather, the stress was on a mystic closeness with nature on the part of the poet, a closeness that, allied to an exacting craft, was considered the best means to achieve genuine poetic insight. Matsuo Bashō (1644-1694) understood this principle to its fullest, as his disciple Hattori Tohō (1657-1730) recorded in his *Sanzōshi*, three notebooks in which he took down his master's various teachings:

"Learn about the pine from the pine, learn about the bamboo from the bamboo" — this dictum of our teacher means that you must forgo your subjectivity. If you interpret "learn" in your own way, you will end up not learning. To "learn" here means to enter the object; then if its esssence reveals itself and moves you, you may come up with a verse. Even if you seem to have described the object, unless [your description] has an emotion that comes out of it naturally, the object and your self will remain separated, and the emotion you have described will not have attained sincerity, because it will be something made up by your subjectivity.

(Tr. Sato)

The means to achieve a mystic union of personal emotion and literary craft was given its first classic statement in the opening lines of Fujiwara no Teika's advice to other tanka poets in the *Eiga Taigai* (An Outline for Composing Tanka) written about 1222 and translated here. Teika, generally considered the greatest critic in the tradition of court poetry, laid down principles that were influential for his contemporaries and for all those who followed:

In emotion, newness is foremost: look for sentiments others have yet to sing, and sing them. In diction, use the old: don't go further back than the Three Anthologies, but use the diction of the masters....

Such sentiments, and the examples of suitable poems Teika provided, helped solidify the tradition that still remains visible in the work of such important modern poets as Masaoka Shiki (1867-1902) or even in the work of Ozaki Hōsai (1885-1926), who strove to create a free-form style of haiku. In more subtle ways, the same concerns are expressed in a writer of modern poetry like Miyazawa Kenji (1896-1933), whose poems seem often to represent a final affirmation of the poetic self as defined through an identification with the great natural forces in the world.

Then too, as the anthology shows, the tradition of Japanese poetry, like others, possesses figures who serve as models to be emulated, despaired over or frowned upon, depending on the poet, his period, and his own sense of vocation. In a sense, most of the poets included here have served as models at one time or another, but among them are those who tower over the others and who cast long shadows, even today.

The earliest of such poets is Kakinomoto no Hitomaro (c. 700), whose moving elegies in the *Man'yōshū* are among the most treasured older poems in the language. A contemporary poet such as Anzai Hitoshi (born 1919) can conjure up, with the full emotional support of his Japanese readers, his own vision of that archaic world in a poem called "Hitomaro." For Anzai and his audience, Hitomaro's name serves not as an archaic reference, but rather as some vital chord that, when struck, still produces strong overtones. In the early Heian period, Ki no Tsurayuki (c. 868-c. 916), the chief editor of the *Kokinshū* and the author of *Tosa nikki* (Tosa Diary), became the first of the great poet-critics whose taste set the directions for tanka poetry. Two hundred fifty years later, the Buddhist priest and recluse Saigyō deepened Tsurayuki's concepts and provided possibilities for a more profound pathos, yet Saigyō's own poems on death owe much in style and mood to models he found in the *Tosa Diary*.

Tsurayuki's role as a poet-critic was taken over in turn by Fujiwara no Teika. The Nō play *Teika*, written about one hundred fifty years after his death and attributed to one of the great poets of the medieval theater, Komparu Zenchiku (1405-1468), indicates Teika's importance for the history of Japanese poetry. His mistress in the play, Princess Shikishi (died 1201), was also an accomplished poet...The play shows the importance of tanka as a source of quotation and inspiration in this high dramatic art. Teika and Saigyo both became important models for the poets who followed them. For a haikai poet like Bashō, Saigyō was still, five hundred years later, the supreme master of tanka poetry, since he was one "who in art follows nature and makes friends with the four seasons." Basho paid Saigyō the compliment of incorporating references to the older poet's work in his own haikai not as an attempt at imitation, but as act of respect to an absolute master....

The traditions of Japanese poetry continue to provide individual inspiration that modern writers value. Kawabata Yasunari (1899-1972), in his 1968 Nobel Prize acceptance speech, chose citations from the poetry of the Buddhist priest Myōe (1173-1232) to exemplify the deeper significance of his own art:

Watching the Moon Go Down

Set now,
and I too will go below
the rim of the hill —
so night after night
let us keep company.

For Kawabata, such a poem showed a warm, delicate compassion, the deep quiet of the Japanese spirit. Even today, the past can inform the present through an act of homage.

Still another source of unity in the tradition can be observed in what might be termed a consistent desire for the cosmopolitan, a penchant for using images and ideas from other civilizations to enrich and enlarge the native tradition. This attitude goes back to before the time of the *Man'yōshū* when an influx of Chinese culture sanctioned the influence of foreign models. At its least effective, such openness may seem to produce a sort of mindless eclecticism, but in the best Japanese poetry this artistic point of view can ground a poem in a more complex view of reality by extending the literary frame of reference. A comparison with the Chinese tradition is particularly striking, since that tradition is remarkably self-contained and has allowed little to enter that lies outside its linguistic and cultural boundaries. For the Japanese, Chinese art and poetry (perfectly or imperfectly understood, depending to some extent on the historical period in question) provided a set of additional points of reference, and of departure, for more than a thousand years. Bashō occasionally paraphrased some of the great Chinese poets because his spirit and his own poetry became richer for this cross-cultural underpinning....

From the *Kojiki*

"Song of a Lady from Mie"

When the emperor held a banquet under a hundred-branch zelkova tree at Hatsuse, a lady from Mie of the land of Ise took up a great wine cup to present to him. At that moment, a leaf fell from the zelkova tree and floated in the cup. The lady, unaware of the leaf, presented the wine. The emperor saw the leaf floating in the cup, struck her down, put a sword to her neck and was about to kill her, when she said to him, "Don't kill me, I have something to say," and sang:

The palace of Sun-White at Makimuku
is a palace on which the morning sun shines,
a palace on which the evening sun casts light,
a palace where bamboo roots grow full,
a palace where roots of trees crawl,
a palace built by firming the good earth with pestles,
a gate of wood of flourishing cypress trees—
growing by the hall of the first fruits,
this zelkova tree has a full hundred branches:
the upper branches cover the heavens,
the middle branches cover the east,
the lower branches cover the villages;
a leaf at the tip of an upper branch
falls and touches a middle branch,
a leaf at the tip of a middle branch
falls and touches a lower branch,
a leaf at the tip of a lower branch
falls and settles like floating oil[1]
in this beautiufl cup, which I,
a child of the silk-cloth Mie, present.
The water rolls and rolls[2]

1, 2. Allusion to the creation of the land as described at the opening of the *Kojiki*.

all this, so awesome,
child of the high-shining sun!
This is the way the story's told.

Because she presented this song, he forgave her for her
offense.

(Tr. Hiroaki Sato)

Princess Nukada (7th cent.)

"When Emperor Tenji"

When Emperor Tenji Commanded the minister of the center,
Fujiwara no Kamatari, to debate the merits of the fragrance of
thousands of flowers on a spring hill as opposed to the color of
hundreds of leaves on an autumn hill, Princess Nukada settled
the question with this poem:

When, after holing up for winter, the spring comes,
birds that weren't singing come and sing,
flowers that weren't blooming bloom;
but the hills are so dense with growth I can't go in and pick the
    flowers,
the grass so thick I can't pick and look at them.
When I look at the leaves of trees on an autumn hill,
I take the yellow leaves and admire them.
I leave the green ones, and I'm sorry,
that's something I regret.
But for me, the autumn hill!

(Tr. Hiroaki Sato)

Prince Otsu (663-686)

An exchange of tanka with Lady Ishikawa

To Lady Ishikawa
In the dripping dew of the foot-wearying mountain I stood
   waiting for you, getting wet in the dripping dew of the
   mountain

Lady Ishikawa Replies
The dripping dew of the foot-wearying mountain where you
   waited for me, getting wet, that's what I'd like to have been

(Tr. Hiroaki Sato)

Yamanoue no Okura (?660-?733)

Longing for His Son, Furhi

The seven types of treasures
people prize and desire—
   what do I have to do with them?
Born of us two,
our son, Furuhi, a pearl,
when the day broke with the morning star
wouldn't leave his bed of white cloth
but, standing or sitting,
   he would play with us.
When the evening of the evening star came,
"Let's sleep," he would say, taking our hands.
"Father, mother, stay near me, don't go away.
Like a marigold I'll sleep in the middle."
He'd say this so lovingly

that we looked forward to the time we'd see him
an adult, for better or worse,
trusting in him as in a great ship.
But unexpectedly a crosswind
swept down and overwhelmed him.
Not knowing what to do, what could be done,
I tucked up my sleeves with a white-cloth sash,
held a clear mirror in my hand
and looked up, begged, prayed to the gods of heaven,
prostrated myself, forehead on the ground, before the gods of
       earth.
  "Whether it is this way or is not,
     is up to the gods,"
I said, pacing up and down, as I begged and prayed.
But he never got better even for a moment;
bit by bit his face lost color,
morning by morning he spoke less,
till his precious life came to an end.
I jumpèd to my feet, stamped, shouted;
I prostrated myself, looked up, beat my chest, grieved.
My son, who I held in my hands, I've let fly away—
the way of this world!

    Envoy

So young he wouldn't know his way. I offer you gifts, messenger
   of the underworld—carry him on your back

                         (Tr. Hiroaki Sato)

Ōtomo no Tabito (665-731)

In Praise of Sake

Don't think about useless things—you should be drinking, it
seems to me, a bowl of raw sake

Choosing "sage" as a name for sake—how good the words of
those great sages of the past![1]

Those seven wise men of the past—what they too wanted, it
seems, was sake[2]

Better than to say things like a wise fellow, it seems, is to drink
sake, get drunk, and weep

I don't know how to say it, what to do about it—the noblest of all,
it seems, is sake

Rather than be a so-so human being, I'd like to be a sake jar and
get steeped in sake[3]

How ugly—take a good look at a man who acts wise and doesn't
drink—just like a monkey!

A priceless treasure it may be, but how can it be better than a
bowl of raw sake?

1. When the Wei dynasty outlawed drinking in third-century
China, secret drinkers referred to raw or unrefined sake as "the
worthy" and refined sake as "the sage."
2. The so-called Seven Sages of the Bamboo Grove, a group of
philosopher-poets of third-century China who often met to
drink and make music.
3. Cheng Ch'üan, a Chinese who loved wine, asked his son to
bury him beside a pottery kiln so that, after his bones had turned
to clay, someone might perhaps mold him into a wine jar.

A gem that gleams at night it may be, but how can it compare to
 drinking sake and opening your heart?

When you're unfilled in ways of worldly entertainment, you
 should, it seems, get drunk and weep

If I enjoy myself in this world, in the world to come I won't mind
 being an insect or a bird

Since all living things die in the end, while I'm in this world I'll
 enjoy myself

To keep silent and act wise—still not as good as drinking sake,
 getting drunk, and weeping

(Tr. Hiroaki Sato)

Takahashi Mushimaro
(dates uncertain)

Tegona of Mama

In the land of Azuma
where the cocks crow,
it took place
far in the past,
though they tell
of it still—
Tegona of Mama
in Katsushika
dressed herself in hemp cloth,
trimmed it with a blue collar,
wove herself a skirt to wear
out of pure hemp,

no comb
for her hair,
no shoes on her feet
when she went abroad,
but what pampered daughtter
done up in
patterns and brocades
could compare to her?
Her face
perfect as the full moon,
when she stood there
smiling like a flower,
men swarmed around her
like summer insects
drawn to a flame,
like ships rowing
for the harbor mouth.
But then,
as though life weren't
short enough already,
what did she do
but take herself off,
laid herself down
where the noise
of the waves is loudest,
in the deeptest part of the harbor!
Though this happened
in an age long ago,
I think of it
as if I had seen it
only yeasterday

Envoy

When I look at the well
at Mama in Katsushika,

I think of Tegona
who used to stand here
drawing water

(Tr. Burton Watson)

Kakinomoto no Hitomaro
(fl. ca. 680-700)

On passing the ruined capital at Omi

Ever since the day
  of the august Emperor[1]
who made his abode
  at Kashihara where rises
holy Mount Unebi,
every sovereign born to us
  had exercised sway
    over all beneath the skies,
each one in his turn,
from the land of Yamato.
But for a reason
  beyond our understanding,
there was a ruler[2]
  who left the sky-filling land,
crossed the mountains
  of Nara where the earth is rich,
and exercised sway
  over all beneath the skies

---

1. Emperor Jimmu, legendary founder of the Yamato clan,
whose traditional dates are 660 B.C.—585 B.C.
2. Emperor Tenji

at Ōtsu Palace,
the place of rippling wavelets
 in Ōmi
    where the water breaks on rocks,
rural though it was,
and distant as the heavens.
But though we are told
  here rose the palace compound
    where dwelt the sovereign,
the godlike Emperor,
and though people say
  here soared the mighty halls,
now haze veils the sky
  above luxuriant growths
    of springtime grasses,
and the spring sun shines weak
  on the site where stood
    the great stone-built palace—
the place I sorrow to see.

   Envoys

It remains unchanged—
Cape Karasaki in Shiga
 of rippling wavelets—
but it will await in vain
  the courtiers in their boats.

sasanami no / shiga no karasaki / sakiku aredo / omiyahito
no / fune machikanetsu

They lie quietly,
the shore waters at Shiga
 of rippling wavelets:
but will they ever meet again
  those whom they knew in the past?

sasanami no / shiga no owada / yodomo to mo / mukashi
no hito ni / mata mo awame ya mo

(Tr. Steven Carter)

Composed when the Sovereign journeyed to the Yoshino Palace[1]

Many are the lands
  in the realm under heaven
    where our Empress reigns,
where holds sway our great Sovereign
  who governs in peace;
yet her august heart inclines
  toward Yoshino,[2]
holding it to be a place
  where the mountain stream
    courses into pure clear pools;
and there in the fields
  where flowers fall at Akizu,
she has erected
  firm pillars of a palace.
Thus the courtiers,
men of the stone-built palace,
align their vessels
  to cross the morning river,
and race their vessels
  to cross the evening river.
Though I gaze and gaze,
never shall I have enough:
palace eternal
  as the flow of the river,

1. The precise date of this excursion is unknown.
2. Yoshino was of special significance to the Empress as the place
where the then-consort of the future Emperor Temmu had
stayed in seclusion just prior to the Jinshin Disturbance.

palace soaring high
  as the towering mountains,
beside the seething cascade.
    Envoy

I shall come again
  to see it—come ceaselessly
as grows velvet moss
  in the Yoshino River,
of which my eyes never tire.

miredo akanu / yoshino no kawa no / tokoname no /
tayuru koto naku / mata kaerimimu

(Tr. Steven Carter)

Composed when the Sovereign journeyed to Yoshino Palace[1]

Our great Sovereign
  who rules the nation in peace,
a very goddess,
thinking to act as a god,
has built splendidly
  a hall towering on high
  by the seething pools
    of the Yoshino River;
  and when she climbs up
    and standing surveys the land,
  the green-wall mountains
  ranging in their serried ranks,
wishing to present
  tribute from the mountain gods,
deck their heads with flowers
  if the season be springtime,
and wear colored leaves
  with the coming of autumn.

1. The precise date of this excursion is unknown.

and eager to give
  food for the august table,
the gods of the stream
  flowing beside the mountains
send out cormorants
  to fish the upper shallows,
send men with scoop nets
  to fish the lower shallows.
ah, this is the reign
 of a god in whose service
    mountains and rivers unite!

  Envoy

A very goddess
  whom the mountains and rivers
    unite in serving,
she is rowed forth in her boat,
rowed forth to the seething pools.

yama kawa mo / yorite tsukauru / kama nagara/ tagitsu
kōchi ni / funade sesu ka mo

(Tr. Steven Carter)

A poem written by Kakinomoto no Hitomaro when Prince Karu[1] took lodging in the fields of Aki

Off to the eastward,
the first shimmer of daylight
  rises on the fields—
and when I turn round to see,
the moon is sinking away.

himugashi no / no ni wa kagiroi / tatsu miete / kaerimi sureba /
tsuki katabukinu

1. The future Emperor Mommu (683-707; r. 696-707).

Written on parting from his wife when he went from Iwami Province to the capital

In Iwami Sea,
minding of rock-creeping vines,
at Kara, the cape
  of wave-chatter like Cathay speech,[1]
upon rocky reefs
  grows the sea-pine of the deep,
upon stony strands
  grows seaweed fair as gems.
Deep as the sea-pine
  was my love for a dear girl,
one who lay yielding
  as fair gemweed yields to waves,
yet only a few
  were the nights of our sweet sleep,
and then I set off;
we parted like creeping vines.
Pain ravaged the heart
  that sits within my breast,
made me turn my head,
look back in ceaseless yearning,
yet only faintly
  could I see her waving sleeve,
glimmering among
  falling leaves in autumn hues
    at Crossing Mountain,
minding of journeying ships.
It grieved me as when
  the moon hides herself from view
as she journeys on
  through cloud rifts at Yakami,

---

1. *Koto saeku kara*, here referring to the "foreign" dialects of the provinces.

hill of cloistered wives.
As my love's sleeve disappeared,
the sky-coursing sun
  declined shining toward day's end,
and then I, the man
  who thought himself stouthearted,
wept into my sleeve—
robe-sleeve spread for sheet at night—
cried until the tears soaked through.

  Envoys

Too swift is the stride
  of the dapple-gray stallion.
I have left behind
  as distant as the heavens
    the place where my love dwells.

aogomà ga / agaki o hayami / kumoi ni zo / imo ga atari o /
sugite kinikeru

You colored leaves falling
  among autumn mountains:
for just a moment
  stop scattering and let me see
    the place where my love dwells.

akiyama ni / otsuru momichiba / shimashiku wa / na
chirimagai so /imo ga atari mimu

(Tr. Steven Carter)

Yamabe no Akahito
(fl. early 8th cent.)

Looking at Mount Fuji in the Distance

Since heaven and earth parted,
godlike, lofty and noble
in Suruga, Fuji the lofty peak—
as I turn and look at the Plain of Heaven,
the light of the coursing sun is hidden behind it,
the shining moon's rays can't be seen,
white clouds can't move, blocked,
and regardless of time, the snow's falling.
We'll tell, we'll go on talking
about Fuji, this lofty peak.

   Envoy

Coming out on the beach of Tago, I look: pure white—on Fuji the
   lofty peak, the snow's falling

Climbing Kasuga Field

On Mount Kasuga of the spring days,
on Mount Mikasa of the high platform,
every morning clouds lie,
cuckoos call, ceaseless and incessant.
Like the clouds my heat lingers,
like those birds I'm in one-sided love,
in the day, all through the day,
in the night, all through the night,
standing or sitting, I brood,
though I cannot meet her.

Envoy

Like the birds that call on Mount Mikasa of the high platform, my
thoughts of love start up as soon as they cease

(Tr. Hiroaki Sato)

Song

Our sovereign familiar with the eight corners,
being a god, rules on high
in Omi Field of Inamino.
There, in coarse-fabric Wisteria Bay,
fishing boats make a commotion, angling for tuna,
many people work, burning seaweed for salt.
Because the bay is good, they fish, yes,
because the shore is good, they burn seaweed for salt, yes.
Clear to the eye why he frequents this place—
this clean, white shore!

Envoys

Because waves in the offing and waves near the shore are calm,
they fish in Wisteria Bay, boats making a commotion

Having pushed down the short reeds in Inamino and slept so
many nights, I miss my home

Through the Akashi marsh, along the tide-bare path, I won't be
able to help smiling tomorrow, for my home will be near

(Tr. Hiroaki Sato)

Two Tanka

I came to this spring field to pick violets. But I loved the field so
much I've slept here all night

In the field I've roped off, thinking to pick spring herbs from
tomorrow, it's been snowing yesterday and today

(Tr. Hiroaki Sato)

Lady Ōtomo no Sakanoue (fl. early 8th cent.)

Love's Complaint

Those sedges in light-flooded Naniwa—
you spoke as intimately as their clinging roots,
you said it would run deep into years, it would last long,
so I gave you my heart, as spotless
as a clear mirror.
                    From that day,
unlike the seaweed that sways with the waves,
I did not have a heart that goes this way and that,
I trusted as one trusts a great ship.
But has a god, a rock-smasher, put us apart?
Or someone of this world interfered?
You used to come but you no longer do,
and no messenger bearing the catalpa branch appears.
Because of this there's nothing I can do.
All through the night black as leopard-flower seeds,
through the day till the red-rayed sun sets,
I grieve, but there's no sign,
I brood, but I don't know what t do.
They speak of "weak women"—I am just that,
weeping loudly like a child,
I go back and forth, waiting for your messenger—
will all this be in vain.

Envoy

If at the outset you hadn't said "It would last long," and made me
    trust you, would I have thoughts like this?

(Tr. Hiroaki Sato)

Lady Kasa (mid 8th cent.)

Eighteen tanka written to Ōtomo no Yakamochi:

My keepsake—
look at it and think of me,
and I will love you
through the long years
strung like beads on a string

Like the crane whose cry
I hear in the dark night,
I hear of you only
as someone far away—
we never so much as meet

I love you,
it's utterly hopeless—
on the Nara hills,
under the little pines
I stand and weep

At my home
the bright dew fades
from evening grasses—
I too will fade away,
so helpless my love for you!

As long as I live
can I forget you?
Each passing day
my love
grows stronger

Eight hundred days
journeying along the shore—
can its sands
outweigh my love,
guardian of the outer island?

The world has so many eyes—
though we're close
as steppingstones in a brook,
I must live with my love unspoken

A person can die of love—
like a hidden scream,
unseen I waste away
each month, each day that passes

Though I only
saw you dimly
as in a morning mist,
I now live with a love
that will cost me my life

I go on loving him—
a man awesome as the waves
of the sea of Ise
that thunder in
upon the shore

When evening comes
I long for you more than ever,
before my eyes
I see you as you looked
when you spoke

If one can die of love,
then a thousand times

I must have died,
died and come alive again

I dreamt
I clasped a sword
to my body—
what sign is this?
does it mean I'll meet you?

If the gods
of heaven and earth
lacked all reason,
they'd let me die
without seeing you

I love you—
do not forget me!
Like winds blowing
over the bay,
never let us cease!

I hear the bell striking,
saying "All to bed!"
but I think of you so,
I could never hope to sleep

Loving someone
who doesn't love you—
it's like kowtowing to the back
of the hungry demon
at the great temple!¹

1. According to Buddhist belief, one who does evil risks being reborn as a hungry demon (*gaki*). Statues of hungry demons were apparently displayed in Nara period temples as a warning, but to pray to such statues was of course pointless and ineffectual.

I can bear
not seeing you
so long as you're near,
but how will I endure it
when you're far away?

(Tr. Burton Watson)

Sami Mansei (dates uncertain)

Tanka

To what shall I compare this world? A boat that rows off
   with morning, leaving no trace behind

(Tr. Hiroaki Sato)

Three Anonymous Poems With Stories (dates uncertain)

It is reported that there was once a young woman who, without letting her parents know, began an affair in secret with a young man. The man, fearful of being scolded by her parents, was somewhat hesitant about the matter. The young woman thereupon composed this poem and gave it to him:

Should you hide in the rock tomb
of Mount Hatsuse,
should it come to that
I'd join you there—
do not doubt me, love!

Legend related that long ago there was a young woman who separated from her husband. She continued to love him and yearn for him over the years, but the husband took another wife and never went to see the young woman. All he did was send her presents. They young woman replied with the following poem of resentment:

I put good rice in water
and brewed wine
and waited,
and all for nothing—
you never even came

According to report, there was once a lady-in-waiting in the personal service of Prince Sai. Nights she was on duty in the prince's palace and had little free time, so it was very difficult for her to meet her husband. But her thoughts turned constantly toward him, for her love for him was very deep. One evening when she was on night duty, she saw her husband in a dream, but when she awoke and reached out to embrace him, her arms encountered only emptiness. Weeping and sobbing, she thereupon intoned this poem in a loud voice. The prince, hearing it, was moved to pity and saw to it that thereafter she would be permanently excused from night duty:

I eat my food
but it has no flavor,
I sleep
but I know no rest—
your love,
my madder-cheeked,
is so hard to forget!

(Tr. Burton Watson)

Two Anonymous Chōka
(dates uncertain)

On Love

This is what
the villagers told me:
"Your beloved husband
that you long for so,
from this mountainside
of Kamunabi
where the yellow leaves
scatter in confusion,
riding a horse
black as leopard-flower seeds,
crossed over the river shoals,
seven shoals in all—
We saw your husband
and he looked so sad!"—
that's what they told me.

    Envoy

I shouldn't have asked,
I should have kept still—
why did they have to tell me
the way you looked!

(Tr. Burton Watson)

On the Roads of Yamashiro

On the roads of Yamashiro
where the chloranthus grows, other women's husbands
ride on horseback,
but my husband

plods along on foot,
and each time I see it
all I do is cry,
whenever I think of it
my heart pains me.
This precious mirror of mine,
a keepsake
from my mother
of the sagging breasts,
this scarf thin as dragonfly wing—
take them, husband,
and buy yourself a horse!

Envoys

At the Izumi River crossing
the shoals are so deep,
my husband's traveling clothes
get soaked right through!

This precious mirror I own
means nothing to me
when I see you
struggling
to make your way on foot

"The Husband Replies"

If I buy a horse,
you must go on foot, love—
Let it be!
Though we walk on stones,
you and I will go together!

(Tr. Burton Watson)

Twenty-Three Anonymous Tanka on Love (dates uncertain)

By the light of the flares
of the fishermen
who fish the sea of Noto
make your way along
while you wait for moonlight

I didn't take
a good look at him
when he left at dawn,
and so for a whole day
all I do is pine

When I love her
so much,
can I watch her pass by
like any other person,
not take her in my arms?

Let me die now,
love,
for in love
not one night, not one day
of peace is mine!

I dusted the bed
with my sleeves
and sat waiting for you,
and while that was going on
the moon went down[1]

1. Once the moon has set, she knows there is little possibility that her lover will come to her.

Flocks of birds are singing
all round my door—
get up! get up!
my husband for a night—
no one must know of this!

Here I thought I was
a big man,
hardly smaller than
earth and heaven—
and yet in love my courage fails

So that no one will see
or blame me,
tonight I'll come to you in dreams—
just be sure you leave
the door unlatched

Like a little boat pushing through reeds
to make the harbor,
so many things block my way—
but I try to reach you—
never think I don't!

As far as sleeping goes
I could sleep with anyone—
but you, who've bent to me
like seaweed in the surge—
it's your word I wait for

I'll not die of love
but go on living, it seems,
a grain of sand
floating on the foam
when the tide comes in

The mere echo
of a horse's hoof
and I go out to see—
in the shadow of the pines,
wondering, could it be you?

If I go
when she's not expecting me,
she'll grin with delight—
I can just picture
how her eyebrows will look!

Straw matting
to sleep on
only one layer thick—
but when I sleep with you
I'm not the least bit cold

Pay no mind to my mother
with he sagging breasts—
if you do
you and I
will never get together

The day I go
to pick arrowhead
in the mountain pond—
let's meet then at least,
whatever my mother may say!

Is he here? Is he here?
But when I went out
to look for him,
light snow was falling
softly over the courtyard

Don't go!
now with the night so far gone,
tonight when
by the roadside
frost falls on the thick bamboo

"For a dead lover":

"My love?" I said,
"he'd never leave me!"
So we slept back to back
like two sticks of bamboo—
now how I regret it!

Like the huts
of the men of Naniwa,
sooty from the reeds they burn,
my wife too is gray with age—
but to me forever new

Though I'm old now,
my strength waning,
how I think of you
who were as close to me
as these white sleeves of mine!

Absurd!
at my age
to mouth such nonsense—
speaking the words of youth,
and I an old man

(Tr. Burton Watson)

"A woman angrily rejects her lover's excuses":

Could a little spring rain
get your clothes so very wet?
And if it rained seven days,
then seven nights
you wouldn't come?

(Tr. Burton Watson)

From the Kokinshū

Preface to the Kokinshū[1] (date uncertain)

Japanese poetry has its seeds in the human heart, and takes form in the countless leaves that are words. So much happens to us while we live in this world that we must voice the thoughts that are in our hearts, conveying them through the things we see and the things we hear. We hear the bush warbler singing in the flowers or the voice of the frogs that live in the flowers or the voice of the frogs that live in the water and know that among all living creatures there is not one that does not have its song. It is poetry that, without exerting force, can move heaven and earth, wake the feelings of the unseen gods and spirits, soften the relations between man and woman, and soothe the heart of the fierce warrior.

(Tr. Burton Watson)

Ariwara No Narihira (825-880)
Eighteen Tanka

Though winds blow,
coloring the
autumn bush clover,
my heart is no grass or leaf
that changes hue

On Nunobiki Waterfall:

Someone must be
unstringing them wildly—
white beads shower down
without pause,
my sleeve too narrow to catch them

1. The opening paragraph is translated. The poets that follow are among the major figures in the anthology and its period.

Before we've had our fill,
must the moon so quickly
hide itself?
If only the rim of the hill
would flee and refuse it shelter!

(Tr. Burton Watson)

Spring

On seeing cherry blossoms at the Nagisa no In[1]

Ah, if in this world
  there were only no such thing
    as cherry blossoms—
then perhaps in the springtime
  our hearts could be at peace.

yo no naka ni / taete sakura no / nakariseba / haru no
kokoro wa / nodokekaramashi

(Tr. Steven Carter)

So fleeting,
that dream of a night
we spent together—
and when I doze off it seems
more insubstantial than ever

(Tr. Burton Watson)

1. A palace anciently located in what is now Hirakata City,
Ōsaka Municipality.

Love

When Narihira went to Ise Province, he met in great secrecy with the lady who was serving as Ise Virgin. The next morning, while he was wondering how to manage a message without a messenger, he received this poem from the Virgin.

Did you come to me?
  Was it I who went to you?
  I am beyond knowing.
  Was it dream or reality?
  Was I sleeping or awake?

kimi ya koshi / ware ya yukikemu / omōezu / yume ka
utsutse ka / nete ka samete ka

His reply:

  I have wandered lost
   in the gloomy darkness
    that is my heart.
  Whether dream or reality,
  let someone else decide.

kakikurasu / kokoro no yami ni / madoiniki / yume utsutsu to
wa / yohito sadame yo

(Tr. Steven Carter)

Written for a woman in Narihira's household to send to a suitor [Fujiwara no Toshiyuki] who complained he was wetting his sleeve with a "river of tears":

A shallow river of tears
if it only wets your sleeve!
When I hear you've washed away
body and all,
then perhaps I'll trust you

Fujiwara no Toshiyuki sent the same woman a letter saying, "I wish I could go to you at once, but since it's raining, I'm afraid that would be difficult." When Narihira heard of this, he wrote the following poem for her to send as her reply:

So much to ask,
so hard to ask it—
do you still care or don't you—
the rain knows my dilemma,
falling in greater torrents than ever

Narihira had been carrying on an affair in secret with a woman who lived in the west annex of the palace of the Gojo Empress, but after the tenth day of the first month, she went into hiding somewhere else. He learned where she was living, but was unable even to send her a letter. In the spring of the following year, on a beautiful moonlit night when the plum blossoms were at their height, he recalled the events of the previous year and went to the west annex, where he lay all night on the rough floorboards and composed this poem:

Surely this is the moon,
surely this spring
is the the spring of years past—
or am I the only one
the same as before?

When Narihira's mother was living in Nagoaka [south of the capital], Harihira was often unable to visit her because of his duties at the palace. Once, in the closing month of the year, a message arrived from her marked "urgent." When Narihira opened it, he found no letter, but this poem:

I'm getting older,
and there's that parting

that won't be put off—
more and more
it makes me want to see you!

Reply:

In this world
there should be an end to
partings that won't be put off!—
for the sake of a son
who'd have you live a thousand years

Written when ill:

In the end
that's the road I'll travel—
I've known that all along—
but I didn't think I'd have to start
this very day

(Tr. Burton Watson)

Felicitations

Composed when there was a fortieth-year celebration for the
Horikawa Chancellor at the Kujō Mansion[1]

Scatter at random,
O blossoms of the cherry,
and cloud the heavens,
that you may conceal the path
old age is said to follow.

sakurabana / chirikaikumore / oiraku no / komu to iu
naru / michi magau ga ni

(Tr. Steven Carter)

1. The Horikawa Chancellor was Fujiwara no Motosune (836 -
91)

In the end I find
I take no pleasure in the moon—
these very moons,
when they pile up,
are what bring us to old age!

(Tr. Burton Watson)

Love

On the day of an archery meet at the riding grounds of the Bodyguards of the Right, Narihira glimpsed a lady's face through the silk curtains of a carriage opposite. He sent her this poem.

How very foolish!
Shall I spend all of today
   lost in pensive thought,
my heart bewitched by someone
   neither seen nor yet unseen?

Mizu mo arazu / mi mo senu hito no / koishiku wa / aya
naku kyo ya / nagamekurasamu

(Tr. Steven Carter)

Neither waking or sleeping,
I saw the night out,
and now spend
all day in thought,
staring at these long spring rains

Pushing home at dawn
through autumn fields of bamboo grass,
my sleeve is wet—
wetter still on those nights
when I return without seeing you

(Tr. Burton Watson)

Sugawara no Michizane (845-903)

On Vacation: A Poem to Record My Thoughts

[Written in 892 in Kyoto, when the poet was a high government official. Officials were given every sixth day off from work, but those of upper rank could request a special five-day leave.]

I put in for a five-day leave,
a little vacation from early duty at the office.
And during my leave where do I stay?
At my home in the Sempū Ward.
Gates bolted, no one comes to call;
the bridge broken, no horses pass by.[1]
Up early, I call the boy to prop up the last of the
                    chrysanthemums.
As the sun climbs higher, I urge the old groom
to sweep and tidy the sand in the garden.
At twilight I take a turn by the eastern fence,
try to wash and dust it, but the bamboo topples over.
When evening comes, I begin thinking of my books,
in rue-scented silk covers, five cartloads.[2]
Spotting the volumes I need, I take them down,
making notes to add on items overlooked.
The cold sound of fallen leaves by the stairs;
in dawn breath, flowers of frost on the flagstones:
at cockcrow I lie down, arm for a pillow,
quietly thinking, grieving for friends far away.
My girls are in the inner rooms helping their mother;
the little boy tags around after Grandpa,[3]

1. His house in the Sempu Ward faced west on a small stream called the Horikawa.
2. The rue was to protect the books from insects. In the fifth month of this year, Michizane had presented his work on Japanese history, entitled *Ruijū kokushi*, to Emperor Uda and was probably preparing additions or corrections to it.
3. In a poem written in Sanuki, Michizane mentions that one of his daughters had given birth to a son in the seventh month of 889, presumably this boy.

but I have duties that cannot be shirked,
I must leave and set out on the long road to the palace.
One sigh brings a sinking feeling in my stomach,
a second sigh and tears begin to flow.
The east already light and still I haven't slept;
glumly I sip a cup of tea.
Heaven is indifferent to my longings for leisure;
even at home I'm busy all the time.
Karma piled up from long ages past
keeps us coming and going in these bitter lives.

(Tr. Burton Watson)

Ono no Komachi (fl. ca. 850)

Love

Topic unknown

> Did you come to me
>   because I dropped off to sleep,
> tormented by love?
> If I had known I dreamed,
> I would not have awakened.

omoitsutsu / nureba ya hito no / mietsuramu / yume to
shiriseba / samezaramashi o

Love

Abe no Kiyoyuki [825-900]. Suggested by the monk Shinsei's sermon during a memorial service at the Lower Isumo Temple;[1] sent to Ono no Komachi

> They are only tears
>   shed for one I cannot see—

1. Located in the Yamashina area, in the Eastern Hills of Kyoto.

those fair white jewels
that will not stay in my sleeve
    when I seek to wrap them up.

tsutsumedomo / sode ni tamaranu / shiratama wa / hito o
minu me no / namida narikeri

Her reply:

Tears that do no more
    than turn into beads on sleeves
        are formal indeed.
Mine flow in a surging stream,
try though I may to halt them.

oroka naru / namida zo sode ni / tama wa nasu / ware wa
seikiaezu / takitsuse nareba

Love

Topic unknown

There is no seaweed
    to be gathered in this bay.
    Does he now know it—
the fisher who comes and comes
    until his legs grow weary?[1]

mirume naki / wa ga mi o ura to/ shiraneba ya / karenade
ama no / ashi tayuku kuru

---

1. This poem is an example of complex rhetorical technique
involving pivot-words (*mirume naki* meaning both "there's no
seaweed" and "you cannot see me") and a string of associated
words: seaweed, bay fisher, and so on.

Spring

Topic unknown

> Autumn nights, it seems,
> are long by repute alone:
> scarcely had we met
>   when morning's first light appeared,
> leaving everything unsaid.

aki no you mo / na nomi narikeri / au to ieba / koto zo to
mo naku / akenuru mono o

(Tr. Steven Carter)

Ki no Tsurayki (ca. 872-945)

Spring

Composed on the first day of spring.

> Soaking my long sleeves,
> I took up in my cupped hands
>   waters that later froze.
> And today, as spring begins,
> will they be melting in the wind?

sode hichite / musubishi mizu no / kōreru o / haru tatsu
kyō no / kaze ya tokuramu

Spring

On a snowfall

> When snow comes in spring—
> fair season of layered haze

and burgeoning buds—
flowers fall in villages
where flowers have yet to bloom.

kasumi tachi / ko no me mo haru no / yuki fureba / hana
naki sato mo / hana zo chirikeru

Spring

Composed by command

Are they on their way
to pick young greens in the fields
at Kasugano—
those girls who call each other
with the sleeves of their white robes?

kasugano no / wakana tsumi ni ya / shirotae no / sode
furihaete / hito no yukuramu

Spring

On seeing cherry blosoms for the first time on a tree planted at someone's
house

Blossoming cherry
who have just this year begun
to understand spring—
would that you might never learn
the meaning of scattering.

kotoshi yori / haru shirisomuru / sakurabana / chiru to iu
koto wa / narawazaranamu

(Tr. Steven Carter)

Lady Izumi (born c. 976)

Twenty-Four Tanka On Love

Unaware of my black hair in disorder, I lay face down, till he first
lifted it—it's him I miss

•

Tonight, as hail falls on bamboo leaves rustling, rustling, I don't
feel like sleeping alone

•

Loving you, my heart may shatter into a thousand pieces, but not
one piece will be lost

•

Someone who did not come to visit for a long time finally did, ·
but again stopped coming:
If you'd left me unhappy and hadn't come, by this time I might
have forgotten all about you

•

Waiting for my two lovers stationed in distant places:
Having waited for this one for this, that one for that, I can no
longer tell which is who

•

In the ninth month, to someone who went home at dawn:
You left, the mist lingered by the hedge, and yes, I had nothing to
do but gaze at the sky

•

Even my pillow, not knowing, won't talk. Don't tell of your
dream of this spring night, my love, as you have seen it

•

Don't tell people how it was, pillow of white cloth; what you
think of me is troubling enough

•

I want to see and be seen by you—if only you were the mirror I
face when I wake each morning!

●

To someone, when I was distressed:
To remember you in the next world, where I will be soon, I'd like
    to meet you just one more time!

●

Sometime in the third month a man spent a whole night talking with
me and went home. The next morning he sent word that he felt
frustrated:
No wonder you're grieved this morning; you didn't even try to
    dream one spring night through

●

To a man I met only briefly:
White dew, a dream, this life, an illusion—all these, by
    comparison, last long indeed

●

There's no color called love in this world, yet how thoroughly it
    has dyed my heart!

●

In the eighth month a man came to see me and left behind a fan with
a painting of dew on bamboo leaves. In returning it a while later:
You rose with eastern clouds and left—the dew on bamboo
    leaves has stayed longer with me.

●

If I should forget you because of this unhappiness, I would not
    consider my heart my own

●

While both he and I had to keep our affair secret, he demurred,
"This is not my heart's desire." Finding it hard that he should be so
resentful:
Aware that your body cannot follow what your heart desires, you
    should show me more understanding

●

To a man who said, "You've forgotten me":
Have I not forgotten you! If I hadn't, I certainly would, if I looked
    into your heart again!

●

A man who used to write to me didn't get in touch with me
for a long time:
Less troublesome than unforgettable: an affair that simply ended
without any acrimony

To a man who left me early in my life:
Whether or not I am as I was— I'd like to ask the one I used to
see, for I can't tell

●

Down the mountain into the path of darkness I've come, so as to
see you just one more time

●

From Prince Atsumichi:
If I speak of love you'll think I am like everyone else, but my
heart this morning is incomparable

In reply:
I don't think you are like everyone else; for the first time I find
myself in troubled thought

From Prince Atsumichi:
I tell myself not to doubt you, never to resent you, but my heart
doesn't follow my heart

In reply:
Don't keep your heart from resenting me; I too doubt you, you
rely on me boundlessly

Elegies for her Daughter, Ko-Shikibu, Who Died in the Eleventh Month, 102

Donating for sutra-chanting a box she used to carry with
her:
That she may know I love her and miss her—clinking a bell,
thinking of her, without a moment's interval

●

> The retired empress Jōtōmon sent word, "Have [Ko-shikibu's]
> Chinese robe with a dew design sent to me; I'd like to use it for
> the cover of my sutra." In having the robe sent to her, I tied
> the following to it:

The dew that formed remains; to what shall I compare that
transient one who faded?

> Jōtōmon's reply:

Had we expected this—that the dew that formed transiently on
the sleeve would be a keepsake?

> The retired empress Jōtōmon sent a roll of fabric as she used
> to do before Ko-Shikibu's death. Seeing "For Lady-in-Waiting
> Ko-Shikibu" written on it:

Bitter—that I should not have decayed under the moss with you,
but found your unburied name!

●

(Tr. Hiroaki Sato)

Laments

Written after the death of her daughter, Koshikibu no Naishi[1], when she
saw the child the latter had left behind

> After leaving us,
> she will be feeling sorry—
> but for which the more?
> No doubt for her own child,
> just as I for my child.

todomeokite / tare o aware to / omouran / ko wa
masaruran / ko wa masarikeri

(Tr. Steven Carter)

1. Also a poet ; she died in childbirth 1025.

"Matters I want settled": three tanka:

Which should I think shouldn't exist in this world, those who
neglect or those who are neglected?

Which is worse, to miss someone dead or to be unable to meet
someone alive?

Which is worse, to love someone far away or see often someone
you don't love?

(Tr. Hiroaki Sato)

Songs from the Ryojin Hisho

Four Songs

The young man came to make you his wife,
posing, he slept with you two nights;
on the third night, around midnight,
    before the break of day,
he picked up his pants and ran away!

You have no heart.
If you said I was nothing
    or that you wouldn't live with me,
I might hate you.
We were torn apart by my father and mother—
they can cut me up or slice me, I won't separate from you,
    that's my fate.

Looking at you my beauty,
I wish I could be a single-root vine
that i could entwine around you from root to tip!

They can cut me up or lice me, I won't separate from you,
that's my fate.

The brocade and rush hat you loved—
it dropped, it dropped
into the Kamo River, into midstream!
I've been looking for it, asking for it,
and now the day has come, the day has come
after rustling, clear autumn night!

Women are at their best
when fourteen, fifteen, twenty-three, or twenty-four;
when they get to be thirty-four or thirty-five,
they're no different from the lower leaves on a maple.

(Tr. Hiroaki Sato)

Fujiwara no Shunzei (1114-1204)

Spring

[From a hundred-poem sequence composed in 1134]

The sound of the wind,
the sight of the rocky crags,
the incoming waves—
all are rough, like this ocean shore;
but what of you, cherry tree?

kaze no oto mo / iwa no keshiki mo / yoru nami mo /
araki isobe ni / ika ni sakura zo

Laments

[From a hundred-poem sequence]

How is it that ducks
 are able to stay afloat
  out on the water,
 while I feel myself sinking
  even here on the land?

mizu no ue ni / ikade ka oshi no / ukaburan / kuga ni dani
koso / mi wa shizuminure

Autumn

Written as an autumn poem for a hundred-poem sequence

Daylight fades away
 and the autumn wind on the fields
  pierces to the soul:
 a quail cries from the deep grass
  of Fukakusa Village.[1]
yu sareba / nobe no akikaze / mi ni shimite / uzura naku
nari / fukakusa no sato

Winter

Written as an autumn poem, when he presented a hundred-poem
sequence

Out on the ice pack
 that glitters with cold moonlight,
 hail is falling,
 shattering my heart
  at Tamakawa Village.

tsuki sayuru / kori no ue ni / arare furi / kokoro kudakuru /
tamakawa no sato

  1. An allusion to [two] poems by Narihira.

Love

A poem on "Love,:" written when there was a contest at the home of
the Regent-Minister of the Right.[1]

> Just to meet with her
> I would exchange this body
> for my next, I thought—
> but O how sad I would be
> the time we were worlds apart![2]

au koto wa / mi o kaete to mo / matsu beki o / yoyo o
hedaten / hodo zo kanashiki

Spring

Written for a five-poem sequence at the house of the Regent-Chancel-
lor.[1]

> Will I see this again?
> A hunt for cherry blossoms
> on Katano Moor—
> petals of snow scattering
> in the first faint light of dawn.

mata ya mimu / katano no mino no / sakuragari / hana no
yuki chiru / haru no akebono

Summer

A poem on the topic "Cuckoo," written for a hundred-poem sequence
requested by the Lay Monk-Former Regent when he was Minister of
the Right.[1]

> Musing on the past,
> I sit in my hut of grass
> amidst night showers.

1. Fujiwara no [Kujō] Kanezane (1149-1207).
2. That is, "worlds apart" in the chain of rebirth.
1. Fujiwara no [Go-Kyogoku] Yoshitsune (1169-1206).
1. Kanezane.

Must you add my tears to the rain,
you cuckoo of the mountain?[2]

mukashi omou / kusa no iori no / yoru no ame ni / namida
na soe so / yama hototogisu

Autumn

Written as part of a hundred-poem sequence.

From beneath the pines
   of the Fushimi Hills
      I look out afar—
as dawn breaks over paddies
   where blows the autumn wind.

fushimiyama / matsu no kage yori / miwataseba / akuru ta
no mo ni / akikaze zo fuku

Winter

Topic unknown

Freezing in one place,
breaking up in another,
the mountain river
   is choked between great boulders—
a voice in the light of dawn.

katsu kori / katsu wa kudakuru / yamakawa no / iwama
ni musubu / akatsuki no koe

2. An allusion to a poem by Bo Juyi (772-846).

Winter

Among poems presented to Cloistered Prince Shukaku as a fifty-poem sequence.[1]

> After a snowfall,
> the *sakaki*[2] on the peak
>   are covered over:
> and polished by the moonlight—
> Kagu's Heavenly Hill.

yuki fureba / mine no masakaki / uzumorete / tsuki ni
migakeru / ama no kaguyama

Winter

Written for The Poem Contest in Fifteen-hundred Rounds.[1]

> Last day of the year:
> as always, I think sadly—
> the last one for me;
> but then here I am this year
>   greeting the day once again.

kyō goto ni / kyō ya kagiri to / oshimedomo / mata mo
kotoshi ni / ainikeru ka na

1. A son of Retired Emperor Go-Shirakawa (1127-92; r. 1155-58); d. 1202.
2. The *sakaki* is an evergreen used as a sacred emblem in Shinto rites.

1. A large contest sponsored by Retired Emperor Go-Toba (1180-1239; r. 1184-98) in 1201-2.

Laments

Written in the autumn, after Teika's mother had passed on and he [Shunzei] went to visit her grave, staying that night in a nearby temple.[1]

> I come so seldom,
> and yet how sad in the night
>   sounds the wind in the pines.
> And she, there beneath the moss—
> does she too hear it, endlessly?

mare ni kuru / yowa mo kanashiki / matsukaze o / taezu
ya koke no / shita ni kikuramu

Love

Sent to a woman on a rainy day

> Overcome by love,
> I gazed out upon the sky
>   above where you dwell—
> and saw the haze parted there
>   by a shower of spring rain.

omou amari / sonata no sora o / nagamureba / kasumi o
wakete /harusame zo furu

(Tr. Steven Carter)

1. Teika's mother (Shunzei's wife) was Bifuku Mon-in no Kaga (d. 1193).

Monk Saigyō (1118-1190)

Seven Tanka

Autumn

Topic unknown

It creates a heart
   even in those among us
who think of themselves
   as indifferent to all things[1]—
this first wind of autumn.

oshinabete / mono o omowanu / hito ni sae / kokoro o
tsukuru / aki no hatsukaze

Autumn

Topic unknown

Even one who claims
   to no longer have a heart[2]
      feels this sad beauty:
snipes flying up from a marsh
   on an evening in autumn.

kokoro naki / mi ni mo aware wa / shirarekeri / shigi
tatsu sawa no / aki no yūgure

---

1. Buddhist monks supposedly severed all connections to the
world.
2. *Kokoro naki mi;* a monk who should no longer feel any attachment to the world.

Autumn

Topic unknown

> Near my little hut
> out in the mountain paddies
> a stag calls out,
> startling me so that I jump —
> and startle him in turn

oyamada no / io chikuku naku / shika no ne ni / odoro-
kasarete /odorokasu kanaAutumn
Topic unknown

> Those crickets calling
> in the chill air of deep night:
> with autumn's advance
> they must be failing—voices
> sounding ever farther away.

kirigirisu / yosamu ni aki no / naru mama ni / yowaru ka
koe no / tō zakariyuku

(Tr. Steven Carter)

> One lone pine tree
> growing in the hollow—
> and I thought
> I was the only one
> without a friend

> Since I no longer think
> of reality
> as reality,
> what reason would I have
> to think of dreams as dreams?

One of a series on scenes depicted in paintings of Hell]

> Did I hear you ask
> what the fires of hell
> are burning for?
> They burn away evil
> and the firewood is you!

(Tr. Burton Watson)

Kamo no Chōmei (1155?-1216)

An Account of My Hermitage

1

The waters of a flowing stream are ever present but never the same; the bubbles in a quiet pool disappear and form but never endure for long. So it is with men and their dwellings in the world.

The houses of the high and the low seem to last for generation after generation, standing with ridgepoles aligned and roof-tiles jostling in the magnificent imperial capital, but investigation reveals that few of them existed in the past. In some cases, a building that burned last year has been replaced this year; in others, a great house has given way to a small one. And it is the same with the occupants. The places are unchanged, the population remains large, but barely one or two survive among every twenty or thirty of the people I used to know. Just as with the bubbles on the water, someone dies at night and someone else is born in the morning. Where do they come from and where do they go, all those who are born and die? And for whose benefit, for what reason, does a man take enormous pains to build a temporary shelter pleasing to the eye? The master in his dwelling is like the dewdrop vying in ephemerality with the morning glory where it forms. The flower may remain after the dew evaporates, but it withers in the morning sun; the flower may droop before the moisture banishes, but the dew does not survive until nightfall.

2

I have witnessed a number of remarkable occurrences in more than forty years since I began to understand the nature of things. Around the Hour of the Dog [7:00 P.M. — 9:00 P.M.] on a very windy night—I believe it was the Twenty-eighth of the Fourth Month in the third year of Angen [1177]—a fire broke out in the southeastern part of the capital and burned toward the northwest. In the end, it spread to Suzaku Gate, the Great Hall of State, the Academy, and the Ministry of Popular Affairs, reducing them all to ashes overnight. Its source is said to have been a temporary structure housing some dancers, located near the Higuchi-Tomi-no-kōji intersection. Spread here and there by an erratic wind, it burned in a pattern resembling an open fan, narrow at the base and wide at the outer edge. Suffocating smoke engulfed distant houses; wind-whipped flames descended to earth everywhere near at hand. The sky was red to the horizon with ashes lit by the fiery glare, and winged flames leaped a block or two at a time in the lurid atmosphere, torn free by the irresistible force of the gale. Everything must have seemed as unreal as a dream to the people in the fire's path. Some of them fell victim to the smoke. Others died instantly in the embrace of the flames. Still others managed to escape with their lives but failed to rescue their belongings, and all their cherished treasures turned to ashes. The value of so much property may be imagined! The fire claimed the houses of sixteen senior nobles, to say nothing of countless others of less importance. It was reported that fully one-third of the capital had been destroyed. Dozens of men and women were killed; innumerable horses and oxen perished.

Al human enterprises are pointless, but it must be counted an act of supreme folly for a man to consume his treasure and put himself to endless trouble merely to build a house in a place as dangerous as the capital.

Again, around the Fourth Month in the fourth year of Jishō [1180], a great whirlwind sprang up near the Nakamikado—[Higashi] Kyogōku intersection and swept all the way to Rokujō Avenue. Not a house, large or small, escaped destruction within the area of three or four blocks where the blast wreaked its full fury. In some cases, entire buildings were flattened; in others, only crossbeams and pillars were spared. Gates were caught up and deposited four or five blocks distant; fences were blown away and neighboring properties merged. And I need hardly mention what happened to smaller objects. Everything inside a house mounted to the skies; cypress-bark thatch and shingles whirled like winter leaves in the wind. Dust ascended like smoke to blind the eye; the terrible howl of the storm swallowed the sound of voices. It seemed that even the dread karma-wind of hell could be no worse. Not only were houses damaged or destroyed, but countless men suffered injury or mutilation while the buildings were being reconstructed. The wind moved toward the south-southeast, visiting affliction on innumerable people.

Whirlwinds are common, but not ones such as that. Those who experienced it worried that it might be an extraordinary phenomenon, a warning from a supernatural being.

Again, around the Sixth Month in the fourth year of Jishō, the court moved suddenly to a new capital.[1] Nobody had dreamed of such a thing. When we consider that more than 400 years had elapsed since the establishment of the present imperial seat during Emperor Saga's reign, surely a new one ought not to have been chosen without exceptional justification. It was more than reasonable that people should have felt disquiet and apprehension.

But complaints were useless. The Emperor, the Ministers of State, the senior nobles, and all the others moved. Nobody remained in the old capital who held even a minor court position. Those who aspired to office and rank, or who relied on the favor of patrons, strove to move with all possible dispatch; those who had lost the opportunity to succeed in life, or who had been rejected by society, stayed behind, sunk in gloom. The dwellings that had once stood eave to eave grew more dilapidated with every passing day. Houses were dismantled and sent floating down the Yodo River, and their former locations turned into fields before the onlookers' eyes.

In a complete reversal of values, everyone prized horses and saddles and stopped using oxen and carriages. Properties in the Western and Southern Sea circuits were sought; those in the Eastern Sea and Northern Land circuits were considered undesirable.

---

1. The move took place soon after the suppression of a preliminary attempt to overthrow the Taira. The new capital was at Fukuhara (now a part of Kōbe), where Taira no Kiyomori had established his principal residence some years earlier.

It happened that something took me to the new capital in Settsu Province. The cramped site, too small for proper subdivision, rose high on the north where it bordered the hills and sank low on the south beside the sea. The breaking waves never ceased to clamor; the wind from the sea blew with peculiar fury. The imperial palace struck me as unexpectedly novel and interesting, situated in the hills as it was, and I asked myself whether Empress Saimei's log house might not have been rather similar.[2]

I wondered where people were erecting the whole houses that were being sent downstream daily, their numbers great enough to clog the river. There were still many empty parcels of land and few houses. The old capital was already in ruins; the new one had yet to take form. Not a soul but felt as rootless as a drifting cloud. The original inhabitants grieved over the loss of their land; the new arrivals worried about plaster and lumber. On the streets, those who ought to have used carriages rode on horseback; those who ought to have worn curt dress or hunting robes appeared in *hitatare*. The customs of the capital had been revolutionized overnight, and people behaved like rustic warriors.

I have heard that such changes portend civil disturbance— and that was precisely what happened. With every passing day, the world grew more unsettled, people lost more of their composure, and the common folk felt more apprehension. In the end, a crisis brought about a return to the old capital during the winter of the same year.[3] But who knows what became of the houses that had been torn down everywhere? They were not rebuilt in their former style.

We are told that the sage Emperors of old ruled with compassion. They roofed their palaces with thatch, neglecting even to rim the eaves; they remitted the already modest taxes when they saw the commoners' cooking-fires emit less smoke than before. The reason was simply that they cherished their subjects and wished to help them. To compare the present to the past is to see what kind of government we have today.

2. The log house was a temporary residence in Kyushu used by Empress Saimei (594-661) when the Japanese were preparing to attack the Korean state of Silla in 661.

3. The rebellions of provincial Minamoto leaders had produced serious military disturbances.

Again, there was a dreadful two-year famine. (I think it was around the Yōwa era [1181-82], but it was too long ago to be sure.) The grain crops were ruined as one calamity followed another: drought in the spring and summer, typhoons and floods in the autumn. It was vain for the farmer to till the fields in the spring or set out plants in the summer; there was no reaping in the fall, no bustle of storage in the winter. Some rural folk abandoned their land and wandered off; others deserted their homes to live in the hills. Prayers were begun and extraordinary rituals were performed, but they accomplished nothing.

The capital had always depended on the countryside for every need. Now, with nothing coming in, people were beside themselves with anxiety. In desperation, they offered all their treasures at bargain rates, but nobody took any notice. The rare person who was willing to trade thought little of gold and much of grain. The streets were overrun with mendicants; lamentations filled the air.

The first of the two years dragged to a close. But just as everyone was anticipating a return to normal in the new year, a pestilence came along to make matters even worse. Like fish gasping in a puddle, the starving populace drew closer to the final extremity with every passing day, until at last people of quite respectable appearance, clad in hats and leggings, begged frantically from house to house. These wretched, dazed beings fell prostrate even as one marveled at their ability to walk.

Countless people perished of starvation by the wayside or died next to tile-capped walls. Since there was no way to dispose of the bodies, noisome stenches filled the air, and innumerable decomposing corpses shocked the eye. Needless to say, the dead lay so thick in the Kamo riverbed that there was not even room for horses and ox-carriages to pass.

With the woodsmen and other commoners too debilitated to perform their usual functions, a shortage of firewood developed, and people who possessed no other means of support broke up their own houses to sell in the market. The amount a man could carry brought less than enough to sustain him for a day. It was shocking to see pieces of wood covered with red lacquer or gold and sliver leaf jumbled together with the rest. On inquiry, one learned that desperate people were going to old temples, stealing the sacred images, tearing away the fixtures from the halls, and breaking up everything for firewood. It is because I was born in a degenerate age that I have been forced to witness such disgraceful sights.

Some deeply moving things also happened. Whenever a couple were too devoted to part, the one whose love was greater was the first to die. This was because he or she put the spouse's welfare first and gave up whatever food came to hand. Similarly, a parent always predeceased a child. One sometimes saw a recumbent child sucking at his mother's breast, unaware that her life had ended. Grieved that countless people should be perishing in that manner, Dharma Seal Ryūgyō of Ninnaji Temple sought to help the dead toward enlightenment by writing the Sanskrit letter "A" on the forehead of every corpse he saw.[4]

The authorities kept track of the deaths in the Fourth and Fifth Months. During that period, there were more than 42,300 bodies on the streets in the area south of Ichijō, north Kujō, west of Kyōgoku, and east of Suzaku. Of course, many others died before and afterward. And there would be no limit to the numbers if we were to count the Kamo riverbed, Shirakawa, the western sector, and the outlying districts, to say nothing of the provinces in the seven circuits.

People say there was something similar during the reign of Emperor Sutoku, around the Chōshō era [1132-35], but I know nothing about that. I witnessed this phenomenal famine with my own eyes.

If I remember correctly, it was at more or less the same time that a terrible seismic convulsion occurred. It was no ordinary earthquake. Mountains crumbled and buried streams; the sea tilted and immersed the land. Water gushed from fissures in the earth; huge rocks cracked and rolled into valleys. Boats being rowed near the shoreline tossed on the waves; horses journeying on the roads lost their footing. Not a Buddhist hall or stupa remained intact anywhere in the vicinity of the capital. Some crumbled, others fell flat. Dust billowed like smoke; the shaking earth and collapsing houses rumbled like thunder. If people stayed indoors, they were crushed at once; if they ran outside, the ground split apart. If men had been dragons, they might have

---

4. In esoteric Buddhism, of which Ninnaji was a center, "A," the first syllable in the Sanskrit syllabary, was regarded as symbolic of the unity of all things.

ridden the clouds, but they lacked the wings to soar into the heavens. It was then then that I came to recognize an earthquake as the most terrible of all terrible things.

The violent shaking subsided fairly soon, but aftershocks followed for some time. No day passed without twenty or thirty earthquakes of an intensity that would ordinarily have caused consternation. The intervals lengthened after ten or twenty days, and then there were tremors four or five times a day, or two or three times a day, or once every other day, or once every two or three days. It must have been about three months before they ceased.

Of the four constituents of the universe, water, fire, and wind create constant havoc, but the earth does not usually give rise to any particular calamities. To be sure, there were some dreadful earthquakes in the past (for instance, the great shock that toppled the head of the Tōdaiji Buddha during the Saikō era [854-57]), but none of them could compare with this. Immediately after the event, people all talked about the meaninglessness of life and seemed somewhat more free from spiritual impurity than usual. But nobody even mentioned the subject after the days and months had accumulated and the years had slipped by.

Such, then, is the difficulty of life in this world, such the ephemerality of man and his dwellings. Needless to say, it would be utterly impossible to list every affliction that stems from individual circumstance or social position. If a man of negligible status lives beside a powerful family, he cannot make a great display of happiness when he has cause for heartfelt rejoicing, nor can he lift his voice in lamentation when he experiences devastating grief. In all that he does, he is ill at ease; like a sparrow near a hawk's nest, he pursues his daily activities in fear and trembling. If a poor man lives next door to a wealthy house, he abases himself before the neighbors and agonizes over his wretched appearance whenever he goes out in the morning or returns in the evening. Forced to witness the envy of his wife, children, and servants, and to hear the rich household dismiss him with contempt, he is forever agitated, constantly distraught.

He who lives in a crowded area cannot escape calamity when a fire breaks out nearby; he who settles in a remote spot suffers many hardships in his travels to and fro and puts himself at grave risk from robbers. The powerful man is consumed by greed; the man who refuses to seek a patron becomes an object of derision.

The man who owns many possessions knows many worries; the impoverished man seethes with envy.

He who depends on another belongs to another; he who takes care of another is chained by human affection. When a man observes the conventions, he falls into economic difficulties; when he flouts them, people wonder if he is mad. Where can we live, what can we do, to find even the briefest of shelters, the most fleeting peace of mind?

3

For a long time, I lived in a house inherited from my paternal grandmother. Later, my fortunes declined through lack of connections, and I found myself unable to remain in society, despite many nostalgic associations. Shortly after I entered my thirties, I moved voluntarily into a simple new dwelling one-tenth the size of the old place. I built only a personal residence, with no fashionable auxiliary structures, and although I managed an encircling earthen wall, my means did not extend to a gate. The carriage-shelter was supported by bamboo pillars, and the house was unsafe in a snowfall or windstorm. The site was near the riverbed, which left it vulnerable to floods, and there was also danger from robbers.

For more than thirty miserable years, I endured an existence in which I could not maintain my position. Every setback during that time drove home the realization that I was not blessed by fortune. And thus, at fifty, I became a monk and turned my back on the world. Having never had a wife or children, I was not bound to others by ties difficult to break; lacking office and stipend, I possessed no attachments to which to cling.

During the next five springs and autumns, I sojourned among the clouds of the Ōhara hills, leading a life devoid of spiritual progress.

Now at sixty, with the dew nearing its vanishing point, I have built a new shelter for the tree's last leaves, just as a traveler might fashion a single night's resting place or an old silkworm spin a cocoon. It is not a hundredth the size of my second house. Indeed, while I have sat around uttering idle complaints, my age has increased with every year, and my house has shrunk with every move.

This house is unusual in appearance. It is barely ten feet square, and its height is less than seven feet. The location was a matter of indifference to me; I did not divine to select a site. I built a foundation and a simple roof, and attached hinges to all the joints so that I could move easily if cause for dissatisfaction arose. There would be no trouble about rebuilding. The house would barely fill two carts, and the carters' fees would be the only expense.

After settling on my present place of retirement in the Hino hills, I extended the eastern eaves about three feet to provide myself with a convenient spot in which to break up and burn firewood. On the south side of the building, I have an open bamboo veranda with a holy water shelf at the west end. Toward the north end of the west wall, beyond a freestanding screen, there is a picture of Amida Buddha, with an image of Fugen alongside and a copy of the *Lotus Sutra* in front. At the east end of the room, some dried bracken serves as a bed. South of the screen on the west side, a bamboo shelf suspended from the ceiling holds three leather-covered bamboo baskets, in which I keep excerpts from poetry collections and critical treatises, works on music, and religious tracts like *Collection of Essentials on Rebirth in the Pure Land*. A zither and a lute stand next to the shelf. The zither is of the folding variety; the handle of the lute is datachable. Such is the appearance of my rude temporary shelter.

To turn to the surroundings: I have made a rock basin in which to collect water from an elevated conduit south of the hermitage, and I gather ample supplies of firewood in a neighboring stand of trees. The locality is called Toyama, "the foothills." Vines cover the paths. The valley is thickly forested, but there is open land to the west.

Aids to contemplation abound. In the spring, lustrous cascades of wisteria burgeon in the west like purple clouds. In the summer, every song of the cuckoo conveys a promise of companionship in the Shide Mountains. In the autumn, the incessant cries of the cicadas seem to lament the transitoriness of worldly things. And in the winter, the accumulating and melting snows suggest poignant comparisons with sins and hindrances.[5]

5. Amida and his attendants were thought to descend, riding on a purple cloud, to escort the believer to the Western Paradise at the moment of death. Possibly because the cuckoo's cry included notes that sounded like *shide*, the bird was considered a messenger from the land of the dead, which lay beyond the Shide Mountains. Sins and hindrances to enlightenment piled up in the course of daily life and were discharged periodically by repentance rites and confessions before a Buddha.

When I tire of reciting the sacred name or find myself intoning a sutra in a perfunctory manner, I rest as I please, I fall idle as I see fit. There is nobody to interfere, nobody to shame me. Although I do not make a point of performing silent austerities, I can control speech-induced karma because I live alone; although I do not make a fuss about obeying the commandments, I have no occasion to break them because mine is not an environment conducive to transgression.

On mornings when I compare my existence to a white wake in the water, I borrow Mansei's style while watching boats come and go at Okanoya; on evenings when the wind rustles the maple leaves, I imitate Tsunenobu's practice while recalling the Xinyang River.[6] If my interest does not flag, I often perform "Song of the Autumn Wind" as an accompaniement to the murmur of the pines, or play "Melody of the Flowing Spring" to harmonize with the sound of the water. I am not an accomplished musician, but my playing is not designed for the pleasure of others. I merely pluck the strings alone and chant alone to comfort my own spirit.

At the foot of the hill, there is a brush-thatched cottage, the abode of the mountain warden. The small boy who lives there pays me an occasional visit, and if I chance to feel at loose ends, I set out for a ramble with him as my companion. He is ten, I am sixty. Our ages differ greatly but we take pleasure in the same things. Sometimes we pull out reed-flower sprouts, pick *iwanashi* berries, heap up yam sprouts, or pluck herbs. Or we may go to the rice fields at the foot of the mountains, glean ears left by the reapers, and fashion sheafs. When weather is balmy, we scramble up to a peak from which I can look toward the distant skies over my old home and see Kohatayama, Fushimi-no-sato, Toba, and Hatsukashi. Nobody owns the view; there is nothing to keep me from enjoying it.

When the going is easy and I feel like taking a long walk, I follow the peaks past Sumiyana and Kasatori to worship at

6. Mansei (8th c.) was the author of a frequently quoted poem on ephemerality: yo no naka o/ nani ni tatoen / asaborake / kogiyuku fune no / ato no shiranami ("To what shall I compare life in this world—the white wake of a boat rowing off at break of day"). Tsunenobu (1016—97) was a major poet known also as an expert lute player. Chōmei alludes to the first two lines of Bo Juyi's "Lute Song": "As I see off a guest at night near the Xinyang River, / The autumn wind rustles through maple leaves and reed plumes."

Iwama or Ishiyama. Or I may traverse Awazu Plain, visit the site of Semimaru's dwelling, cross the Tanakami River, and seek out Sarumaru's grave.[7] On the way home, I search for cherry blossoms, pick autumn leaves, gather bracken, or collect fruit and nuts, depending on the season. Some of my trophies I present to the Buddha; others I treat as useful souvenirs.

On peaceful nights, I long for old friends while gazing at the moon through the window, or weep into my sleeve at the cry of a monkey. Sometimes I mistake fireflies in the bushes for fish lures burning far away at Maki-no-shima Island, or think that a gale must be scattering the leaves when I hear rain just before dawn. The h*orohoro* call of a pheasant makes me wonder if the bird might be a parent; the frequent visits of deer from the peaks attest to the remoteness of my abode.[8] Sometimes I stir up the banked fire and make it a companion for the wakefulness of old age. The mountains are so little intimidating that even the owl's hoot sounds moving rather than eerie. Indeed, there is no end to the delights of the changing seasons in these surroundings. A truly reflective man, blessed with superior powers of judgment, would undoubtedly find many more pleasures than the ones I have described.

4

When I first began to live here, I thought it would not be for long, but five years have already elapsed. My temporary hermitage has gradually become a home, its eaves covered with rotted leaves and its foundation mossy. Whenever I happen to hear news of the capital, I learn that many illustrious personages have breathed their last since my retreat to these mountains. And it would be quite impossible to keep track of all the unimportant people who have died. A great many houses have also suffered destruction in recurrent conflagrations. Only in my temporary hermitage is life peaceful and safe. The quarters are cramped, but I have a place

---

7. Semimaru and Sarumaru were semilegendary poets.

8. Gyōki (Gyōgi): yamadori no / horohoro to naku / koe kikeba / chichi ka to zo omou / haha ka to zo omou ("When I hear the voice of the pheasant, mountain bird, crying *horohoro*, I think, 'Might it be a father? Or might it be a mother?'"). Saigyō: yama fukami / naruru kasegi no / kejikasna ni / yo ni tōzakaru / hodo zo shiraruru ("To see at close hand deer grown accustomed to me deep in the mountains is to know my remoteness from the affairs of the world").

where I can lie at night and another where I can sit in the daytime. There is ample room for one person. The hermit crab likes a small shell because it knows its own size; the osprey lives on the rocky coast because it fears man. It is the same with me. Knowing myself and knowing the world, I harbor no ambitions and pursue no material objectives. Quietude is what I desire; the absence of worries is what makes me happy.

Men do not usually build houses for their own benefit. Some build for wives, children, relatives, and servants, some for friends and acquaintances, some for masters, for teachers, or even for household goods, treasures, oxen, and horses. But I have built for myself this time, not for anybody else. Because of present conditions and my own situation, I possess neither a family to share my dwelling nor servants to work for me. If I had built a great house, whom would I have lodged in it, whom would I have established there?

Friends esteem wealth and look for favors; they do not necessarily value sincere friendship or probity. I prefer to make friends of music and nature. Servants prize lavish rewards and unstinting generosity; they do not care about protection, affection, or a safe, tranquil existence. I prefer to make my own body my servant. How do I do it? If there is work to perform, I sue my body. True, I may grow weary, but it is easier than employing and looking after someone else. If there is walking to do, I walk. It is burdensome, but less so than worrying over horses, saddles, oxen, and carriages. I divide my body and put it to two uses: it suits me very well to employ hands as servants and feet as conveyances. My mind understands my body's distress: I allow the body to rest when it is distressed and use it when it feels energetic. I use it but do not make a habit of pushing it to extremes. If it finds a task irksome, I am not perturbed. It is surely a healthful practice to walk constantly and work constantly. What would be the point of idling away the time? To make others work creates bad karma. Why should I borrow their strength?

It is the same with food and clothing. I hide my nakedness under a rough fiber robe, a hemp quilt, or whatever comes to hand; I survive by eating starwort from the fields and nuts from the peaks. Because I do not mingle with others, I need not chide myself for having felt ashamed of my appearance. Because I posses little food, I find coarse fare tasty.

I do not describe such pleasures as a means of criticizing the wealthy; I merely compare my own former life with my present existence. "The triple world is but one mind."[9] If the mind is not at peace, elephants, horses, and the seven treasures are trash; palatial residences and stately mansions are worthless. I feel warm affection for my present lonely dwelling, my tiny cottage. My beggarly appearance is a source of embarrassment on the infrequent occasions when something takes me to the capital, but after my return I feel pity for those who pursue worldly things. If anyone doubts my sincerity, let him consider the fish and the the birds. A fish never tires of water, but only another fish can understand why. A bird seeks trees, but only another bird can understand why. It is the same with the pleasures of retirement. Only a recluse can understand them.

5

The moon of my life is setting; my remaining years approach the rim of the hills. Very soon, I shall face the darkness of the Three Evil Paths. Which of my old disappointments is worth fretting over now? The Buddha teaches us to reject worldly things. Even my affection for this thatched hut is a sin; even my love of tranquility must be accounted an impediment to rebirth. Why do I waste time in descriptions of inconsequential pleasures?

As I reflect on these things in the quiet moments before dawn, I put a question to myself: You retired to the seclusion of remote hills so that you might discipline your mind and practice the Way, but your impure spirit belies your monkish garb. Your dwelling presumes to imitate the abode of the honorable Yuima, but yu are worse than Suddhipanthaka when it comes to obeying the commandments. Is this because you let yourself be troubled by karma-ordained poverty or has your deluded mind finally lost its sanity?

The question remains unanswered. I can do no other than use my impure tongue for three or four repitions of Amida's sacred name. Then I fall silent.

Late in the Third Month of the second year of Kenryaku [1212]

Set down by the monk Ren'in in the hermitage at Toyama[10]

(Tr. Helen McCullough)

9. *Kegon Sutra:* "The triple world is but one mind. Outside mind there is nothing; mind, Buddha, and all the living, these three are no different."

10. Ren'in was Chōmei's Buddhist name.

Fujiwara no Teika (1162-1241)

An Outline for Composing Tanka[1]

In emotion, newness is foremost: look for sentiments others have yet to sing, and sing them. In diction, use the old: don't go further back than the Three Anthologies,[2] but use the diction of the masters, including those ancient poets in the *Shinkokinshū*.[3] In style, learn the good tanka of gifted masters: don't ask if they're ancient or modern, but look at appropriate tanka and learn their style. As for the sentiments and diction of the poets of recent times, respectfully ignore them: try hard not to adopt the diction of the poets of the last seventy to eighty years. To use much of the same diction as that of ancient poets is an old practice; but if you borrow from an ancient tanka, you must compose a new one. To borrow as many as three units out of the five[4] is quite excessive and results in a lack of novelty; to borrow two units plus three or four syllables is admissible. Considering this further it is quite mindless to borrow from an ancient tanka when composing on the same subject: flower alluded to and flower sung of, moon alluded to and moon sung of. When you allude to a tanka on one of the four seasons and sing of love or a miscellaneous subject, or allude to a tanka on love or a miscellaneous subject and sing of one of the four seasons, then no one would criticize your borrowing from an ancient tanka.

1. Believed to have been prepared for Prince Kajii no Miya Sonkai-hō in 1222. A passage of instruction followed by an anthology of exemplary tanka, *Eiga taigai* (An Outline for Composing Tanka), is similar to *Kindai shūka* (Good Tanka of Modern Times), which Teika prepared for the shogun and poet Minamoto no Sanetomo in 1209.

2. First three of the tanka anthologies compiled by imperial order: the *Kokinshū* the *Gosenshū* (951), and the *Shūishū*. (c.1005).

3. Eighth imperial anthology of tanka (1205), of which Fujiwara no Teika was one of the six editors. It includes tanka from the *Man'yōshū*; hence, "ancient poets."

4. A tanka consists of five syllabic units: 5, 7, 5, 7, 7. Allusion in tanka, a practice not all discouraged, most often took the form of direct borrowing of words and phrases, and duplication of up to three of the five units was not uncommon.

cuckoo on the foot-wearying mountain [5]

Mount Yoshino on Miyoshi Plain [6]

katsura *tree on the eternal moon* [7]

cuckoos call in May [8]

someone who walks along the spear-adorned road [9]

Things like these [the five phrases cited above] may be used frequently with impunity.

spring has come before the year's end [10]

surely this is the moon, surely this spring [11]

wind under cherry trees as petals scatter [12]

faintly, on the bay of Akashi [13]

' 5. Five tanka begin with the phrase in the Three Anthologies alone; none of Teika's does.

6.An anonymous tanka in the *Goesenshū* (no. 117) begins with the phrase; none of Teika's does.

7. A tanka by Mibu no Tadamine in the *Kokinshū* (no. 194) and another by Sugawara no Michizane's mother in the the *Shūishū* (no. 473) begin with phrase; Teika has left one beginning with the phrase (*Shūi gusō*, no. 2209). *Katsura* is a tree, *cercidiphyllum japonicum.*

8. an anonymous tanka in the *Kokinshū* (no. 469) and another anonymous one in the *Shūsisū* (no. 125) begin with the phrase; so do at least two pieces by Teika (nos. 1855 and 1888).

9. A tanka in the *Shinkokinshū* (no.232) begins with the phrase; it is by Teika.

10. The opening tanka of the *Kokinshū*, by Ariwara no Motokata, begins with the phrase.

11. See Ariwara no Narihira's tanka beginning with the phrase on p. 296. It is among the more famous pieces by the poet, and tops the fifth volume on love of the *Kokinshū*.

12. A tanka by Ki no Tsurayuki in the *Shūishū* (no 64) begins with the phrase. The tanka is often quoted as exemplary.

13. A tanka attributed to Kakinomoto no Hitomaro in the *Kokinshū* (no. 409) begins with the phrase. The tanka is often quoted as exemplary.

Things of this sort [the four phrases cited above], though of only two units, may never be used.

Always keep in mind the tones of ancient tanka and steep your mind in them. The ones you should especially follow are the especially skillful tanka in the *Kokinshū, The Tales of Ise,*[14] the *Gosenshū,* the *Shūishrū,* and the collections of the Thirty-Six Poets:[15] poets such as Hitomaro, Tsurayuki, Tadamine,[16] Ise, and Komachi. though he was not a tanka poet, grasp and play lovingly with the first and second books of Po Chü-yi's *Collected Writings*[17] so as to know the truth of the matter, such as the feel of the season and the ups and downs of society; he is deeply empathetic to the heart of tanka.

In tanka, there are no teachers. Simply make old tanka your teachers. Those who steep their minds in the old style and learn their diction from the masters—who of them will fail to sing?

(Tr. Hiroaki Sato)

14. A collection of episodes, each incorporating one to several tanka, which is believed to have taken its present form around 900.

15. Those chosen as preeminent by Fujiwara no Kintō (966—1041).

16. Mibu no Tadamine (c. 860—c. 920).

17. The Chinese poet Po Chü-yi (772—846) greatly influenced the Japanese poets of the time. The first two books consist of poems.

Anonymous (date uncertain)

A Tale of Brief Slumbers

Utatane ni	In a brief slumber
koishiki hito wo	I caught sight of my beloved,
miteshi yori	and now I cling to
yume chō mono wa	each passing dream.[1]
tanomisometeki	

These words of the poet Ono no Komachi expressed but a trifling fancy in comparison to the passion that rejects even life itself. Among the many tales of long ago is one extraordinary account of such a love.

The story I am about to tell occurred in the not-too-distant past. There was once a prominent minister well regarded at court. Of his many children born to several consorts, one son was Master of the Crow Prince's Household; another younger son held the rank of prelate and was head priest of Ishiyama Temple. The Minister had but a single daughter, sister to the Prelate, whom he cherished beyond measure. He considered sending her to serve at court and had already begun the preparations for her presentation when he realized that she would be surrounded by a bevy of imperial consorts and ladies of the bed chamber. In such an atmosphere, even if she were to receive imperial favor, she would be subjected to fierce jealousy, and he feared lest she become withdrawn and sink into depression. As he vacillated over the decision, certain presentable suitors called with offers to marry and care for her, but he was reluctant to give his precious daughter to anyone at all.

Soon the girl blossomed into the full flower of maidenhood and radiated such an array of charms that she was a pleasure to behold. Her father treated her with special consideration, inviting young ladies of excellent qualities to serve her. At times she lived happily, deriving amusement from the many diversions afforded by the spring flowers and autumnal foliage. Other times, however, the weight of her father's duties led him to neglect her, and, her

1. *Kokinshū* no. 553, by the famed poetess Ono no Komachi.

mother having passed away, the girl perforce spent long hours in lonely idleness.

Near her rooms grew a late-blooming wild cherry tree, adorned with blossoms far outlasting those of other flowering trees. As the spring days slipped away, she found solace in these flowers and lamented their final descent to earth. One lonely afternoon, as the long rains gently fell and droplets ceaselessly pattered on the eaves, she left off her aimless plucking at the koto and lay down, falling off into a deep sleep.

Suddenly, it seemed that someone appeared before her, proffering a branch of flowing wisteria deeply fragrant despite the dew still clinging to it. Attached to the branch was a slip of paper tinted in the same pale lavender hue as the wisteria. Assuming that this lovely offering was a message from the Kamo Priestess,[2] the girl casually picked it up. In a man's hand was written:

Omoine ni	Yet more fleeting than a daydream
miru yume yori mo	from the slumbers of love—
hakanaki wa	the vision of another,
shiranu utsutsu no	a reality yet unknown.
yoso no omokage	

The traces of ink were well modulated and the hand remarkable, revealing that the poem had been written by no ordinary person. She gazed at it with admiration, her heart in turmoil, wondering who might have sent it. This was a most unexpected dream!

This vivid vision had been so beautiful and the traces of his brush so lovely that her heart was quite captivated, and she yearned to see more. She sat lost in bemused contemplation until night fell. Lamps were brought in, and she played at *go* with attendant Chūnagon and nursemaid Ben. Though she tried to maintain interest in the game, she was wholly preoccupied by thoughts of the unknown man in that fleeting dream and overwhelmed by a sense of unreality. In a daze, she pulled over the movable screen to take a brief nap.

There at her side was a figure wearing a soft courtier's robe

2. As later becomes apparent, the girl is on friendly terms with several members of the imperial family. The Kamo Priestess was always selected from offspring of the imperial or princely families.

layered over a crimson robe and trousers of pale lavender lined with green. The color and quality of his dress were so elegant and his fragrance so profoundly penetrating that she was quite entranced. They lay together with an intimacy as of long association. When she cast a glance at his face, her heart throbbed wildly. So radiantly handsome and charming was he, possessed of such refinement and a host of appealing features, that he brought to mind the shining Prince Genji of tales of old. Indeed, the very sight of him led her to think that even a man could possess the proverbial hundred charms.[3] Mute in her agitation, tears streaming down, she tried to move away, but he grasped her hand and addressed her.

"The anguish of my love cannot but have moved you to pity—did you not even look at the faint traces of my brush? Your failure to respond caused me such distress that I was compelled to come. Do you not know the expression 'a slave to love?' The bonds linking a man and woman are not only of this life but are fated from past lives as well. So often in the past has unrequited longing led to terrible retribution! If you and I were to leave our love unconsummated in this world, it would wander aimlessly on the dark path to come. Would this not be a lamentable fate?"

He tearfully spoke on, though unable to pour out all that was in his heart. Somehow he seemed to know that she was not unmoved, though he could not possibly hear her response. All too soon there came the faint sound of the cock's call of dawn. "the cock must be well accustomed to the resentment of departing lovers," she heard him say dispiritedly.[4] Just one encounter could not possibly suffice for the full exchange of lovers' intimacies. Sensing something oppressing her, she looked up to see that the sun had risen high in the sky. With a sense of utter unreality, she arose, but was not at all herself.

How terribly confusing was this dream arisen from slumbers beneath the spring blossoms! It had always been said that, in a love dream, the object of yearning appeared in one's own dream, but

---

3. A common description of female beauty, based on a description of the legendary beauty Yang Kuei Fei in "The Song of Unending Sorrow": "If she but turned her head and smiled, there were cast a hundred smiles, / And the powder and paint of the Six Palaces faded into nothing" (Birch, ed., *Anthology of Chinese Literature*, p. 266).

4. It was customary for lovers to depart at dawn, which was signaled by the cock's crow.

she had also heard that a soul could wander afar to visit the dreams of the beloved,[5] as exemplified in the lines of Princess Shikishi, "the one I would see even in a dream."[6] What kind of dream had this been? Who had appeared before her? What unknown sender had offered these blossoms of affection? Should others realize that she was lying lovelorn in the shadows of the tree of laments, sleeves damp with tears, they would regard it as deeply sinful.[7]

When her lover Fujiwara no Norimichi ceased to call on her, Ko Shikibu passed long empty months in melancholy. Suddenly he came to visit, and she was beside herself with joy. When it came time for him to depart, she stitched a thread on the sleeve of his cloak as a momento. By daylight, however, she saw the thread caught in a tree in the garden and realized that he had not really come. Her own excess of longing had summoned before her the image sheltered in her heart.[8]

Who was it that loved her both in dream and in reality? Although there was no way to communicate her longing to him, her heart remained in turmoil. "How did I sleep that night such as to see him?" she wondered as she lay on her lonely bed.[9] Her own fragrance wafting up served as the only reminder of that vision. She so yearned for him, and dwelled so constantly on him, that presently she completely lost her ability to distinguish reality from dream. The thought of anything else—even things she had previ-

5. The text is distinguishing between two kinds of dream appearances: the love dream (*omoine*), in which one falls asleep yearning for another and consequently dreams of that person, and the case in which one's spirit leaves one's sleeping body and appears in the dreams of another.

6. *Shinkokinshū* no. 1124: "Yume nite mo / miyuran mono wo / nagekitsutsu / uchinuru yoi no / sode no keshiki wa" (Lamenting for the one / I would see even in a dream / my sleeves of evening / drenched with tears).

7. This passage is somewhat unclear, particularly the line stating that, should others see her, it would be "deeply sinful" (tsumibukaki). It may be that the term is used weakly, in the sense of "undesirable"; otherwise, it is difficult to see how the girl's sad plight would be all that sinful, unless, of course she had been pledged already to another.

8. This legend of Ko Shikibu, the daughter of the famed poetess Izumi Shikibu, is recounted in several sources, among them episode 26 of the *Ima monogatari* (*Tales of the Present*).

9. A reference to *Kokinshū*. no. 516: "Yoi yoi ni / makura sadamen / kata mo nashi / ika ni neshi yo ka / yume ni mienu" (Night after night / I shift my pillow around / how did I sleep that night / that I saw him in my dreams?)

ously liked—was distasteful to her. As time passed, she weakened and became increasingly distraught, unable so much as to glance at food. Deeply concerned, her father and attendants offered prayers and commissioned services for her recovery. Day and night the halls were filled with the commotion of rituals and sutra recitations, but she remained sunken in her own reveries. That her father should worry so on her behalf became to her a source of further anguish, and she grew even worse.

Shocked to hear of her condition, her brother the Prelate came to conduct services on her behalf. Some hope lay in the particularly effective vow of salvation for all sentient beings made by the Savior Kannon of Ishiyama; there had been much talk of the miracles she[10] performed. He promised that the girl would make a pilgrimage to Ishiyama if her condition were sufficiently relieved to permit the journey. To everyone's vast relief, her health improved, most probably owing to the innumerable prayers on her behalf.

Soon she was making hurried preparations for a journey to Ishiyama. She chose to travel without carriage or fanfare, limiting her retinue to Chūnagon, her nurse, and four of five close attendants, for her petition was just as weighty as that of Lady Tamakazura, who had traveled far on foot to Hatsuse Temple.[11]

When she arrived, she was impressed by the singular beauty of the place. From the foot of the cliffs stretched a moon-bathed expanse of rippling waves; the cliffs were covered by deep layers of moss—untold aeons must have passed since they were mere pebbles.[12] The ancient garden was suffused with the silence of another world, and all the hardships of her journey were forgotten as she gazed at it. She prayed fervently and prostrated herself in supplication. Entreating that her many afflictions be vanquished, intoning loudly the prayer, "Thy great vow is as deep as the

---

10. The Kannon was frequently envisioned as female. See, e.g., the description of the Ishiyama Kannon in *The Tale of Ikago*.

11. In *The Tale of Genji*, the orphaned Tamakasura makes a pilgrimage to petition the gods of Hatsuse for help in locating her father. At Hatsuse, she meets her mother's former maidservant, now in the household of Genji; thereafter her fortunes change for the better.

12. The Japanese believed that pebbles grew to boulders over the ages.

seas,"[13] she paid homage with all her soul.

Late at night, she finally completed her worship. The room adjoining her own was said to have sheltered Murasaki Shikibu when writing *The Tale of Genji*, and the girl was curious to see this unusual place. Suddenly she heard a refined voice from within. It seemed that a certain general of the left was summoning a middle captain. Then the voice of the Middle Captain responded.

"Why did you come here to pray when the annual court appointment ceremonies[14] were nigh, when you had pressing obligations both public and private? I cannot but wonder why you have wet your sleeves in these autumnal dews to come here. It defies all reason! You have not told me the least thing about why we are here, and it pains me to feel such a gulf between us. It seems that you are atoning for some sin you have committed—please tell me," he entreated sadly.

"Well, you know that one should not speak of dreams at night,"[15] replied the General, "but you are so concerned, and there is no longer any point in concealing it. I have entrusted the Buddha with my prayers for a clear resolution to my longings."

His manner of speaking was precisely that of the man who had visited her dreams. Her heart was thrown into turmoil, and she was desperate for a glimpse of him. Her attendants were already fast asleep, fatigued from the long journey. The lamp had been extinguished, and light shone brightly from the next room. Peering in through the crack in the door, she saw an elegant man dressed in hunting garb sitting forlornly. He was identical in every respect to the man of her dreams. Thinking that she must be dreaming again, she listened on, suppressing the dark storms in her heart.

"In China and in Japan, people have been guided by dreams, one seeking on Fugan Plain,[16] another on the shores of Akashi.[17] In these and other cases, their dreams have coincided with reality. At the end of the third month of last year, I received a poem, apparently from a woman, attached to a lovely branch of wisteria:

13. From chap. 25 of the Lotus Sutra, which describes the limitless compassion of the Bodhisattva Kannon.
14. *Tsukasameshi no jimoku*, an annual three-day-long ceremony held in the fall, at which court appointments were conferred.
15. Apparently, contemporary superstition had it that speaking of one's dreams at night was unlucky.

Tanome tada
omoiawasuru
omoi ne no
utsutsu ni kaeru
yume mo koso are

I wake to find
our tryst but a reverie—
would that dreams too
come back to life

Ever since then, we have visited each other nightly for almost two years. We have vowed the eternally fresh passion of intertwined branches of two trees and the ever-constant love of two birds sharing one wing.[18] Throughout my service at court and in the privacy of my own affairs, through the beauty of the changing seasons, I have been living solely in the hope that my dreams might be realized. Consumed with the thought of it, I could attend to nothing else; I am no longer myself and have weakened in body and spirit. I have rested all hope on this pilgrimage."

The girl was profoundly moved to hear him alternately laughing and crying as he poured out his tale of love and sadness. This indeed was the dream she had seen and the reality behind it! She desperately longed to pull open the sliding door that separated them and to converse of their nightly pledges. Yet such forwardness was inappropriate for a woman, and she was forced to repress the urge.

She was at the end of her wits. Those ephemeral dreams had rendered her unable to forget him; now she had heard the same tale about dreams of love and seen the same face of her dreams. All this had come to an end as empty as the open sky, for there was no way to bridge the gap between them, even for a moment. She had no way of predicting his reaction should she burst in and pour out her raging emotions, so she was unable to speak out or go to his side. For her, this stolen glimpse must be their only encounter. Her

16 Legend has it that Emperor Yin, founder of the Shang dynasty, was led by a dream to discover a loyal minister living there.

17. In the *Tale of Genji*, the old priest of Akashi is bidden in a dream to seek someone on the shores of Akashi. There he finds Genji, who subsequently weds his daughter.

18. See the ending of *The Little Man*, in which love is described in the same terms borrowed from "The Song of Unending Sorrow." (Tales of Tears and Laughter, tr. Skord, p. 124).

only recourse lay in becoming a fisherwoman[19] in the waters, trusting that the ever-flowing currents of love would unite them in the world to come. Thus she bravely resolved to die.

After her mother's death, she had relied solely on her father and looked to him for protection; he in turn had loved her dearly. Should she commit the grave sin of predeceasing her parent, somber skies must darken the path she would tread in the hereafter.[20] As he awaited her return on the morrow, he would be unaware that the brief full tide of her life would soon recede—with what sorrow would he receive the tidings, and how he would mourn! Still her resolution wavered not. Sadly, she remembered those who had served her for so long and her friends at court—the Kamo Priestess, the Empress, the various imperial princes and princesses. Regrettably, shallow rumors would cling to her unhappy name in the wake of her death. Numerous considerations gave her pause, but her resolve was strengthened by the prospect of meeting her beloved in the world to come. She lit the lamp and wrote a letter to her father, her eyes so blurred by tears that she was barely able to see. "Do not grieve. Alas, the dews on the young clover of spring[21] are fleeting, yet all must die in the end."

Dawn finally broke. Chūnagon and the others read the sutras, the girl's own faintly whispered prayers barely audible. As her attendants admired the dawn breaking over the waters and mountains, she reflected on their grief should they discover the slightest dewdrop of her heart's intentions. It was indeed sad, but she had been granted a glimpse of the reality behind her dream vision and the knowledge that his feelings mirrored hers. This had to be a manifest token of the Kannon's expedient means, a trustworthy guide to the world to come that lent her courage to face the end with serenity. Hoping that the sin of dying before her parent might prove to be a kind of inverse karma,[22] she prayed that she and her beloved might share a lotus leaf in perfect nuptial harmony in the Pure Land. Though this was her own heart's desire, it was none-

19. A reference to a poem in the *Kokin waka rokujō* anthology: "Kono yo ni te / kimi wo mirume no / kata karaba / koyo no ama to narite / kazuken" (If in this world I may not reap / the grasses of seeing you / then I shall become a fisherwoman / in the one to come). The first oblique reference to her intention to drown herself.
20. Parents were thought to guide offspring down the dark path after death.
21. The message incorporates a pun on *ko hagi*, "young/child" and "bush clover," retained in English as "of spring" (offspring).

theless very sad.

Her party hastened to depart before the sun rose higher. Her brother's wetnurse, now bent with age, lived close to the nearby Seta Bridge. She had implored them to come visit, saying, "I live so near to where you will be passing. It won't do to let this rare opportunity go to waste...if I could only see you. Please come— then you can continue your journey by carriage." For one with intentions such as hers, visiting a place near the water provided a good pretext.

Her heart composed, the girl walked calmly as a lamb to slaughter,[23] yet, the closer she drew to the bridge, the more foreboding the water seemed. What retribution from another life had led her to the depths of this watery grave? Now that the moment of death was on her, she imagined her father's terrible desolation after his only daughter had departed the world before him. Among the many examples of sad events that flooded her mind was the line of verse, "I know not where I go in the hereafter...,"[24] and she was obliged to brush away the torrent of tears coursing down her face lest someone remark them. In the middle of the bridge, she paused, wavered indecisively, then leaped into the waters below.

"What has she done!" screamed her nurse in shock, standing transfixed in utter horror. Unable to restrain her tears, lacking even the presence of mind to jump in after her, her only thought was somehow to rescue her mistress, and she screamed for help at the top of her lungs.

Just then there appeared an elegant boat bearing a number of gentlemen dressing in hunting costume, who wondered at her hysterical sobbing. Overjoyed to see them, the nurse wildly screamed out, "Someone has just jumped in. Can you help?" stamping her feet in the frenzy of her emotion. Moved by pity for her, they

22. *Gyakuen*, lit., "reverse karma," here refers to the doctrine that religious ends can be achieved even through ostensibly wrong causes.

23. *Hitsuji no ayumi*, lit., "the paces of a sheep (to its death)," an expression derived from the Nirvāna sutra, similar to the English "a lamb to slaughter."

24. See n. 20 above. An allusion to a poem written on her sickbed by Ko Shikibu no Naishi, daughter of Izumi Shikibu: "Ika ni semu / ikubeki kata mo omoezu / oya ni sakidatsu / michi wo shiraneba" (What shall I do? / I know not where I go / along the path I walk / before my parents). In *Kokon chōmonjū*, vol. 5, no. 175; also referred to in *Shasekishū*, vol. 5, no. 9, and *Mumyō zōshi*.

resolutely let down some men familiar with the ways of the water, who dragged up the girl.

That the girl should be rescued from the watery depths was indeed a true witness to the message of the Lotus Sutra.[25] Miraculously, her robes bore not a trace of moisture, as if they had been dry for many a long year.

The boat bore none other than the General, who, having completed his seven days of prayer, was on his way home. After the lady had been safely bundled aboard, the General regarded her closely. She was not yet twenty years old, charming and innocent, with striking eyes and features that brought to mind a far-off white-wreathed mountain cherry in the misty dawn light. Her face was modestly averted, and her abundant hair spilled down luxuriantly, nary a wisp astray, filled with the dewy grace of a willow.[26] He felt that his customary dream was but an ephemera compared to this glowing reality. They spoke together without tiring, as if they had known each other for years. One might expect that a woman of such tender years would be embarrassed at having been pulled up in this manner, but she felt not a trace of reserve, for this was the same man dear to her in her dream life.

The love they shared was so strong that it flourished even in the darkness of a jet-black dream; how much more now that they were able to meet in reality! The revered Kannon had led them to realize their long-standing karmic bond. They lived happily ever after, wanting for nothing, assisted by the excellence of the reign, and their legendary prosperity extended even to their children and grandchildren.[27]

I should like to write on further, but I intended to tell only the story of a couple brought together in a dream through the manifestation of the Savior Bodhisattva's vow, and I shall leave the embellishment to another. To ramble on further would be a waste of ink, so I shall put aside my brush.

(T. Virginia Skord)

25. In the Kannon chapter of the Lotus Sutra, it is stated that, if one is swept off by a great river and calls on the Kannon, he shall find a shallow place.

26. A metaphor of female beauty, derived from "The Song of Unending Sorrow."

27. In the Japanese text, their prosperity is likened to that of "Fujinoura," a reference to the chapter of the same name in *The Tale of Genji* which describes the full flowering of Genji's fortunes.

Komparu Zenchiku (1405-1468)

TEIKA, a Nō play

[Believed to have been written by Komparu Zenchiku (1405-1468), the play is based on the love affair that is supposed to have existed between Fujiwara no Teika, here called Sadaie at times, and Princess Shikishi, here called Shokushi. Sadaie and Shokushi are different but legitimate readings of the the same ideographs.]

PERSONS

> Traveling Priest
> His Two Companions, also Priests
> "Woman of the Place"
> Chorus
> "Man of the Place"
> Ghost of Princess Shokushi

TIME AND PLACE

Act I, first half: near the Hut of Intermittent Showers in Sembon, Kyoto, one early winter evening with intermittent showers; second half: in front of Princess Shokushi's grave, later the same evening.
Act II: in front of the same grave, late at night with the moon shining.

ACT I

(The stage assistants bring out a large construction representing a grave mound and place it upstage, in front of the musicians. As the music begins, the TRAVELING PRIEST and his COMPANIONS enter quietly and stand side by side near front apron. Then they face one another.)

PRIEST & COMPANIONS

The northern showers come out of the mountains,
the northern showers come out of the mountains,
but seem to have no place to settle.

PRIEST

(*He faces front.*) I'm from a northern province, and I am a priest. Since I've never seen the capital, I have now decided to go there.

PRIEST & COMPANIONS

(*They face one another.*)
When the winter began,
in traveling robes, early in the morning,
in traveling robes, early in the morning
we left, and came away over mountain after mountain,
far and near, with clouds coming and going
(*The* PRIEST *indicates he is walking.*)
till
we came to the flowering capital,
we came to the flowering capital
where the last crimson leaves hold our eyes.
(*He indicates arrival.*)

PRIEST

(*He faces front.*) Hurrying along I've reached a place called Upper Capital. (*Saying,* "Let me look around," *he goes to stage center and stands there. In the meantime, his* COMPANIONS *have taken their seats at front left corner. The* PRIEST *faces front.*)

Curious:
it's around the tenth of the tenth month,
and the treetops are all seared by winter;
but the crimson leaves remaining on the branches,
though only here and there, the way they look—
the scenery moves me more in the capital,
the view is different this evening.
A shower has started! I think I'll stand by this hut until it clears up. (*He starts toward front left corner.*)

WOMAN OF THE PLACE

(*Calling to the* PRIEST *from offstage, she enters quietly.*) Tell me—tell me, why are you standing by that hut?

PRIEST

(*He turns to face the* WOMAN *at front left corner.*) I'm standing here because of the shower that just started. What do you call this place?

WOMAN

(*As she walks on the bridgeway leading to the stage.*) It's known as the Hut of Intermittent Showers, a place with a history. I thought you were standing there because you knew the story—that's why I asked the question.

PRIEST

Indeed, I see a plaque up there, and it has "Hut of Intermittent Showers" written on it. A coincidence, perhaps, but an interesting one. Would you tell me what kind of person built it?

WOMAN

Lord Fujiwara no Sadaie. Though it's within the capital, this place is so desolate, and the showers so moving, that he built this hut and every year wrote tanka on the subject, they say. (*She stops walking and faces front.*) Such is the history of the place, and by coincidence you've happened by, so you might preach the Law and pray for the peace of his soul—
    I thought I'd make that request,
    and gave you a full explanation.
(*She resumes walking and comes on stage.*)

PRIEST

I see, Lord Sadaie built it.
    Well, now, I wonder
    which tanka of his caused this hut
    to commemorate the "showers."

WOMAN

    I must say that's hard to settle.
    In the season of showers
    every year, he wrote about them,
    and I can't say with conviction, "This is it."
Nevertheless, on the topic, "Intermittent showers know their time," he wrote:
        "No falsity
    in this world: another tenth month—

whose sincere heart has caused
the showers to begin again?"[1]
Considering that he wrote "At my house" in the headnote to it, it
may be the tanka in question.

PRIEST

How those words
affect me!
True, with intermittent showers, no falsity
in this world where they stay on,

WOMAN

but the one who's no more! We speak
such words now, in this transient world,

PRIEST

Because our ties from another life have not decayed.
We "shelter under the same tree,"

WOMAN

"drink from the flow of the same river."[2]

PRIEST

As if to urge us to realize it,

WOMAN

Just then,
(*During the* CHORUS *chanting that follows,* the MAN OF THE PLACE
enters inconspicuously and takes his seat near right corner upstage.)

CHORUS

here a shower starts
on the old house, the shower of the past,
on the old house, the shower of the past,
and we know how the one with a clear heart
must have felt. The world of dreams
never settles. On Sadaie's[3]
  eaves,

---

1. No. 2305 in Teika's anthology of his own poems, *Shūi gusō.*
2. The two last phrases are believed to be popular sayings of
the time.
3. Pun on the name Sadaie, which means "settled house" or
"settling the house."

the shower falls at dusk—
thoughts of old move me to tears.
The garden and the hedges, no longer separate,
grass bushes, grown ever wilder,
are all seared, dew seldom forming on them.
How desolate this evening,
how desolate this evening!

(*While looking off into the distance, the* WOMAN *steps backward to rear right corner and turns to face the* PRIEST.)

WOMAN

This happens to be the day I offer prayers for someone who is dead, and I am going to her grave. Would you mind coming with me?

PRIEST

Not at all. I'll be glad to come with you. (*The* WOMAN *moves a few steps forward and turns to the grave mound; the* PRIEST *does the same.*)

WOMAN

Look at the grave mound here.

PRIEST

It's strange. The marker looks very old, but the way kudzu vines crawl all over it and cling to it—I can't even tell its shape. Whose marker is it?

WOMAN

It's Princess Shokushi's grave. Those kudzu vines are called "Teika vines."

PRIEST

How odd. Why are they called "Teika vines"?

WOMAN

Princess Shokushi was, at first, a vestal of the Kamo Shrine, but soon left that position.[4] Then Lord Teika fell in love with her, and their love for each other, though secret, was deep. Soon afterward, Princess Shokushi died. Teika's attachment then turned into vines and crawled over her grave, clung to it. So, in their suffering, unable to separate,

---

4. Shikishi was made *saiin* (vestal, priestess) of the Kamo Shrine in 1159, but because of illness she left the position in 1169.

they lust for each other, a delusion,
of which I will tell you more, if you are kind enough to offer prayers
for them.(*She goes to stage center and takes her seat; the* PRIEST *returns
to his seat.*)

CHORUS

Unforgettable, though it was long ago;
"the depth of her heart, Mount Secret
I went over to visit in secrecy"[5]—the dew on the grass
by the path—my telling you this is as purposeless.

WOMAN

Now, "string of beads,
if you must break, break. If you last longer,

CHORUS

my resolve to keep it secret"[6] will weaken,
she felt, and as pampas grass shows its tufts in fall,
began to betray her affair,
when it was cut short and fell apart.

WOMAN

"I did not feel at all before then,"

CHORUS

and "my heart since"[7] has remained astray.
"Know the grief
of the sleeve dyed mountain indigo
that decayed from frost to frost throughout
its life"[8]— full of tears, those past days;
to do without the distress of longing she made ablutions,
she became vestal of the Kamo Shrine,

---

5. Allusion to the tanka in section 15 of *The Tales of Ise:* "If only
there were a path on Mount Secret by which to visit in secrecy,
so I might see the depth of her heart."
6. Shikishi's tanka (*Shinkokinshū*, no. 1034), quoted with the
last part slightly changed..
7. Allusion to Fujiwara no Atsutada's tanka (*Shūishū*, no.
710):"Compared with my heart since meeting you, I did not
feel at all before then."
8. *Shūi gusō*, no. 2579, "Thoughts near the Kamo Shrine,"
written in 1210.

that was what she became,
but the god did not accept it.[9]

Her vow with someone
betrayed its colors[10]—that's what saddens us.
    She tried to hide it, in vain in this world
    of vanity; her affair came to light,
    the rumors grew as vast
    as the sky with its terrifying sun,
    so that the path to the clouds was cut
    and the figure of the maiden could not be kept,[11]
    a painful thing for both of them.

WOMAN

                    Indeed, "I grieve,
    I long for you, but there's no way of meeting you:

CHORUS

    you are a cloud on Katsuragi peak"[12]—
the feeling that moved him to write it,
        we understand, because of that attachment
        his body turned into the Teika vines,
        and here, where her remains are, from long ago
        he's stayed inseparable, vines with crimson leaves,
                            color scorching,
                            clinging,
        a tangle of hair, bound, binding.
                        This delusion
                        that faded and has returned
                        like frost or dew—
    please save me from it.
    As we listened to the story of log ago,
    soon it's the end of another day, darkening;

9. Allusion to an anonymous tanka (*Kokinshū*, no. 501): "To stop longing I made ablutions in the Mitarashi River, but the god has not accepted them."
10. Allusion to Taira no Kanemori's tanka (*Shūishū*, no 622): "I kept my longing secret, but it betrayed its colors, till someone asked if I was brooding."
11. Allusion to Yoshimine no Munesada's tanka(*Kokinshū*, no. 872, "On seeing Gosechi dancing princesses": "Wind of heaven, blow shut the past to the clouds, so the figures of the maidens may stay a while."
12. *Shūigusō*, no 2483, quoted with the last part slightly changed.

mysterious—would you tell us who you are?

WOMAN

Who am I, you ask.
the remains of my dead body have decayed
under miscanthus and frost, only my name staying on, all to
no avail.
(*She turns to the* PRIEST.)

CHORUS

Placed under grass though you may be,
show your colors, your name.

WOMAN

I would hide it

CHORUS

no longer now:
I am no other than Princess Shokushi.
(*She rises to her feet and, with her eyes fixed on the* PRIEST, *walks toward him slowly, firmly.*)
I have been visible to you till now,
but my true figure is like heat haze,
(*She faces front*)
and even my form left in stone
(*She retreats backward t the grave mound*)
is invisible under the kudzu vines.
(*She walks toward the* PRIEST.) Please help me out of this suffering.
(*She circles back to the grave mound and disappears into it.*)
As soon as she said it, she disappeared,
as soon as she said it, she disappeared.

INTERLUDE

(*The* MAN OF THE PLACE *leaves his seat, announces himself, indicates that he has come across the* PRIEST, *and takes his seat at stage center. In response to the* PRIEST'S *questions, he tells the story of the affair between* FUJIWARA NO TEIKA *and* PRINCESS SHOKUSHI *in some detail. He says, among other things that the kudzu vines that started growing on* SHOKUSHI'S *grave mound soon after* TEIKA'S *death used to be cut and removed, but they would immediately grow back; the cutting was continued until some holy person said that the vines were a manifestation of* TEIKA'S *attachment to the* PRINCESS *and therefore should be left alone. When the* MAN *learns about the woman the* PRIEST *has just met, he says she must be* SHOKUSHI'S *apparition, urges the* PRIEST *to offer prayers to lay her troubled soul to rest, and returns to his original seat. He exits inconspicuously after the* GHOST OF PRINCESS SHOKUSHI *enters in Act II.*)

ACT II

PRIEST & COMPANIONS

The evening passed, and now the moon is out.
The evening passed, and now the moon is out.
This late, when winds blow through pines, under desolate
clumps of grass she lies, a drop of dew.
Although our thoughts are many as our rosary beads,
how fortunate this chance to pray for her,
how fortunate this chance to pray for her.
    (*Gloomy, foreboding music is played.*)

GHOST OF PRINCESS SHOKUSHI

(*In the grave mound, in a low voice*)
                    Is this a dream?
In this dark reality, on Mount Real,
I trace by the moonlight
the path buried under the vines.
    (*In a high, painful tone*)
                    Once in the past,
a pine wind or the moon through vines
moved us to exchange words;
pillows laid side by side
in green curtains, on a scarlet bed,

PRIEST

we loved each other
in many ways. But in the end,

GHOST

the blossoms and crimson leaves[13] scatter away;

PRIEST

a cloud in the morning,

---

13. Echoes Teika's "As I look out."

GHOST

rain in the evening, [14]

CHORUS

that is an old story, yes
but my body now,

(*Quietly, with emotion*)
and dreams, reality, illusions,
all have become part of the transient world,
leaving not a trace.

(In *a different tone, reflectively*)
Yet, here I am, under the grass—
not in a hut covered with burdock,[15]
but with the Teika vines over me.
Look at this, look at me, holy priest.

(*The stage assistants remove the cloth covering the grave mound, revealing the emaciated* GHOST OF PRINCESS SHOKUSHI. *She is seated on a chair, stiff, looking down, indicating that she is under the spell of Teika's passion.*)

PRIEST

How painful it is to look at you, the way you are. How painful it is.
(*He joins his hands in prayer.*)
"The Buddha's undifferentiated preaching
Is like the rain, all of one flavor;
But beings, according to their nature,
Receive it differently."[16]

GHOST

Look at me.
(*She turns her face to the* PRIEST.)
I stand and sit, uselessly as waves.
Suffering as I am even after death,
I'm bound by the Teika vines;

14. An old Chinese legend tells of an amorous encounter between a mortal ruler and a mountain goddess; as the goddess took her leave, she said, "At dawn I am the morning clouds, at evening I am the passing rain."
15. Such a hut was a traditional abode for a hermit.
16. From Chapter 5, "The Parable of the Herbs," of the Lotus Sutra.

suffering as I am
without a break—
                    I'm grateful to you.
What you have kindly recited now is from the "Parable of the
Herbs," is it not?

PRIEST

Indeed, you are right.
The wonderful Law overlooks no grass or tree.
Sever yourself from the vines of attachment,
    and become a buddha.

GHOST

O, how grateful I am,
yes, indeed, indeed!
this is the heart
of the wonderful Law!

PRIEST

(He turns to face front.)
We receive the blessings
of the universal dew.

GHOST

"Not a second

PRIEST

not a third,"[17]

CHORUS

(Somewhat forcefully)
the one rain, the one Law,
sprinkles,
and all turn moist,
grasses, trees, the land,
becoming buddhas.
Having that opportunity

17. From the passage, "In the buddha-lands of the ten directions / There is only the One-vehicle Law, / Not a second, not
a third, / Except the expedient teachings of the Buddha," in
Chapter 2, "Expedient Devices," of the Lotus Sutra.

(*Growing quieter*)
the Teika vines,
tears shed on them
　　in large drops,
unbind themselves, spread
　　(*The* GHOST *indicates she is being freed*)
　　　　and I, tottering,
like a cart with feeble wheels, leave the burning house.[18] (*Rising to her feet, she steps out of the mound.*) How grateful I am. (*She tuns toward the* PRIEST *and joins her hands in prayer.*)
In gratitude, may I then
flutter the flowery sleeves, which I once had
above the clouds,[19] and bring back the past,
a dancing princess in the Omi robe?[20]

GHOST

How embarrassing I look,

CHORUS

Dancing.
(*She dances a slow, quiet dance.*)

GHOST

How embarrassing I look, dancing.

GHOST

How embarrassing. I am embarrassed.

GHOST

The way I was,

CHORUS

my face was like the moon.

GHOST

but it began to cloud often,

CHORUS

18. The "burning house" is a Buddhist metaphor for "this world." See Chapter 3, "A Parable," of the Lotus Sutra.
19. "Above the clouds" is a metaphor for the imperial court.
20. The "Omi robe" is official festival attire, used also by dancer-princesses.

and my eyebrows painted crescent-shape

GHOST

lost their beauty, in tears.

CHORUS

Even after I faded like dew,
(*She circles back to the rear right corner, then goes to stage center.*)
I was pitilessly covered with vine leaves, and am now like the
goddess of Kazuraki.[21] I'm ashamed of it, but can't help it. (*She sees
the* PRIEST *and hides her face with her fan.*)
 Because we can meet only at night,
 before this dream ends,
so saying, she returned to the place where she had been. (*She walks
to the grave.*) Then the vine leaves crawled over her, clung to her,
those Teika vines. (*She settles in the grave mound.*) And before we knew
it, she was buried, she was gone. (*She covers her face with her fan and
lowers her body.*)

(Tr. Hiroaki Sato)

21. The ugly goddess of Kazuraki was so ashamed of her looks
that when ordered by an exorcist to build a stone bridge, she
would work only during the night when no one was around.
As a result, she could not finish the bridge in time, and the
angry exorcist bound her with vines.

Suggestions for Further Reading

Arberry, A. J. *Classical Persian Literature*. London: G. Allen & Unwin, 1958.

Brown, Edward Granville. *A Literary History of Persia*. Cambridge, Eng: The University Press, 1956.

de Bary, Wm. Theodore, ed. *Approaches to the Oriental Classics*. New York: Columbia University Press, 1959.

Dimock, Edward C., Jr., et al. *The Literatures of India: An Introduction*. Chicago: University of Chicago Press, 1978

Frankel, Hans. *The Flowering Plum and the Palace Lady: Interpretations of Chinese Poetry*. New Haven: Yale University Press, 1976.

Gibb, Hamilton Alexander Rossken. *Arabic Literature: An Introduction*. 2nd ed. London: Oxford University Press, 1974.

Gordon, Leonard A. and Barbara Stoler Miller. *A Syllabus of Indian Civilization*. New York: Columbia University Press, 1971.

Hightowner, James Robert. *Topics in Chinese Literature: Outlines and Bibliographies*. Cambridge: Harvard University Press, 1962.

Keene, Donald. *Japanese Literature: An Introduction for Western Readers*. New York: Grove Press, 1955.

Konishi, Jin'ichi. *A History of Japanese Literature*. Ed. Earl Miner. Trans. Aileen Gatten and Nicholas Teele. 2 vols. Princeton, NJ: Princeton University Press, 1984-1986.

Levy, Reuben. *An Introduction to Persian Literature*. New York: Columbia University Press, 1969.

Liu, James J. Y. *The Art of Chinese Poetry*. Chicago: University of Chicago Press, 1962.

— *The Interlingual Critic: Interpreting Chinese Poetry*. Bloomington: Indiana University Press, 1982

Najib Ullah. *Islamic Literature: An Introductory History with Selections*. New York: Washington Square Press, 1963.

Renou, Louis. *Indian Literature*. Trans. Patrick Evans. New York: Walker, 1964.

Rimer, J. Thomas. *A Reader's Guide to Japanese Literature*. Tokyo; New York: Kodansha International, 1988.

Ueda Makoto. *Literary and Art Theories in Japan*. Cleveland: Press of Case Western Reserve University, 1967.

Watson, Burton. *Shih Poetry: From the Second to the Twelfth Century*. New York: Columbia University Press, 1971.

Winterniz, M[oriz]. *A History of Indian Literature*. Trans. S. Ketkar and H. Kohn. 2 vols. New York: Russell & Russell, 1971.